TREATY CRUISERS

TREATY CRUISERS

The World's First International Warship
Building Competition

Leo Marriott

Pen & Sword
MARITIME

First published in
Great Britain in 2005
By Pen & Sword Maritime
An imprint of Pen and Sword Books Ltd
47 Church Street
Barnsley
South Yorkshire
S70 2AS
England

ISBN 1 84415 188 3

Typeset in the UK by Mac Style, Scarborough, N. Yorkshire.
Printed and bound in the UK by CPI UK.

Pen & Sword Books Ltd incorporates the imprints of Pen & Sword Aviation, Pen & Sword Maritime, Pen & Sword Military, Wharncliffe Local History, Pen & Sword Select, Pen & Sword Military Classics and Leo Cooper.

For a complete list of Pen & Sword titles please contact
Pen & Sword Books Limited
47 Church Street, Barnsley, South Yorkshire, S70 2AS, England
E-mail: enquiries@pen-and-sword.co.uk
Website: www.pen-and-sword.co.uk

Contents

Glossary   vi

PART ONE   *The Rules*   1

CHAPTER ONE   *Introduction*   3
CHAPTER TWO   *The Naval Treaties*   9

PART TWO   *The Contestants*   17

CHAPTER THREE   *Britain and the Commonweatlth*   19
CHAPTER FOUR   *France*   38
CHAPTER FIVE   *Germany*   45
CHAPTER SIX   *Italy*   50
CHAPTER SEVEN   *Japan*   58
CHAPTER EIGHT   *United States*   69

PART THREE   *The Final Test (Cruisers at War)*   87

CHAPTER NINE   *Atlantic, NW Europe and Trade Protection*   89
CHAPTER TEN   *The Mediterranean*   103
CHAPTER ELEVEN   *The Pacific and Indian Oceans*   115
CHAPTER TWELVE   *South-West Pacific*   123
CHAPTER THIRTEEN *Victory in the Pacific*   137
CHAPTER FOURTEEN *Review*   149

Appendix I   Technical Data   153
Appendix II   Construction Programmes   160
Appendix III   Eight Inch Guns   164
Appendix IV   Aircraft Deployed Aboard Heavy Cruisers   168

Index   177

Glossary

AA	Anti-Aircraft
AR	Air Ranging (radar)
AW	Air Warning (radar)
bhp	Brake horsepower
cal	calibre
CT	Conning Tower
DCT	Director Control Tower
Desron	Destroyer Squadron (US Navy)
D/F	Direction Finding (Radio)
DNC	Director of Naval Construction
DP	Dual Purpose (relating to guns capable of use against both surface and aerial targets)
ft	feet (unit of measurement)
GW	General Warning (radar)
HA	High Angle
HA/LA	Combined High Angle and Low Angle
HACS	High Angle Control System
HE	High Explosive
HMAS	Her Majesty's Australian Ship
HMS	Her Majesty's Ship
HP	High Pressure
hp	horsepower
IJN	Imperial Japanese Navy
in	inch (unit of measurement)
kt/kts	knot/knots
lb	pound weight
LP	Low Pressure
MG	Machine Gun
mm	millimetre (unit of measurement)
MTB	Motor Torpedo Boat
nm	Nautical mile (6080 ft)
oa	overall
pdr	pounder
pp	Between perpendiculars
RAN	Royal Australian Navy
RN	Royal Navy (United Kingdom)
RNZN	Royal New Zealand Navy
RPC	Remote Power Control
shp	Shaft horsepower
SR	Single Reduction
SR	Surface Ranging (radar)
SW	Surface Warning (radar)
TF	Task Force
TG	Task Group
TT	Torpedo Tube
US	United States
USN	United States Navy
USS	United States Ship
wl	Waterline

PART ONE

The Rules

CHAPTER I

Introduction

When war broke out in 1939 the world's navies consisted of a mixture of warships that mostly fell into two basic categories. First there were many ships which had been designed or built during the First World War and, although many had been modernised, they were, nevertheless, at least 20 years old in 1939 and inevitably lacked many of the refinements of the newer ships. Second there were the ships built between the wars, particularly from 1922 onwards, whose basic design was constrained by the clauses of the Washington Naval Treaty which was signed in that year. This laid down the total tonnage of warships in each category permitted to each of the world's major naval powers and, more specifically, set limits on the size and armament of each individual class of warship. Apart from one or two exceptions, the building of battleships was deferred for at least ten years and so some of first major warships to be built to the treaty limitaions were heavy cruisers limited to a standard displacement of 10,000 tons and guns of an 8in maximum calibre. These limits were an arbitary set of figures designed to allow the Royal Navy to retain their *Hawkins* class cruisers then under construction.

However, the politicians and naval staffs at the Washington Conference had inadvertanty come up with a standard which was immediately regarded not as the maximum allowable, but as the minimum which should be built. Within twelve months of the signing of the treaty, the navies of Britain, France, Italy, Japan and the United States were all in the process of laying down new cruisers armed with 8 inch guns and intended to be just within the permitted 10,000 ton limit. Thus the stage was set for a fascinating technological competition which continued right up to the outbreak of the Second World War by which time the treaty limitations had lapsed and navies were free of restrictions. Although not a signatory of the Washington Treaty, Germany nominally accepted the technical limitations when she signed the Anglo German Naval Treaty of 1935 and thereby became a late entrant to the competition. Nearly all the significant naval actions fought during the war were between ships of the Treaty era and so each was well tested in battle, with varying and sometimes unexpected outcomes. It was not until late 1943 that significant numbers of major warships (i.e. battleships, aircraft carriers and cruisers), whose design was free of treaty restrictions and incorported wartime experience, started to join the fleets, by which time the focus of naval action had moved to the Pacific and the drive against Japan.

This book will look specifically at the 8 inch gunned, 10,000 ton cruiser which came into being as a direct result of the Washington Naval Treaty, and other subsequent treaties and accords. It will compare their designs and try to to assess how they performed in service. Before doing that, it will be useful to look at the negotiations and bargaining which went on at the various conferences in order to understand the objectives of the varying participants and to gauge whether the outcome was as they expected. Inevitably, the ships displayed something of their countries national character, both in appearance and capabilities, but also by the degree to which the treaty limitations were observed. The result is perhaps a useful object lesson to those who would today put their faith in various arms limitaions and treaties as a way of ensuring peace in a troubled world.

However, we should not forget the men who went to war in these ships. Whatever the technical merits of each class, or the aims of their political masters, when these cruisers went into action there was no lack of bravery, courage and devotion to duty in any of the navies concerned. Whether we think of the HMS *Exeter* slugging it out with the pocket battleship *Graf Spee*, Japanese cruisers inflicting a crushing defeat on the American and Australian ships off Savo Island because of their infinitely superior tactics and training, the USS *Salt Lake City* holding her own against a superior Japanese force, or the stately British *County* class ships which played their parts in the destruction of the *Bismarck* and the *Scharnhorst*, the crews of all these ships endured the horrors of war with a fortitude and bravery which we can only admire.

Evolution of the Cruiser

The origin of the cruiser as a type of fighting ship goes back to the days of the sailing navies when battles were fought between rows of heavily armed line-of-battleships. In the Royal Navy such ships were classified by a rating system which depended on the number of guns carried. A first rate ship, such as Nelson's HMS *Victory*, carried well over a hundred guns including 36 and 42 pounders while the backbone of the fleet was the famous 74 gun third rate ship armed with 24 and 36 pounders. However, a smaller class of ship had also evolved that was fast and manoeuvrable and carried between 20 to 44 relatively light 9 and 12 pounder guns. Termed as Frigates, these ships acted as scouts ahead of the main fleet but were also employed on many other important duties for which a ship of the line was too large or too slow. These duties included convoy protection as well as seeking out and destroying enemy merchant shipping. While engaged on such tasks, the Frigate would cruise independently, not constantly beholden to the orders of a squadron commander or Admiral, and consequently were often termed as cruisers.

The great technological advances of the mid 19th century completely changed the nature of every type of warship. Briefly, these changes included the adoption of iron and then steel in place of wood for the construction of warships, the adoption of steam power to supplement and then replace sails as a source of power, and the adoption and refinement of shell-firing breech loading guns capable of accurate fire at much greater ranges. Initially, such changes were directed at the larger warships so that, for a while, the new steam powered battleships were faster than the older sailing frigates. However, once the new technology filtered down, steel hulled steam frigates began to appear and the term cruiser began to be more commonly applied. A major influence on cruiser design was the Armstrong shipyard at Elswick on the River Tyne. Built in the 1880s for foreign navies, the *Elswick* cruisers, as they were known, were revolutionary for their time, being both fast and heavily armed, and their design features were soon incorporated in Royal Navy cruisers. By the late 19th century two distinct cruiser types had evolved. One was the so called protected cruiser in which such armour protection as was provided consisted mainly of an armoured deck to cover the machinery, magazines and other vital spaces. The armament and upper decks were mostly unarmoured. Such cruisers were intended mainly for trade warfare and were not intended to work in support of the battlefleet. This task was allocated to the armoured cruiser which, as it name implies, was much better protected including an armoured belt above and below the waterline as well as protection to the guns and control positions. Some armoured cruisers were larger than contemporary battleships and, on paper at least, were formidable warships, although their battle record in the First World War was unspectacular. Some of the protected cruisers were also very large, the ultimate examples being the British 14,000 ton HMS *Powerful* and HMS *Terrible* launched in 1895 and armed with two 9.2in and sixteen 6in guns. They were also armed with lighter, quick firing guns and with torpedoes and could make 22 knots. The slightly smaller *Diadem* class of eight ships displaced 11,000 tons and dispensed with the 9.2in guns. These and similar ships were known as First Class Protected cruisers while smaller ships such as the 5,600 ton *Highflyer* class armed with 6in guns were designated as Second Class. Finally, there were even smaller Third Class Protected Cruisers displacing around 3,000 tons and carrying 4.7in guns as their main armament.

By contrast, the Armoured cruisers grew in size and power during the 1890s and the early years of the 20th century. The last to be built for the Royal Navy (*Defence*, *Minotaur* and *Shannon*) were

HMS Archer, *an early type of trade protection cruiser which retained a sailing capability.* Maritime Photo Library

launched in 1906/07 and on a displacement of 14,600 tons carried an armament of four 9.2in and ten 7.5in guns as well as several 12 pdrs and five 18in torpedo tubes. However, these were the last large heavy gun cruisers to be built for the Royal Navy until after the First World War and the emphasis was now turning to fast, light cruisers, also known as scout cruisers, which were needed to lead and protect the flotillas of destroyers being built to take advantage of another technological development, the torpedo. In order to work with destroyers, high speed was essential and this demanded high installed power in long slim hulls, leaving little space for armament which initially comprised 4in guns but later standardised on 6in guns. During the First World War, their design was standardised to some extent, resulting in the excellent C class cruisers which were built in several versions, many of which survived to give sterling service in the Second World War. An enlarged version with an extra 6in gun became the D class which entered service in 1918. Later, a further stretch resulted in the E class which were armed with seven 6in guns and could make 33 knots, the fastest conventional cruisers ever built for the Royal Navy.

During the early part of the First World War, German cruisers such as *Emden* and various disguised Armed Merchant Cruisers played havoc with allied shipping until they were finally hunted down and sunk. However, this experience gave rise to a requirement for a large heavily armed cruiser for trade protection duties. The result was the *Hawkins* class although no ships were completed until after the end of the war. Although lightly armoured, they displaced almost 10,000 tons and were intended to

HMS Terrible, *pictured in 1898, was one of two ships which represented an extreme development of the protected cruisers. At over 14,000 tons displacement, they were considerably larger than the later Washington Treaty cruisers.* Maritime Photo Library

be armed with 7.5in guns. As will be seen, their existence was to have a significant effect on the outcome of the various political manoeuvrings after the war which ultimately resulted in the construction of the heavy cruisers that are the subject of this book.

In the years leading up to the First World War, Britain's obvious rival for maritime supremacy was Germany and, indeed, the naval arms race in the early part of the Twentieth Century was undoubtedly one of the factors that led to the War. The German Navy was particularly strong in light cruisers that were well built and armed with excellent 4.1in guns. They did not build many large armoured cruisers and those that were completed mostly had a similar experience to their British counterparts. The largest was the 15,500 ton *Blücher* armed with twelve 8.2in guns and she was sunk in January 1915 at the Battle of Dogger Bank.

French cruiser development was specifically directed towards commerce raiding and by 1914 the bulk of her cruiser force consisted of large armoured cruisers that were generally not up to the standards of the British and German ships. Also, France only had a few old protected cruisers and, crucially, none of the light scout cruisers which were to prove so successful in other navies. More critical was the fact that no new cruisers were completed during the war so that by 1918 the French cruiser force was out of date and relatively ineffective.

During the First World War, Japan was an ally of Great Britain and America and her navy was heavily influenced by British trends in warship construction, particularly in the construction of light scout cruisers although none were actually completed until after 1918. However, Japan was an early advocate of armed cruisers with 8in guns and had actually finalised the design of such ships before the Washington Treaty negotiations were completed. Across the Pacific, the US Navy did not accord a high priority to cruiser construction while pursuing its aim of parity with the Royal Navy because it did not have the requirement to protect extensive trade routes resulting from Britain's status as a major colonial power. At the start of the First World War a total of twelve armoured cruisers, most at least ten years old, and a handful of ancient protected cruisers was all that was available to the US Navy. They did have three experimental scout cruisers, launched in 1907, although it is interesting to note that the first flight of an aeroplane from the deck of a ship took place aboard one of these, USS *Birmingham*, in November 1910. Surprisingly, no new cruisers were completed during the war although 10 new light cruisers of the *Omaha* class (7,000 tons, twelve 6in guns, 34 knots) were approved when America entered the war in 1917. However, none had even been laid down until after the end of hostilities and the first examples did not enter service until 1923

In the aftermath of the First World War the success of the light scout cruiser led to its continued construction by Britain, America and Japan although neither Italy or France had any under

HMS Caradoc *was a typical example of the very successful C class light cruisers built during the First World War.* Author's collection

HMS Hawkins. Maritime Picture Library)

construction or projected. Britain, however, persisted with the larger *Hawkins* class and Japan was following suit with the 8in armed *Furutaka* class which was specifically intended as a counter to the British ships. The US Navy General Board was considering a number of draft proposals for large 8in armed cruisers but none had been laid down at that time. However, there were significant construction plans by most of the major navies for other classes of warships, notably new large battleships and battlecruisers, and despite the end of hostilities the cost of these programmes was relentlessly rising. It was this situation which led to the convening of a conference on naval armaments in Washington in 1921 and the outcome of this was to have a profound effect on future cruiser construction.

CHAPTER II

The Naval Treaties

The Washington Treaty

At the start of 1919 the Royal Navy possessed 120 cruisers of all types while the US Navy had only around 35; Japan had 26, France 29 and Italy 17. These figures are not entirely realistic as they include many obsolete cruisers dating from the nineteenth century and many of these were subsequently scrapped. Nevertheless, the overwhelming strength of the Royal Navy is clearly apparent and this was one factor which influenced US Naval planners in their quest for parity. In 1916 the US Government had sanctioned a massive building programme which included six *South Dakota* class battleships, six *Lexington* class battlecruisers, ten *Omaha* class light cruisers and large numbers of destroyers. In the post-war era the General Board considered proposals for further construction in addition to these ships. In the meantime, Japan laid down four *Kaga* class battleships and four *Akagi* class battlecruisers and proposed a further construction programmes intended to produce a fleet of twenty-seven modern capital ships by 1927. Faced with this situation the Royal Navy, then still the world's most powerful navy, needed to take action if it was not to be overtaken. Although it held an overwhelming numerical advantage, none of its ships, apart from the battlecruiser *Hood*, had been built late enough to take advantage of the lessons learnt at the battle of Jutland. Consequently, the First Sea Lord, Admiral Beatty, proposed the construction of four new battleships and battlecruisers in the 1921 programme and a further four in the following year's estimates.

It was quite obvious that the World's major powers were engaging in a serious naval arms-race in which the size, power and cost of each ship was spiralling almost uncontrollably upwards. However, there were two factors which acted as a brake on these grandiose plans. The first was cost. Britain in particular was trying to recover from four years of total war and there was enormous pressure to reduce spending on all aspects of defence expenditure. The Royal Navy was forced to lay up significant numbers of ships although many of these were obsolete and would perform no useful function in any new war. In addition, the British Government in 1919 declared that all estimates for military expenditure should be based on the premise that no major war would occur for ten years. Known as the ten year rule, this was perpetual in concept so that at any future date it would still be assumed that there would be no war for ten years ahead. This rule was only abandoned in 1932 and was a constant restraint on naval expenditure during the intervening years.

The United Sates was not as financially constrained as Britain but on the other hand there was a strong pacifist and isolationist movement which was opposed to the continuing expenditure on naval and military arms. President Wilson who had taken America into the war in 1917 was a strong supporter of the Treaty of Versailles and the formation of a League of Nations. However, the US Senate voted against both and America did not ratify the treaty or become a member of the League (consequently it was to prove an ineffective body in its attempts to counter aggression and the outbreak of conflict). Wilson was replaced by President Harding in the 1920 election and his administration realised that it was necessary to show that America was still committed to actively working for world peace. In 1921 the US administration became aware that the British government was planning to call an international conference to discuss Pacific and Far Eastern affairs. The American, regarded this part of the world as their legitimate sphere of influence and therefore did not relish the idea of such a meeting. However, the Harding administration was under pressure from a populist movement calling for a world general disarmament conference and, therefore, it was keen to debate the concept of a limitation on naval armaments. As a result, the Americans forestalled the British initiative by formally proposing a naval limitation conference to be held in Washington in 1921 and the whole concept was made more acceptable by broadening its scope to include Pacific and Far Eastern affairs in the discussions. The invitation to attend was limited to Britain, Japan, France and Italy as the major allied powers, although other nations including China, the Netherlands, Belgium and Portugal were invited to attend the forums related to the Pacific and Far East where they were all interested parties. A notable omission was Russia which was both a naval power and had obvious interests in the western Pacific.

The participating nations immediately set about establishing the position they would adopt at the conference. The Royal Navy, with its worldwide commitments was adamantly opposed to any limitations based on total tonnage as they perceived that their requirements, particularly in cruisers, were legitimately greater than other nations. Their opinion was also that restricting the size of individual ships would present insurmountable technical difficulties and it was therefore determined that the only acceptable limitations would be in actual numbers of capital ships. It was also decided that the British Empire Delegation, as it was officially termed, would press for the complete abolition of submarines. This was understandable as Britain had come close to losing the war due to the depredations of the German U-boat fleet (and, indeed, would do so again twenty years later in the Second World War. However, it was tacitly accepted that this was an unrealistic demand which would find little support from the other participants.

The US Navy General Board, tasked with framing the American position, effectively decided that it was not prepared to reduce construction programmes until parity with Royal Navy had been achieved in categories of warships. This, effectively, would result in an increase in naval construction, hardly the outcome which the President had in mind. Consequently, a small committee was set up to consider a more drastic and imaginative response and as result of these deliberations a new set of proposals was drawn up. However, these were a closely guarded secret so that Secretary Hughes could present them with maximum effect at the plenary opening session of the Washington Conference on 12th November 1921. Hughes was a born showman and his presentation of the American proposals was masterly and incredibly effective. The basic proposals were sweeping and breathtaking and briefly were as follows:

i)   All projected or approved capital ship building programmes should be immediately abandoned.
ii) Existing capital ship strengths should be reduced by the scrapping of older ships.
iii) The existing relative strengths of the major naval powers should be established as the relative proportions of strength after the implementation of the above proposals.
iv) The agreed measure of naval strength should be the total capital ship tonnage (i.e. not numbers) and that the tonnage of auxiliary ships (such as cruisers) should be in the same proportions as the capital ships.

Of these points, the last was very much counter to the British position at the time. Hughes also made more specific proposals and suggested that the US would scrap fifteen capital ships then under construction, and also fifteen old pre-dreadnought battleships, and suggested that other nations, notably Britain and Japan, should take similar action. This would result in the US Navy retaining eighteen capital ships for a total of 501,000 tons), the Royal Navy twenty-two (604,000 tons) and Japan ten (300,000 tons). There were more detailed technical proposals including a 35,000 ton limit for individual capital ships, no new capital ships should be built in the next ten years and any existing ship could not be replaced until it was at least twenty years old. Finally, he proposed that the British total should fall to 500,000 tons as ships were replaced, the same as the United Sates, and that Japan should remain at 300,000 tons.

Needless to say, these far ranging proposals had a considerable impact and, after getting over their initial surprise the delegates welcomed them in principle. However, there were numerous points that needed clarification and compromise before a final treaty draft could be produced. Much of the discussion covered capital ships and resulted in some exceptions to the proposal to scrap all new construction arising from the Japanese desire to complete their *Mutsu* class battleships armed with 16in guns. This resulted in the US Navy being permitted to retain two *West Virginia* class ships, also armed with 16in guns and as Britain did not possess any 16in gun ships, she would be allowed to construct two new 35,000 ton battleships (*Nelson*, *Rodney*). A potential sticking point on the capital ship negotiations was the attitude of the French who were incensed at the suggestion that their capital ship tonnage should be only 175,000 tons and initially demanded 350,00 tons. However, they were eventually persuaded to accept this figure but as a consequence refused to countenance similar limitations in any other categories and also insisted on a large submarine fleet of 90,000 tons. Italy was only concerned to maintain parity with France and was happy to accept the lower limit.

There was also considerable discussion about aircraft carriers, a totally new class of warship, but it is appropriate at this point to look at proposals regarding cruisers. Britain had already stated that it could not agree on mere parity with the US or any other navy in respect of cruisers due to its massive trade protection commitments. However, as a compromise, the Admiralty agreed that if cruisers were to be restricted by tonnage then the Royal Navy would require 450,000 tons and that the US and Japan should be restricted to 300,000 and 250,000 tons respectively. Even if this was accepted, the Admiralty still expressed reservations as many of their cruisers would be in urgent need of replacement before the proposed replacement date (seventeen years) as they had been subjected to arduous war service. The fact that it was to prove virtually impossible to agree total tonnage limits led to proposals to limit cruisers on a qualitative basis (i.e. setting limits on their individual displacement and calibre of armament). This suggestion appears to have been originally proposed by the British delegation who proposed a 10,000 ton upper limit and guns of 8in maximum calibre. Although these figures resulted from a desire to retain the *Hawkins* class then under construction and whose characteristics approached these criteria, they were also very much in accord with American requirements for large cruisers to operate over the vast distances of the Pacific. The Japanese, with the *Furutaka* class already under development, were also content with the British proposal which was consequently adopted by all participants with little debate and unanimous agreement. Almost certainly, however, none of the delegates realised that they were firing the starting gun to a major naval construction race, an odd outcome to what was supposed to be a naval limitation treaty. Nor was it immediately realised that all the signatories would immediately take the 10,000 ton upper limit as the minimum size which they were prepared to build. Also, there was no quantitative limitation of cruiser numbers (or those of destroyers and submarines) and nations were free to build as many as they wished.

The Washington Conference was formally concluded on 6th February 1922 when the Treaty for the Limitation of Armament was signed in the closing plenary session. In fact, the conference actually produced no less than nine treaties as well as twelve resolutions, but the Limitation Treaty was the one which encapsulated all the major naval construction limitations. Apart from naval affairs, the conference had also discussed Far East and Pacific affairs although in some instances this had also involved elements of the naval discussions. A typical example was the Japanese position concerning the retention of the battleship *Mutsu* and their overall permitted tonnage. In order to accept the 300,000 ton overall limit Baron Kako, leader of the Japanese delegation, suggested that the other powers would need to agree to a maintenance of the existing position in respect of fortifying islands in the Pacific. Although there was, as might be expected, considerable discussion over the status of bases in the Pacific and Far East (including Singapore, the Philippines and Hawaii), the end result was favourable to the Japanese and the ramifications became all too plain in 1941. The negotiations which led to the resulting Four Power Pact continued well after the main Conference and it was not signed until 13th December 1922.

In the immediate aftermath of the Washington Conference the wholesale scrapping of the older battleships began while, in Britain, work began on the two new battleships. As far as cruisers were concerned, the Royal Navy immediately put in hand plans to lay down the first of the *County* class cruisers which were built to the 10,000 ton, 8in gun limits mandated by the treaty. It appears that virtually no consideration was given to the possibility that smaller and more lightly armed cruisers might better meet the Navy's requirements. Instead it was noted that the US Navy was adopting the 8in gun and Japan was also to build similar ships. A requirement for at least seventeen 10,000 ton heavy cruisers was foreseen (to be completed by 1928) but in the event only thirteen were built (including two for the Australian Navy) as well as the two smaller *York* class. This demand was driven by the need to match the then Japanese construction programme, but a long term plan identified that the Royal Navy needed a total of at least seventy cruisers of which up to forty-eight might be large 8in armed cruisers.

Across the Atlantic, the US Navy decided that they needed at least sixteen heavy cruisers (very close to the British requirement) with the first eight to be laid down in the 1924 fiscal year. However, Congress did not authorise construction of the cruisers until the end of the year and the first was not laid down until 1926. In contrast France and Italy were much quicker off the mark; France laying down two ships in 1922/23 and Italy followed with her first two in 1925. However, the first to enter the race, and the reason why Britain and America were quick to join in, was Japan who had laid down the two *Furutaka* class almost as soon as the ink was dry on the treaty in 1922, and followed up with two similar ships in 1924, while four 10,000 ton *Myoko* class were laid down in 1924-25. Thus, as a direct result of the Washington Conference designed to reduce naval armaments, all five signatories had embarked on major construction programmes of heavy cruisers. This was partly as a result of the strict limitations on the larger capital ships which all but precluded construction of these types. By the mid 1920s the US Navy was working steadily towards parity with the Royal Navy and in 1926 decided that they needed a total of no less than twenty-four heavy cruisers The General Board proposed that the 1928 programme should include no less than eight such ships, these being in addition to the eight which had been approved at the end of 1924 (although some of these had not then been started).

Geneva Conference 1927

While these building programmes were under way, the League of Nations began sponsoring a series of Disarmament Conferences, the first of which took place in 1926. Arising from discussion of naval matters at these meetings, President Coolidge of America proposed a new Naval Armament Limitations conference which was eventually held in Geneva in June and July, 1927. By far the most significant point of discussion by the delegates was the limitation of cruiser tonnage. The Americans proposed that cruisers, destroyers and submarines should be subject to overall tonnage limitations in the same proportion as already established for capital ships and suggested a figure of around 300,000 tons for the US and Royal Navies. Within this limit, there would be no restriction on the size or armament of individual ships. Again this ran entirely counter to British proposals which were against overall limitations and the Royal Navy was beginning to come round to the idea that smaller and more lightly armed cruisers might suit their requirements. They therefore put forward the idea that the 10,000 ton upper limit should be reduced and the construction of "Washington" type cruisers would cease. The Japanese, who by this time were well advanced in the construction of several large cruisers, were at that time happy to agree to an embargo on any further construction. Faced with British objections, the Americans stated that they would consider raising the total permitted tonnage to 400,000 tons although in their case 250,000 tons of the total allowable would be allocated to twenty-five of the current 10,000 ton type cruisers while the remainder, although smaller, would still be armed with 8in guns. Against this the Royal Navy had stated that it needed seventy cruisers of all types for a total tonnage of over 560,000 tons, well in excess of the American proposals. The negotiations dragged on throughout July and into

August but finally the Conference broke up without any agreement as the Americans were insistent on their need to build up to twenty-five heavy cruisers and would not consider abandoning them to build more lightly armed cruisers. However, the British could not see their way clear to reduce their tonnage requirements based on seventy cruisers of both types. During the conference, Anglo-Japanese relations had been relatively cordial and this may also have been a reason for American intransigence.

The First London Treaty 1930

With no cruiser limitations imposed, all five major powers continued to lay down and build the 10,000 ton ships. However, by the time the London Naval Conference was convened in January 1930 there was a considerable change in attitudes. In Britain a Labour government under Ramsey MacDonald was in power and with a strong programme for social reform they looked at a reduction in naval expenditure as one way of releasing the necessary finance as well as furthering the cause of world peace. This view was shared by President Hoover in America and the two leaders met in October 1929. As a result it was agreed that both sides would aim for parity in all classes of warships including cruisers. Here Hoover, against the advice of his naval staff, suggested that the US Navy would only complete eighteen heavy cruisers and the British fifteen although the latter would retain greater numbers overall and be permitted a higher total tonnage. A complex yardstick formula was worked out whereby the age and size of a particular cruiser would affect its nominal tonnage for treaty limitations. By this means the tonnage disparity between Britain and the United States could appear much less than it actually was. More significantly, MacDonald stated that the British requirement could be reduced to fifty cruisers but this appears to have been an entirely political idea and was not supported by the Naval Staff who insisted that seventy was the minimum. After returning home MacDonald subsequently had negotiations with representatives of Italy, France and Japan.

After these preliminary encounters, the London conference opened 23 January 1930. One of the most significant points debated was that the "holiday" in building capital ships agreed at the Washington Conference and due to expire in 1931 should be extended until 1936 (although France and Italy were permitted to proceed with replacement tonnage already allowed under the Washington Treaty). In respect of cruisers, after long and tortuous negotiations it was agreed that the US Navy would complete eighteen heavy cruisers, Britain fifteen and Japan twelve although the latter could replace her four small 8in cruisers (*Furutaka* and *Aoba* classes) with larger ships in 1943. In order to limit the British numbers to fifteen (which included two RAN vessels) it was announced that two *County* class cruisers already ordered (*Northumberland* and *Surrey*) would not be built and a projected third ship was also cancelled while a third *York* class cruiser projected in the 1929-30 building programme was also cancelled. The Japanese already had their twelve ships in service or under construction and so, in theory, they would build no more while the Americans would cease building Washington cruisers when their existing programme was completed. In terms of tonnage the British agreed that by 1936 their total heavy cruiser tonnage would reduce to 146,800 tons which meant that the four *Hawkins* class cruisers would have to be scrapped or demilitarised by then. In another step to reduce the size of cruisers, two distinct types were defined under the terms of the treaty, Type A armed with guns of more than 6.1in (155mm) calibre and Type B armed with guns of 6.1in (155mm) calibre or less. Total tonnage limits were then placed on each category as follows:

	Type A	Type B	Total
Britain	146,800 tons	192,200 tons	339,000 tons
US Navy	180,000 tons	143,500 tons	323,500 tons
Japan	108,400 tons	100,450 tons	208,850 tons

Within this tonnage, older vessels could be replaced by new construction after sixteen years if they had been laid down before 1920 but newer vessels could only be replaced when twenty years old.

However, the British delegation, consisting of politicians rather than naval staff, also agreed to restrict their new construction replacement of over age Class B cruisers to 91,000 tons. The effect of this pointless gesture was that by 1936 almost a third of its light cruiser tonnage would be over age. While the US Navy accepted no such restrictions, a timescale for the completion of their eighteen Type A cruisers was laid down. On the assumption that fifteen would have been completed by 1935, it was specified that the sixteenth would not be laid down before 1933 for completion in 1936 with the seventeenth and eighteenth then following at yearly intervals so that the last would not commission before 1938.

The above rules and limits concerning limitations on cruiser tonnage did not apply to France and Italy as both refused to accept any change to their rights under the Washington Treaty. In practice this made little difference as neither country had the resources to build up to the scale of the other three signatories and in fact their last heavy cruisers were laid down in 1930 (Italy) and 1931 (France). When Britain and Japan completed their existing construction programmes they would both have built up to their limits and, in theory, only the United Sates would continue construction until 1938. After that, no more heavy cruisers would be built except as replacements. As will be seen, things did not quite work out that way.

The Second London Conference 1935–36
In the early 1930s the League of Nations continued to work for further disarmament and a Conference was held in Geneva in 1932 although this did not result in any changes to the existing naval limitations despite suggestions that 8in cruisers should be abolished and cruisers generally limited to 7,000 tons displacement. The next major event was the Second London Naval Conference held in 1935. Again the deliberations were tortuous and marked by the fact that Japan withdrew from the conference, effectively giving notice that she no longer accepted any previously imposed limitations. Various issues were discussed including a British proposal to restrict the main armament of battleships to 14in calibre and, although this was adopted, it was with the proviso that it was accepted by all of the original Washington Treaty signatories. As Japan had withdrawn this did not occur and subsequently Britain was the only nation to build post Washington battleships with 14in guns. As far as cruisers were concerned, the main outcome was that no further Washington Treaty heavy cruisers would be built and future light cruisers would be restricted to 8,000 tons. Although the US Navy accepted the latter provison, it was only on condition that their existing 10,000 ton *Brooklyn* class could be completed and they reserved the right to resume the construction of heavy cruisers under certain circumstances. The Conference ended in March 1936 and was ratified by Britain, France and the United Sates at the end of that year. Italy subsequently agreed to accede to the Treaty in 1938 although this was a token gesture by that time. An interesting footnote to the Conference was that discussion took place in 1936 between Britain and the USSR with the objective of allowing the latter to accede to the treaty as a signatory. This never happened, although the Russians agreed to accept the 8,000 ton cruiser limitation and gave notice of their intention to build seven such vessels.

Anglo German Agreement 1935
Prior to the London Conference, Britain had also held bilateral discussions with Germany in May 1935. Concerned at the rise of German military power under Hitler, Britain sought to limit any challenge to her naval power as Germany, having thrown aside the Versailles Treaty was not bound by any of the other treaties. Admittedly, it would take decades for Germany to match the Royal Navy in terms of numbers if that was their intention but the British government was of the opinion that a negotiated agreement to limit the size of the German fleet was a worthwhile objective. The talks progressed smoothly and agreement was quickly reached to the effect that Germany could build up to 35% of the British tonnage in any category, except submarines where they were permitted up to 45% (and 100% if they considered it necessary). Although no timescale was laid down over which

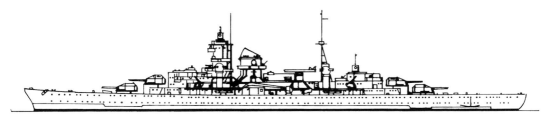

Admiral *Hipper, 1940. (Germany)*

these figures could be attained, the British expressed a hope that the rate of construction would be at a relatively modest pace. Implicit in the agreement was that Germany would accept the Washington and London Treaty restrictions on the size and armament of various warship types. Under the terms of the Anglo German agreement, the *Kriegsmarine* was entitled to build 51,380 tons of heavy cruisers (i.e. five 10,000 ton ships) and 67,270 tons of light cruisers. At the time of the signing of the agreement two heavy cruisers (*Admiral Hipper* and *Blücher*) had already been ordered in secret. Subsequently, their existence was revealed and a third (*Prinz Eugen*) was ordered in November 1935. Two more were subsequently ordered but these were to have been armed with 5.9in guns. However the Germans informed the British government at the end of 1938 that these would be upgraded to 8in cruisers in view of the proposed Russian construction of heavy cruisers. At the same time they formally gave notice of their intention to increase the submarine fleet to parity with the British. By that time Britain, the United Sates and France had agreed to increase the maximum allowable tonnage of battleships to 40,000 tons and they could be armed with 16in guns. Attempts were made to get the Germans to agree to these limitations but they refused to accept this. For all practical purpose the Anglo German agreement was now ineffective.

End of the Treaties
By the time the London Treaty had been ratified, the effective control of warship building by treaty limitations was almost at an end. At the end of 1936 Japan gave formal notice that she would withdraw from the process at the end of 1938 and would no longer accept the treaty limitations after that date. In 1937 the capital ship "holiday" introduced at the Washington Conference and extended at the first London Conference came to an end and in that year Britain, America, and Japan all laid down new battleships, while France and Italy had already done so. After 1938 Japan was able to increase her total of 8in heavy cruisers at a stroke, converting all four of the 10,000 ton *Mogami* class light cruisers by the simple expedient of removing the five triple 6in turrets from each ship and replacing them with five twin 8in mountings instead. Two more large cruisers (*Tone* and *Chikuma*), were converted while under construction so that by 1941 Japan had not twelve but eighteen heavy cruisers and had achieved parity with the US Navy. This of course was the very situation which the various treaties had sought to prevent. By 1940, with the war raging in Europe and the London and Washington Treaties in abeyance, the US Navy initiated the largest ever heavy cruiser programme with the laying down of the first of the *Baltimore* class of which some two dozen were planned.

Retrospective consideration of the treaties shows that they were not a total failure and did, for a while, keep naval construction within reasonable bounds. The emphasis on building to a given displacement gave the impetus to a variety of technical developments in order to reduce weight and these had an overall beneficial effect on warship design. In the field of cruisers, the Washington Treaty was inadvertently directly responsible for the building of the type of cruiser which forms the subject of this book. The later London Treaties also defined that characteristics of subsequent light cruiser design and construction. It is interesting to observe the trend of warship design under the influence of war conditions and freed from any treaty restrictions. In virtually every class of warship the trend was for increased size, cost, and complexity and this is no more clearly shown than by the heavy cruiser. While those at the outbreak of war were nominally within the 10,000 ton limit, the last US heavy cruiser to be built (completed after the war) had almost doubled in size. Thus at least the treaty restrictions had reduced the economic burdens on the relevant national budgets and so achieved one of the original objectives. However, in several instances the treaty limits were not wholly observed and this undoubtedly put those nations which had complied with the rules at some disadvantage when war came. This was particularly true of the Royal Navy which in the years between the wars steadily gave away the overwhelming advantage in numbers and technical expertise which it had held at the end of the First World War. In many cases this was as a result of altruistic gestures intended to set an example to other nations who mostly chose not to make any such reciprocal moves. Admitedly, political and economic forces would have led to a substantial reduction in the size of the Royal Navy, but this would have been quite enough without the self imposed restrictions (such as 14in guns for battleships) with which it also had to contend.

PART TWO

The Contestants

CHAPTER III

Britain and the Commonwealth

No sooner was the ink dry on the Washington Treaty than the Royal Navy began serious work on designs for a new cruiser. Having secured an upper limit of 10,000 tons and an 8in gun armament in order to retain the *Hawkins* class cruisers then under construction, it was quickly realised that other navies were already planning to build right up to those limits. There could, therefore, be no question of building anything smaller or more lightly armed even though such ships might better meet British requirements for trade protection cruisers. It was quickly established that the basic requirements of the new cruisers would be an armament of eight 8in guns in four twin turrets, a speed of 33 knots, and a hull with high freeboard in order to ensure good sea keeping qualities. Almost equally as quickly it was realised, and confirmed by the DNC in a report dated July 1923, that to incorporate all of these requirements in a ship displacing 10,000 tons would leave a very small margin for armour protection. A number of sketch designs were offered but in each case only around 820 tons of armour was incorporated and this was not enough to provide adequate protection to all the vital compartments including the machinery spaces and magazines.

HMS Berwick *was the first of the* County *class be completed, in July 1927. As originally designed the funnels were relatively short and this photo clearly shows how smoke could affect the bridge and fire control systems.* Maritime Photo Library

A wartime view of HMS Berwick *showing all aircraft handling facilities, including a hangar fitted in 1937–38, removed to make room for radar equipment and additional AA guns.* S. Goodman Collection

Inevitably, the various options to reduce weight were investigated but, with no concessions accepted in respect of the main armament, it was only by reducing installed power and machinery weight that any significant results could be obtained. By accepting a speed of only 31 knots, power requirements fell from the original 100,000 shp to 75,000 shp and the number of boilers required was reduced to eight. In total, these changes resulted in a saving of around 400 tons and although not all of this was utilised for improved protection, nevertheless, the final weight of armour rose to 1,025 tons. The original scheme had allowed only for protection of the magazines and shell rooms, with the machinery spaces being left unarmoured. This was a serious weakness which was addressed when the additional allowance became available, although the resulting scheme was rather complex. The fore and aft 8in magazines had 4in sides with 2.5in bulkheads and crowns, with an additional 0.5in plating above the crowns. In both magazines the armour tapered to only 1in around the shell rooms at the base of the turrets. The secondary magazine amidships had 3in sides and 1.5in bulkheads and crowns with supplementary thin plating in each case. A 1.375in armoured deck covered the machinery spaces including the boiler rooms at lower deck level. A side strake of 1in armour ran down to 18in below the light displacement waterline and this was closed off by bulkheads of similar thickness fore and aft. Above the lower deck was a mixture of 0.75in and 1in plating up to main deck level while the steering gear had a sloping 1.5in roof and 1in bulkheads. The main armament turrets received 2in faces and crowns, and 1.5in sides and rears while the barbettes were given only 1in protection. In theory, this scheme was expected to protect the magazines and machinery spaces from 8in shellfire striking at angles up to 40 degrees, although resistance to plunging fire was not so good and, as was

HMS Cumberland *was the first of the* Kent *class to undergo a major modernisation refit which included the addition of a large hangar and a fixed athwartships catapult. To keep weight within the treaty limitations, the quarterdeck was cut down by one deck aft of Y turret. HMS* Suffolk *was similarly altered.* Maritime Photo Library

to be demonstrated, it was virtually ineffective against bombing attacks. Finally, the hull incorporated a modest anti-torpedo bulge amidships.

As work progressed the Admiralty Engineer in Chief was able to redesign the machinery so that power output could rise to 80,000 shp without any increase in weight and this, together with an 8in reduction in beam and a 27in increase in length combined to raise speed to 31.5 knots. Also, the hull was generally built to robust standards and the high freeboard contributed to a high initial stability in the event of flooding so that these factors provided some degree of secondary protection.

The main armament was fixed at eight 8in guns in four twin turrets equally disposed fore and aft, although these were of a new design capable of elevating to 80 degrees for AA barrage fire. This feature, little used in practice, produced unnecessary complications which initially caused many problems and took many years to eradicate. The secondary armament was relatively light, consisting only of four single 4in guns although these were at least on high angle mountings. The light AA armament should have introduced the new quadruple 2 pdr pom-pom mounting, two of which were to be fitted. However, only single 2 pdrs were available at the time of building and four single guns were carried for some time until the multiple mountings later became available. Although this weapon was to prove not as effective as expected in the econd world War, it was nevertheless in advance of other navies and showed that the threat of air attack was being taken seriously. There were also two quadruple 0.5in machine guns mountings intended for AA defence. Finally, there were two quadruple 21in torpedo tubes in trainable mountings, carried on either beam abaft the funnels at upper deck level. The requirement to carry an aircraft for scouting and spotting purposes was well understood but in order to ensure that the ships were within the treaty tonnage limitations it was decided that one would not be embarked initially although provision for a trainable catapult abaft the funnels was included in the design.

Mention of the funnels highlights the distinctive recognition feature that readily distinguished these ships from any of the other treaty cruisers. For some reason it had been decided that the uptakes from the eight Admiralty three drum boilers should be trunked into three separate funnels. The fore and aft pair of boilers were linked to relatively slim funnels while the centre four uptakes were brought to a

HMS Cornwall *(shown here in 1938) and HMS* Berwick *also had the hangar fitted although in their case the quarterdeck was not cut down.* Maritime Photo Library

HMS Kent *at Plymouth in late 1941 following a refit. Type 279 radar is on the foremast and a Type 284 gunnery radar on the main director.* S. Goodman Collection

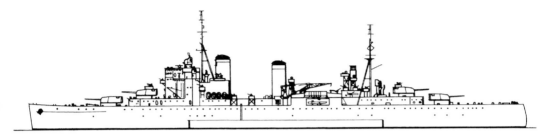

HMS London, *as reconstructed, 1943. (Great Britain)*

broader funnel between the other two. All three were raked aft, and together with the high freeboard lines of the hull the overall result was rather stately and old fashioned when compared to the rather dashing lines of the Italian and French ships and the solid workmanlike appearance of the American cruisers. In fact there was no reason why the uptakes should not have been led more conventionally to two funnels as was in fact done when HMS *London* (q.v.) was modernised. Of two similar vessels built for the Spanish Navy, one had two funnels and the other had the three combined into one massive and distinctive single funnel. Nevertheless, the Royal Navy retained the three funnelled layout in all three groups of their 10,000 ton heavy cruisers. The first *Kent* class to be completed, HMS *Berwick*, had relatively short funnels as originally designed but it was quickly found that smoke and fumes severely affected the 4in guns on the shelter deck and also the after control position so that they were raised by an additional 15 ft and this modification was incorporated in all subsequent Royal Navy vessels. The first Australian ship, HMAS *Australia* was also completed with short funnels but these were subsequently heightened by 18 ft and her sister, HMAS *Canberra*, was similarly modified before completion.

HMAS Canberra *running trials in 1928. This view emphasises the extra funnel height of the Australian ships.*
Maritime Photo Library

HMAS Australia *passing through the Canal in 1935.* US Navy Historical Branch

The original building programme was ambitious and the Royal Navy planned to build no less than seventeen 10,000 ton cruisers with eight to be laid down under the 1924 programme. The general election of that year returned the first Labour Government and they immediately slashed the programme by half, although they later relented to the extent that five ships were eventually approved for the 1924/25 programme and work began on all five in 1924. Known as the *Kent* class, they were all named after English counties and inevitably they and their successors were generically referred to as the *County* class even though the later ships differed in many respects. In addition to the five ships ordered for the Royal Navy, Australia ordered two identical ships which were laid down in 1925 under a scheme to strengthen the Commonwealth Navies.

By scrupulous consideration of all aspects of the design, the final displacement was calculated to be 9,942 tons, just within the treaty limit. This figure was made up as follows and the percentage of total displacement allocated to each item is also indicated.

Hull	5,570 tons	56.02%
Machinery	1,826 tons	18.36%
Protection	992 tons	9.98%
Armament	986 tons	9.92%
General Equipment	568 tons	5.72%

According to these figures there would be only a small margin of 58 tons available so it was something of a bonus that inclining trials on the completed ships showed them to be around 250 tons below the 10,000 ton limit. There were several reasons for this but it mostly related to savings in hull weight by the use of high-tensile steel milled to very tight tolerances and the first use of aluminium in a warship for the fabrication of non-supporting structures. Even the use of fir planking on the decks instead of the traditional teak played a small part in weight and the fact that the deck stanchions were hollow instead of solid showed the lengths to which they were required to go in order to keep down the weight. One item that ran against this trend was the weight of the main armament twin Mk.I mountings which, at 205 tons, were each 50 tons heavier than the original estimate, adding a total of 200 unwanted tons. Fortunately, savings in other departments contributed to the overall reduction.

The 250 available tons allowed for the fitting of a catapult and crane to permit operation of a single aircraft, and an increase of the 8in ammunition stowage. This had originally been reduced to 100 rounds per gun, but was now raised to 125 or 150 rounds. Provision for an additional motorboat for those vessels designated as flagships was also made. These alterations were incorporated in all five British ships by 1932 and, in addition, a much needed high angle control system for the 8in guns was also fitted. In the mid 1930s more extensive modifications were proposed that were intended to improve the armour protection, increase the 4in and light AA armament, and allow for the operation of more aircraft. A 4.5in armour belt was added abreast the machinery and magazine spaces, and similar protection was applied to the generator spaces and the vital transmitting station. The boiler room fans also received 4in armour protection. In all, this totalled an extra 288 tons. The secondary armament was increased to eight 4in guns (either singles or in four Mk.XIX twin mountings) and the originally planned two quadruple 2 pdr pom-pom mounts replaced the temporary single 2 pdrs. The aircraft arrangements were ambitious with the existing training catapult removed and replaced by a fixed athwartships catapult abaft the funnels while a large hanger capable of housing two aircraft (a third occupied the catapult) replaced the after control position. The total weight of all these changes was expected to be around 442 tons, but was partly offset by the removal of the original catapult and also the torpedo tubes. Nevertheless, the total displacement rose to around 10,300 tons although by this time it was unofficially accepted, at least by the signatories of the 1930 London Treaty, that heavy cruisers could exceed the 10,000 ton limit by around 300 tons as a result of modernisation and refits.

Although these changes were put in hand from 1935 onwards, their application differed from one vessel to another. *Cornwall* and *Berwick* were refitted more or less as planned with four twin 4in

HMS Suffolk, *1941. (Great Britain)*

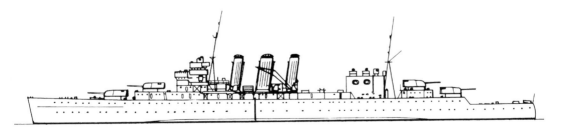

mountings replacing the four singles and also receiving two new eight-barrelled pom-poms instead of the former quadruple mountings. *Cumberland* and *Suffolk* were the next to be taken in hand but in the former only the after 4in guns were replaced with twin mountings while *Suffolk* retained four single 4in guns but these were in new shielded mountings. In order to reduce weight, these two ships had their quarterdeck cut down aft of Y turret, giving them a distinctive appearance. All the above four ships received the new hangar and catapult but the fifth ship, *Kent*, retained the training catapult, although this was of a new type capable of handling the Walrus amphibian that was now standard equipment for cruisers. She had previously received extra single 4in guns and no further additions were made, although she did later receive two eight-barrelled pom-poms.

Following the outbreak of war, subsequent modifications mostly centred on efforts to improve the effectiveness of the light AA armament. Initially, this took the form of additional 20mm guns as they became available and all the ships received ever more effective radar equipment. In fact *Berwick* had been one of the very first Royal Navy warships to be fitted with radar, receiving an experimental set as early as 1936. The capabilities of new radars, together with the ongoing need to increase the AA armament led to the removal of aircraft facilities and the hangar during 1942-43. Prior to that all five *Kent* class had standardised on a secondary armament of eight 4in guns in twin Mk.XIX mountings. The addition of radar equipment led to tripod masts replacing the tall pole masts in all ships by mid 1942.

As might be expected, all five ships saw arduous war service and, despite their elderly appearance, mostly gave a good account of themselves although *Cornwall* was overwhelmed and sunk off Ceylon by Japanese carrier-based aircraft in April 1942. The rest survived the war and all except *Cumberland* were laid up and scrapped in 1948/49. *Cumberland* herself soldiered on as a training and trials vessel and eventually had all her original armament removed so that new weapons, such as the automatic 3in and 6in mountings for the new post-war Tiger class cruisers, could be tested. She eventually decommissioned and was broken up in 1958 after a career spanning 30 years.

The two Australian vessels, HMAS *Australia* and *Canberra*, were completed in 1928 and initially were identical to the Royal Navy vessels except for their slightly higher funnels. Their subsequent updating lagged behind the British ships so that, for example, an aircraft and catapult was not fitted until the mid 1930s and a major refit of HMS *Australia* did not commence until 1938. She then received the additional armour to protect the machinery spaces and transmitting station. The 4in armament was increased to four twin Mk.XIX mountings carried lower down at upper-deck level instead of on the shelter deck. By reducing the clutter around the base of the funnels, this modification noticeably emphasised the taller funnels. The trainable catapult was removed and replaced by a fixed athwartships installation, and provision was made for two additional aircraft to be carried although no hangar was provided. Two multiple 0.5in machine-gun mountings were fitted but these were replaced in 1942 by 20mm guns and the light AA armament was subsequently increased substantially. *Australia* perhaps saw more action than any of her sister ships, initially in the North and South Atlantic, and later in the Pacific where she was involved in some of the major campaigns in conjunction with US forces. In 1944 the aircraft facilities were removed and tripod masts stepped to carry new radar and communications equipment. She was hit by kamikazes in October 1944 and again in January 1945. As a result of the damage sustained she underwent a major refit in the UK in which X turret was removed (this was actually lifted out at Sydney before proceeding to the UK) to make way for two additional eight barrelled pom-pom mountings and a twin 40mm Bofors gun. This refit was not completed until after the end of the war and the *Australia* ended her days as a training ship until being decommissioned and laid up in 1954. She was eventually towed back to the UK and broken up at Barrow in Furness in 1956.

HMAS *Canberra* underwent a refit from February 1941 to May 1942 along similar lines to *Australia* although the eight 4in guns remained in single mountings. Her subsequent career was sadly all too brief. Operating with the US Navy in support of the Guadalcanal landings, she was one of several allied cruisers sunk by Japanese forces in the Savo Island night action on 8/9 August 1942.

Post-war, HMS Devonshire *was retained as a cadet training ship. Much armament was removed although the forward 8in turret was retained. B turret was replaced by a deckhouse containing additional accommodation and classrooms.* Author's collection

HMS Devonshire *after refit in 1944.* S. Goodman Collection

Even while the *Kent* class ships were under construction, the Royal Navy pressed ahead with plans for more 10,000 ton cruisers in the 1925/26 programme when a further four ships of the *London* class were ordered (*London, Devonshire, Shropshire, Sussex*). Although superficially similar to the *Kents*, they introduced a number of improvements intended to overcome the perceived shortcomings of the earlier ships. These shortcomings included unsatisfactory protection, a speed less than staff requirements and a lack of aircraft. Various schemes were considered, all of which required compromises in one aspect or another but the final outcome was to delete the anti-torpedo bulge and slightly increase the length and reduce the beam so that speed rose to 32.25 knots with the same machinery installation. Armour protection remained substantially unaltered but some of the internal spaces were rearranged so that, for example, the transmitting station and principal low-power supply room were moved to a protected position formally occupied by the small arms and 2 pdr magazine. The latter was moved to a protected position amidships.

To reduce potential blast effects when the main armament was trained aft of the beam, the bridge was moved aft by 15 ft and this necessitated a similar rearrangement of the funnels. Armament was unchanged, comprising eight 8in in twin turrets and four 4in AA in single mountings. The torpedo armament of eight 21in tubes in two quadruple mountings was retained although, carried at upper deck level, some problems were experienced because of the height of the deck above the sea. Although the need for aircraft was recognised, it was not until 1931/32 that the four *London* class received their catapult and an aircraft and all four were without these facilities when completed in 1929. Almost immediately after completion, all four ships received an HACS atop the after control position.

By the mid 1930s there were proposals to substantially modernise these ships by replacing the machinery with lighter units of higher output, improving the protection and rebuilding the superstructure along the lines of the new *Southampton* class light cruisers then under construction. In the event, the pressing need for warships of all types brought about by the impending hostilities prevented all but HMS *London* being so modified. As it was, all four received an increase in the 4in secondary armament by the addition of four additional single mountings in 1936/37 as well as two quadruple 0.5in machine-gun mountings abreast the fore funnel. *Sussex* and *Shropshire* also received an additional HACS on the fore bridge. During the Second World War *Devonshire, Shropshire* and *Sussex* all had their 4in single guns replaced by four twin mountings (c.1941/42) and two or four eight-barrelled pom-poms were also fitted. As the war progressed 20mm guns in single and twin mountings were fitted in increasing numbers so that, for example, by 1945 HMS *Sussex* carried thirty-two 2pdrs and twenty-six 20mm guns. HMS *Shropshire* had been transferred to the RAN in 1943 following the loss of HMAS *Canberra* and the threat from kamikaze attacks resulted in her carrying fifteen 40mm Bofors instead of the lighter 20mm in *Sussex*. All ships received continuous upgrades in radar equipment and in 1945 HMS *Devonshire* was fitted with Type 293 SW, Type 281 AW, and Types 282 and 285 AR. In 1944, *Devonshire* and *Sussex* had X turret removed so that the light AA armament could be boosted by the addition of two quadruple 2pdr mountings and their High Angle (HA) directors. Aircraft facilities were also removed and these two ships also lost their torpedo tubes. Although as completed the *London* class ships were slightly under the treaty limits at around 9,750 tons, the various wartime additions took the standard displacement up to around 10,900 tons.

During the war *Sussex* was severely damaged by bomb attack while refitting at Glasgow in September 1940 and did not recommission until August 1942. Subsequently, she served in the Atlantic and Far East. She was retired in 1949 and scrapped the following year. As related, *Shropshire* was transferred to the RAN in 1943 and served with distinction and participated in the final surrender of Japan in September 1945. Thereafter, she remained with the RAN until 1949 when she was paid off and was subsequently scrapped in the UK in 1954/55. *Devonshire* had the longest active career; after wartime service in the Atlantic, Arctic and Indian oceans she was converted to a training ship in 1949 and served in that role until 1954 when she was sold and scrapped at the end of the year.

HMS London *in 1937. Note the Walrus seaplane carried on the catapult.* Wright and Logan Collection

Despite all the alterations and modifications, these ships retained the basic *County* class outline with their distinctive three funnelled silhouette. However, the lead ship of the class, HMS *London*, underwent a major modernisation refit between March 1939 and February 1941 in which her appearance was completely altered. The basic changes were along the lines of those applied to the *Kent* class and included the addition of a 4.5in armour belt abreast the machinery compartments and magazines and the upgrading of the 4in battery to four twin Mk.XIX mountings at shelter deck level. Externally, the most noticeable change was the trunking of the boiler uptakes into two well-spaced upright funnels. This made room for a new and enlarged bridge superstructure which incorporated twin hangars in its after section, similar to the *Fiji* class light cruisers then under construction. A fixed athwartships catapult was installed between the funnels and a total of three aircraft could be embarked. The area aft of the funnels, previously occupied by the training catapult, was converted to a boat deck and two cranes were sited abreast the after funnel where they could handle both aircraft and boats. Two eight barrelled pom-pom mountings were fitted atop the hangars on either side of the fore funnel and two quadruple 0.5in machine-gun mountings were fitted atop B turret, with another two on X turret. The eight 21in torpedo tubes were retained. Fire control arrangements were enhanced with a new Director Control Tower (DCT) above the bridge and the after 8in DCT fitted on a raised pedestal abaft the mainmast. Two HA.DCT were installed on either side of the bridge. Finally, tripod masts replaced the previous tall polemasts. During the rest of the war, *London* received several extra light AA guns and by 1945 was armed with sixteen 2pdr, four single 40mm and twenty 20mm (four twin and twelve single) guns.

A post-war view of HMS London *showing how the modernisation carried out in 1939–41 had completely transformed her appearance. Although the characteristic high freeboard hull was unaltered, the massive bridge structure and twin straight funnels gave the ship an impressive profile.* Wright and Logon Collection

When this modernisation was completed, HMS *London* presented an imposing appearance and, from a recognition point of view, could be confused with a *Fiji* class light cruiser at a distance, giving a potential tactical advantage. However, all was not well beneath the external façade. The *County* class hull had been carefully designed to treaty limits and consequently the structure was optimised for the original design and layout. The redistribution of weights arising from *London*'s modernisation produced a new set of stresses not envisaged by the designers. The result was that a weakness of the upper hull led to split seams and worked rivets, and there were cracks in the upper deck around the enlarged boiler uptakes. It was, therefore, necessary to reinforce the upper hull by strengthening the sheer strake and reinforcing frame brackets and parts of the hangar structures. This added 63 tons weight but also resulted in a transfer of the stress paths to the lower part of the hull so that leaks developed in the shell plating. This in turn resulted in flooding and fuel contamination during operations to cover Arctic convoys in 1942 and the ship had to be withdrawn from service in 1942/43 for a further refit in which external butt straps were fitted to the outer hull below the bilge keels. This effectively solved the problems and she subsequently joined the Eastern Fleet for the rest of the war. She saw further service in the Far East in the post-war period and was in action against Chinese Nationalist forces in support of HMS *Amethyst* in 1949 when that frigate made her famous dash to freedom after being bottled up in the Yangtse river for several months. Later that year she returned to the UK for decommissioning and was scrapped in 1950.

The four *London* class were built under the 1925/26 programme and the subsequent 1926/27 programme allowed for two more of the same class, although in the event various changes resulted in a separate sub group known as the *Norfolk* class. The two ships, *Norfolk* and *Dorsetshire*, were laid down in 1927 and completed in April and September 1930 respectively. The main change planned for these ships was the adoption of a new Mk.II twin 8in mounting which was expected to be some 20 tons lighter than the Mk.I mounting in all earlier *County* class ships. Unfortunately, this saving was not realised and, in fact, at 220 tons the Mk.II ended up heavier than the earlier version which weighed in at around 210 tons in the *London* class and slightly less in the *Kent* class. Consequently some planned improvements to the armour protection could not be incorporated and the only addition was to extend the 8 inch magazine protection (4in sides and 3in crowns) to the adjacent shell rooms. This took the total weight of armour to 1,060 tons representing an increase of 100 tons over the preceding *London* class. As completed the *Norfolk* class had a standard displacement of 10,060 tons. The 4in guns were moved forward to breast the funnels and the bridge and after superstructure were slightly lower but in almost every other respect they were identical to the *London* class and subsequent modifications echoed those incorporated in the other *County* class cruisers. Almost as soon as they were completed aircraft facilities were added together with an HACS. In 1933 *Norfolk* and *Dorsetshire* received two quadruple 0.5 machine-gun mountings carried on a raised platform between the first and second funnels. A more extensive refit in 1936/37 resulted in an additional HACS, the two now being carried either side of the bridge while the 4in battery was increased to four twin Mk.XIX mountings. An upgraded EIVH catapult was fitted and two quadruple 2 pdr mountings shipped abreast the after control position. As a result of these changes displacement crept up to 10,400 tons. *Dorsetshire* subsequently was little modified apart from the addition of some single 20mm guns before she was sunk by Japanese aircraft off Ceylon in April 1942, although prior to that she had a

HMS Shropshire *in 1937. This ship was transferred to the RAN in 1943 as a replacement for the Canberra, which was sunk at the Battle of Savo Island in August 1942.* Maritime Photo Library

A view of the midships section of HMS Norfolk *in 1932. The two portside single 4in guns on open HA mountings can be seen but note that no catapult is fitted at this stage.* Maritime Photo Library

HMS Norfolk *in June 1943. Aircraft facilities have been removed and a type 273 radar lantern has been fitted where the catapult was previously sited. Note the torpedo tubes trained to starboard.* S. Goodman Collection

moment of glory when her torpedoes finished off the German battleship *Bismarck* in May 1941. *Norfolk* received more extensive modifications and by September 1945 she had lost X turret so that the light AA armament comprised no less than six four-barrelled 2 pdr pom-poms, ten single 40mm Bofors, and twenty-two 20mm guns in twin mountings — a truly formidable volume of fire and an interesting comparison with the four single 2 pdrs originally fitted! The increase in armament was matched by an extensive radar outfit which now included Type 277 SW, Type 293 GW, Type 274 SR, and Type 282 AR. *Norfolk* spent most of the war with the Home Fleet based in Scapa Flow where she was damaged by air attack in March 1940. Subsequently she took part in the *Bismarck* action, being one of the ships that first sighted the battleship and was then involved in the entire action over a period of several days. While acting in support of Arctic convoys, she also took part in the action which resulted in the sinking of the battlecruiser *Scharnhorst* off North Cape on Boxing Day 1943. After the war she was flagship of the C in C East Indies until 1949 when she was laid up and then scrapped the following year.

As it turned out, HMS *Dorsetshire* was the last *County* class cruiser and the last 10,000 ton cruiser built for the Royal Navy. Two further *Norfolk* class (*Northumberland* and *Surrey*) had been planned, one in the 1927/28 programme and another for 1928/29 programme. However, the first was deferred for

Two modified County *class cruisers were built for the Spanish Navy and commissioned in 1936. Originally, they featured a single broad funnel but in 1952 the surviving vessel,* Canarias, *was rebuilt with a twin funnel layout as shown here. She was finally scrapped in 1978.* Maritime Photo Library

HMS York *in 1931. The noticeably tall bridge was intended to provide a view over an aircraft and catapult that was intended to be fitted atop B turret, although the catapult installation subsequently proved impracticable.*
Maritime Photo Library

twelve months and both were not ordered until March 1929. However, the 1929 general election returned a Labour government which immediately suspended them before construction had begun and then cancelled them in January 1930. This secision was partly as an economy measure but also as a political gesture for the forthcoming London Naval Conference. As ever, evolution would have determined that these ships would not have been exact repeats and, certainly, further improvements to the armour protection would have been incorporated. The long term building programme drawn up in 1925 under which the *County* class had been built envisaged a further vessel in the 1929/30 programme but this was never ordered, although by then some work had been done on a number of sketch designs, some of which featured an increased main armament of ten 8in guns in five twin mountings. In order to achieve this increased armament within the 10,000 ton limit, it would have been necessary to substantially reduce the weight allocated to armour protection and the Royal Navy was understandably not in favour of such a retrograde step. To provide space for fifth turret, the boiler uptakes were trunked into two funnels and a Q turret squeezed in between the aftermost funnel and the aircraft catapult. An alternative scheme still featured only two funnels, but the bridge was moved aft to make room for a third turret on the forecastle, the arrangement being very similar to the Japanese *Myoko* class then under construction. The American *Pensacola* class also carried ten 8in guns and these developments no doubt prompted the British designs. In the event, the Royal Navy fundamentally revised its approach to cruiser construction and no more 10,000 ton heavy cruisers were built and, as will be seen, the trend was to smaller and more lightly armed ships which could be built in greater numbers. Nevertheless, the Royal Navy had still completed an ambitious construction programme and by the end of 1930 had commissioned no less than eleven large heavy cruisers and another two had been built for the Royal Australian Navy. By comparison, at the same time the US Navy had only completed five, Japan eight (of which four were the much smaller *Furutaka* and *Aoba* classes), Italy two and France three.

While the construction of these ships was a fine achievement, it had always been accepted that with its commitment to worldwide trade protection the Royal Navy needed substantial numbers of cruisers and that the these need not be as large, or heavily armed, as the Counties. Already the 1925 plan had envisaged a smaller edition of the *County* class armed with only six 8in guns and this was known as a Class B cruiser (as opposed to the Class A 10,000 ton cruisers). It was intended to order one ship in the 1926/27 programme and two in each of the following three years. Financial and political constraints combined to reduce these numbers but the first ship, HMS *York* was ordered in 1927 and one of the ships in the 1927/28 programme, HMS *Exeter* was ordered the following year. However the second ship in that year's programme was cancelled as were both ships in the 1928/29 programme, while only one of the 1929/30 programme was authorised but this order was eventually transferred to a new type of 7,000 ton 6in gun armed cruiser.

Design work on the Class B cruiser began in 1925 on the basis that, although the main armament would be reduced to six 8in guns, the ships would otherwise retain all the other features and capabilities of the *County* class. The machinery installation was identical with four boilers in each of two boiler rooms connected to four Parsons geared turbines for a speed of 32.5 knots on an output of 80,000 shp. The boiler uptakes were trunked into a wide fore funnel and a much slimmer second funnel, both of which were raked aft. Machinery spaces were protected by a 3in armoured belt closed off by 1in bulkheads while the magazines received up to 4in side armour and 2.5in crowns. The transmitting station had 1in side armour, turret faces and crowns 2in, turret sides and rear 1.5in and the barbettes 1in. This was similar in scale to the *Kent* class. The Mk.II 8in mounting designed for these ships was intended to be lighter than its predecessor but, as already related, it actually turned out to be heavier. Nevertheless, weight saving in other departments resulted in a final standard displacement of 8,500 tons. Although the hull was similar in form to the *County* class, it was 50 feet shorter and the upper deck was cut down aft of the bridge. Initial secondary armament was four single 4in QF Mk.V guns carried at upper deck level abreast the trunked fore funnel, and two single 2 pdr guns. Triple 21in torpedo tubes were carried on either beam at main deck level abreast the funnels. The aircraft arrangements were, initially, rather unusual. It was intended that two aircraft would be carried, one conventionally on a catapult abaft the funnels but the other was intended to operate from a platform atop B turret. For this reason, a high bridge structure was necessary in order that its view forward was not obstructed. In the event, the B turret structure was not strong enough to support the aircraft and it was deleted although the distinctive high bridge was retained.

HMS *York* was laid down in May 1927 and completed in May 1930. In a subsequent refit the forecastle side plating was extended aft as far as the torpedo tubes and quadruple 0.5in machine gun mountings installed on the shelter deck abreast the bridge. During the war she received a few single 20mm guns. After taking part in the Norwegian campaign, she was transferred to the Mediterranean Fleet in mid 1940 and was lost during the battles which raged around Crete in the spring of 1941. In fact her demise was a drawn out affair: she was severely damaged on 26 March in a unique attack by Italian radio controlled explosive motor boats. The damage was so severe that she had to be beached at Suda Bay on Crete's northern coast. There, strenuous efforts were made to repair her but when almost completed she had to be abandoned in the face of the German capture of the island at the end of May. She was blown up and scuttled on 22 May, 1941.

The second Class B cruiser was HMS *Exeter* which was laid down in August 1928 and completed in July 1931. The interval between the laying down of the two ships allowed some changes to be

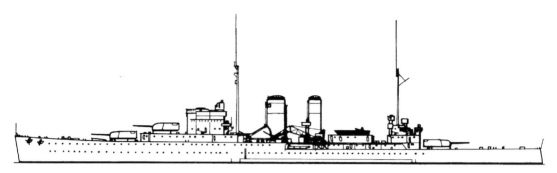

HMS Exeter, *1939. (Great Britain)*

made to the design so that *Exeter* was not an exact sister of the earlier ship. The most obvious external difference was the lower and more compact bridge superstructure made possible by the deletion of the aircraft facilities on B turret. This, in turn, meant that the funnels, which had been raked in *York* to keep exhaust gases away from the bridge, could now be straight, as were the two masts. The mainmast was moved forward so that it was stepped in the centre of the after superstructure instead of aft as in *York*. A less obvious difference was that armour protection to the magazines was improved and the DCT above the bridge was armoured, necessitating a one foot increase in beam to retain stability margins. Two aircraft were carried, mounted on fixed catapults that were angled to port and starboard abaft the after funnel, although these facilities were not fitted until after the ship had commissioned. Armament outfit was exactly the same as *York* except that the 8in guns were carried in Mk.II* mountings which could only elevate to 50 degrees so that their use for AA defence, always a dubious asset, was no longer required. As with *York*, her forecastle plating was extended further aft after completion but otherwise she was little altered when she went to war in 1939. On 13 December she was involved in the first major naval action of the war when she met the German pocket battleship *Graf Spee* off Montevideo. Seriously damaged in this engagement, *York* was able to make the Falkland Islands where temporary repairs were made to enable her to return to the UK where she arrived in February 1940. Repairs and refitting took another twelve months and she did not recommission until March 1941 when her appearance was altered as a result of many modifications. The bridge superstructure was enlarged and modernised and now carried a radar equipped HA.DCT abaft the main armament director, the latter fitted with Type 284 SR Radar. Short tripod masts carrying Type 279 AW radar replaced the original polemasts. The secondary armament was increased to eight 4in guns in Mk.XIX twin mountings disposed in projecting sponsons abreast the bridge and between the funnels. Light AA firepower was boosted by the addition of two four-barrelled 2 pdr pom-poms at the forward end of the after superstructure, while single 20mm guns were positioned atop B and X turrets. A new training catapult enabled a Walrus amphibian to be carried instead of the Seafox seaplanes.

Following her return to service, *Exeter* was dispatched to the Far East following the Japanese entry into the war and in February 1942 formed part of a scratch British, American and Dutch force deployed to protect the Dutch East Indies from a Japanese invasion. In the Battle of the Java Sea (26 February) she was damaged by an 8in shell and returned to Surabaya for repairs before attempting to escape to the west though the Sunda Straits, accompanied by two destroyers. Intercepted by Japanese cruisers, she was overwhelmed and sunk on 1st march.

Exeter and *York* were the last 8in gun cruisers built for the Royal Navy. By the time of the London Navy Treaty in 1930, it was accepted that British needs for large numbers of cruisers could best be met by smaller and more lightly armed cruisers. The result was the *Leander* class, similar in many respects to the *York* class but slightly smaller and armed with eight 6in guns. The trend continued with the even smaller *Arethusa* class with only six 6in guns and this line of development resulted in the *Dido* class with a dual purpose armament of 5.25in guns. However, developments abroad, particularly with the Japanese development of large 10,000 ton cruisers armed with no less than fifteen 6in guns led to a return to larger dimensions with the 9,000 ton *Southampton* class (twelve 6in guns) and the slightly smaller 8,500 ton Fiji class.

Nevertheless, there were tentative plans in 1940 for a new class of heavy cruisers to be armed with eight 8in guns and twelve 4in AA guns. Freed from the restraints of the various treaty restrictions, their standard displacement would have been around 18,750 tons with some 4,660 tons devoted to protection including a 4.5in main belt and a 2–3in armoured deck. Unofficially referred to as the *Admiral* class, up to four ships were planned, but the heavy workload already engaging all available shipyard capacity, coupled with priorities accorded to other projects meant that they were never ordered or laid down. Even if they had been, given the outcome of other cruiser orders placed after 1940 it is unlikely that they would have been completed in time to see any action.

CHAPTER IV

France

Prior to the outbreak of war in 1914, France had an ambitious naval construction programme underway but in the event very few of the planned ships were actually completed. This was partly due to the fact that much of France's heavy engineering industry was located in the north- east of the country which had been overrun by German advances, and also that subsequent war production was directed to bolstering the Army in the defence of the homeland. By 1918 the lack of new ships, coupled with the heavy wartime losses, meant that French naval strength was severely reduced and even the few ex-enemy ships passed over as reparations did little to restore the situation. Even so, the first post-war construction programme, authorised in 1922, only provided for three light cruisers (*Duguay Trouin* class) although 18 destroyers and 12 submarines made up the balance. It was

Dusquense in 1930. The seaplane is a pre-production Gourdou-Leseurre GL810 embarked for catapult trials.
Marius Bar

The heavy cruiser Tourville *at Toulon in 1945. The aircraft catapult has been removed while the mainmast and fore topmast have been struck. AW and SW radars are fitted and the light AA armament boosted by the addition of several 40mm and 20mm guns.* Marius Bar

not until the 1924 programme that two heavy cruisers were authorised and inevitably they had to be designed to the limits imposed by the Washington Treaty. The lead ship, *Dusquense*, was laid down at Brest in October 1924 while her sister ship, *Tourville*, was laid down at Lorient in March of the following year.

The French naval architects quickly realised, as had their counterparts in other countries, that the design of a 10,000 ton cruiser was going to require some painful compromises. An additional complication was that there was no existing 8 inch gun which could be utilised and one had to be designed from scratch, together with its twin mounting. The resulting ships were fast, comparatively well armed, but almost totally devoid of armour protection. What there was consisted of 30mm plating around a central citadel containing the machinery and magazines, together with similar protection to the turrets, conning tower and sections of the main deck. This was only splinter protection and would have been easily penetrated by shellfire, let alone aerial bombing. However, much of the weight saved was utilised by the machinery system comprising nine Guyot boilers supplying high pressure steam to Rateau-Bretange single reduction geared turbines driving four shafts. The machinery was arranged on the unit principle to minimise the effects of battle damage and this resulted in the boiler uptakes being grouped into two well-spaced raked funnels which contributed to the ship's handsome and balanced outline. Total output was 120,000 shp for a design speed of 33.75 knots, although this was handsomely exceeded under trial conditions when over 35 knots was recorded. Even in war trim at full load, these ships could maintain 30 knots at only half power, making them among the fastest of the treaty cruisers but compared to British, American and Japanese cruisers, their range of 4,500nm at 15 kts was much less.

Armament comprised eight 203mm/50cal M1924 guns mounted in four twin turrets evenly distributed fore and aft. Secondary armament was on the light side with eight single 75mm guns amidships together with eight 37mm M1925 semi-automatic AA guns in four twin mounts.

Suffren, *the lead ship of the* Suffren *class; as completed in 1930.* Marius Bar

Dupliex, *completed in 1932, differed from her sister ships in a number of respects. In particular, the secondary armament of eight 90mm guns was carried in twin mountings . Note the HACS abreast the fore funnel in this 1940 view.* Marius Bar

Additional AA defence was provided by 13.2mm machine guns. On the other hand, a heavy torpedo armament consisting of four triple mounts for 21.7in (550mm) torpedoes was installed port and starboard at maindeck level. Provision was made for two aircraft launched from a trainable catapult abaft the after funnel. Initially these were Gourdou-Leseurre GL-812 or GL832 floatplanes, but by 1939 these had been replaced by the Loire-Nieuport 130 flying boat, similar in size and specification to the British Walrus.

Both ships were completed in December 1928 and embarked on a typical cruiser career of training and exercising, interspersed with long cruises. Few alterations were made and it was appreciated that their light armour limited their usefulness in some situations. Consequently, there was a serious proposal in 1935 to convert them to light aircraft-carriers carrying up to 14 aircraft each. This idea was not pursued and instead two large purpose built carriers (*Joffre* class) were projected but these were never completed. As with most French warships, their early war career was brief and both were interned at Alexandria after the fall of France in June 1940, remaining there for almost exactly three years. Eventually they came over to the Allied cause and sailed to America in the summer of 1943 where they were extensively refitted. This work involved the removal of the aircraft and their handling facilities, the torpedoes removed, and the light AA armament considerably boosted by the addition of eight 40mm and sixteen 20mm guns. Their combat effectiveness was considerably enhanced by the addition of radar. *Dusquesne* assisted in the Normandy operations in 1944 while *Tourville* was based at Dakar and then Toulon, ending the war as a depot ship for escort vessels. Both saw service in support of post-war operations in Indo China before being laid up in 1947 and being used for various purposes including base and accommodation vessels. *Dusquense* was scrapped in 1955 but *Tourville* survived until 1963, making her one of the longest lived of the once numerous Washington Treaty cruisers.

The 1925 programme originally included two further 10,000 ton cruisers but in the event only one, *Suffren*, was authorised and a further single cruiser was then included in the construction programme for each of the next three years. These four ships were known as the *Suffren* class but as improvements were progressively incorporated in each, there were some significant variations within the class. The basic design to which the *Suffren* was constructed superficially resembled the earlier *Duquesne* class but the need for improved armour protection was realised and the only way this could be incorporated in the tonnage limitation was by reducing the installed power. Consequently, a three shaft layout was adopted, reducing power by 25% to 90,000 shp but even so designed speed was still 30 knots and *Colbert* (the second ship) actually reached over 33 knots in trial conditions. This reduction in weight allowed armour protection to be increased to 50mm on the main belt although this did not completely cover the machinery spaces and the remaining longitudinal bulkheads were only 25mm. There was 25mm over the upper and main decks, and 30mm to the turrets and control tower. In all this amounted to 951 tons or armour, more than double the 450 tons of protection in

Suffren, *1940. (France)*

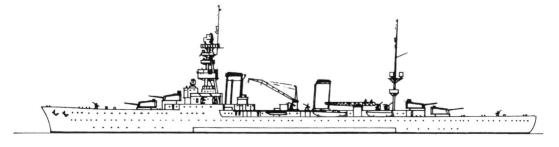

A 1941 photo of Foch *showing a modified tripod foremast. Note the nationality colours on B turret and the Loire 130 seaplane on the catapult.* Marius Bar

The heavy cruiser Algérie *was thought by many to be the best of the Washington Treaty cruisers. Certainly she had a handsome profile as illustrated in this 1937 photo.* Marius Bar

Duquesne and *Tourville*. While this represented a significant increase, it still gave only limited protection against 8in shellfire or aerial attack, and in the remaining ships there were further increases including 54-60mm on the main belt which completely covered the machinery spaces, although the standard 30mm hull plating was reduced to 20mm in partial compensation. Nevertheless, the weight of armour protection had now risen to 1,374 tons. Both *Suffren* and *Colbert* were equipped with auxilliary coal fired boilers and the coal bunkers on either beam provided additional protection for the after boiler room and engine rooms. In the third ship, *Foch*, the auxiliary boilers were removed and the space used for additional oil bunkerage, but the coal bunkers were retained for protection. In the fourth and final ship, *Dupliex*, main deck protection was increased to 30mm and this together with other improvements took the total to 1,553 tons. The rearrangement of the armour protection resulted in small variations in the hull dimensions of each of these ships.

There were other differences within these four cruisers. While all carried two aircraft catapults instead of the single installation in the *Duquesne* class, those aboard *Suffren* were abaft the funnels. In subsequent ships they were amidships between the funnels and a new pattern crane was fitted. This latter arrangement allowed three aircraft to be embarked instead of two. The secondary AA armament was successively improved from eight single 3in (75mm) guns in *Suffren* to eight single 3.5in (90mm) in *Colbert* and *Foch*, and finally eight 3.5in in four M1930 twin mountings in *Dupliex*. All four ships carried the standard 8in (203mm) M1924 gun as main armament.

All four were built at Brest Navy Yard and were laid down at approximately 12 month intervals between April 1926 and November 1929. *Suffren* was completed on 1st January 1930 and the final ship, *Dupliex*, on 20th July 1932. *Suffren* had an active career until she was interned at Alexandria in 1940 and from 1943 was employed in the Atlantic searching for commerce raiders. After some post-war service in the Far East, she was laid up at Toulon in 1947 and finally scrapped in 1974. *Colbert*, *Foch* and *Dupleix* were all scuttled at Toulon in November 1942 when German forces occupied Vichy France.

France's final 8in cruiser was the *Algérie*, a single ship authorised under the 1930 programme. Whereas improvements in the previous six Washington type cruisers resulted in successive changes to the same basic design, the *Algérie* was driven by a new requirement to be protected against 6in (155mm) shellfire from the new, fast Italian light cruisers then under construction. Together with the lessons learnt from the earlier ships, this led to an entirely new design and produced a ship which was considered by many to have to have been the best of the Washington Treaty cruisers, at least from a technical standpoint. The earlier cruisers were distinguished by a raised forecastle deck and twin well-spaced funnels resulting from the unit arrangement of the machinery. In the new ship the forecastle deck was removed to save weight and the unit machinery abandoned so that the boiler uptakes were trunked into a single squat funnel. This increased the area of upper deck available for armament and aircraft operations. Installed power was reduced to 84,000 shp to save weight and after some debate a four shaft layout was adopted. Improvements in superheated steam technology meant that only six boilers (instead of eight) were required and these were installed in three boiler rooms. Not only was the machinery installation much lighter (some 275 tons being saved) but it was much more compact so that the length of the main armour belt could be reduced.

The *Algérie* had 2035 tons of armour protection but its distribution was much more effective than the incremental ad hoc improvements made to the earlier ships. The main belt (110mm) was now carried externally and its height reduced to save weight. An armoured 80mm deck covered the magazines, shell rooms and machinery spaces while protection for the turrets faces and control tower was 100mm, with 70mm being applied to the turret sides and crowns. The main armament remained unchanged at eight M1924 8in (203mm) guns in twin turrets fore and aft, but the secondary armament featured new M1930 100mm/45 dual purpose semi automatic guns disposed in six M1930 twin mountings at shelter deck level. AA defence was supplement by four single M1925 37mm and sixteen

Algérie in 1942, shortly before she was scuttled at Toulon in November of that year. The mainmast has been moved to the searchlight tower in order to make space for additional superstructure carrying several light AA guns. Marius Bar

13.2mm machine guns in four quadruple mounts. Finally, there were six 21.7in (550mm) torpedo tubes in two triple mountings disposed on either beam at upper deck level.

Aircraft arrangements comprised a single catapult on the port side between the funnel and the searchlight platform. This carried a single GL-812 floatplane (later replaced by a Loire 130) while a second aircraft was then stowed on the starboard side of the shelter deck. These aircraft were handled by a large crane mounted in front of the searchlight tower while a smaller crane abaft the tower handled the substantial numbers of ship's boats that were carried as a result of the *Algérie*'s intended role as a force flagship. Laid down at Brest in 1931, she commissioned in September 1934 and was immediately designated as flagship of the 1st Light Division (encompassing most of the other heavy cruisers) and also of the 1st Squadron, France's main fleet in the Mediterranean. Despite her undoubted technical worth, her operational career was brief and, along with other ships of the Mediterranean Squadron, she was scuttled at Toulon in November 1942.

CHAPTER V

Germany

U nder the provisions of the Versailles Treaty, Germany was not permitted to build heavy cruisers, although in the 1920s construction of light cruisers proceeded. These were allowed as replacements for the obsolescent cruisers retained under the treaty but were restricted to 6,000 tons maximum standard displacement. However the *Deutschland* class *panzerschiffe* (armoured ship), of which the first was launched in 1931, were built as replacements for old pre-dreadnought battleships and were, therefore, much larger. Nominally built within the 10,000 ton limit set by the Versailles Treaty, they were armed with six 11in guns and were theoretically capable of outfitting any of the 10,000 tons 8in heavy cruisers built to the Washington limits. Although popularly known as "pocket battleships", they were more akin to cruisers in terms of their planned operational role against enemy maritime trade and, indeed, they were officially redesignated as heavy cruisers in 1943.

Nevertheless, Germany recognised the need for more conventional heavy cruisers and in the early 1930s secret planning began on a new design. Initially, there was some debate as to whether the main armament should comprise eight 8in (203mm) or twelve 5.9in (150mm) guns but ultimately, in order

Admiral Hipper, *as completed in 1939 with a straight stem and no funnel cap.* MPL

This model of the Admiral Hipper *clearly shows the ship's underwater lines with a bulged hull, and also the triple screw layout.* Author's collection

to keep pace with foreign construction, particularly the British and French ships, the 8in main armament was adopted. Similar debates concerned the propulsion system; the choice being between diesels (as in the very successful *panzerschiffe*) or steam turbines in which a German lead in high pressure steam turbines could be fully exploited. Another possibility would have been a mixed diesel and steam turbine system as already installed in the light cruisers. Ultimately the high pressure steam turbines were selected, although, in the light of the ship's most likely role as a commerce raider, this was not entirely logical.

The appearance of the *Deutschland* class had prompted France to lay down two 26,000 ton battlecruisers (*Strasbourg* and *Dunkerque*) and consequently the *Kriegsmarine* decided to lay down two similar vessels (*Scharnhorst* and *Gneisenaü*) in response. As a result of this the fourth *Deutschland* class already announced in the 1934 programme was dropped and the order transferred to the one of the new battlecruisers, although this change was not made public at the time. The officially announced programme for that year also included another light cruiser and some escort sloops. However, the accession of Hitler to power in 1933 led to a massive expansion of all service arms and the 1934 programme also included two heavy cruisers as well as sixteen destroyers and twenty-eight submarines although again these plans for extra ships were not made public at the time. It was not until 1935 that Hitler officially repudiated the Versailles Treaty and, as already related, the British Government therefore negotiated a separate Naval Treaty under which the German Navy was voluntarily limited to 45% of the Royal Navy total tonnage in any particular class of warship. Assuming the German ships were built to Washington Treaty limitations then, allowing for the two

The Blücher *was the first of Germany's major warships to be completed with the so called 'Atlantic' bow. This modification was subsequently extended to the* Admiral Hipper *which originally had a straight stem.* WZB

heavy cruisers already laid down, a further three could be ordered. In fact, the Germans were not actually bound by the Washington limits but kept up the pretence of working within them. The outcome was that a third heavy cruiser, *Prinz Eugen*, was ordered in 1935, and two more, *Seydlitz* and *Lutzow*, in 1936.

The first pair (*Hipper* and *Blücher*) were launched in 1937 and both were completed in 1939 before the outbreak of hostilities. The main armament of eight 8in guns was carried in twin turrets equally disposed fore and aft. The secondary battery consisted of no less than twelve 4.1in (105mm) AA guns carried in six twin mountings and controlled by four HA directors (initially only two in *Admiral Hipper*). Both the gun mountings and the directors were fully stabilised and the fire control system was one of the most advanced of its time. For close range AA fire twelve 37mm SKC/30 semi-automatic guns were carried in six twin mountings and a total of twelve 21in torpedo tubes was also shipped in four triple mounts. Abaft the single broad funnel was a hangar which could house two aircraft while a third could be carried on the catapult which was between the hangar and the mainmast.

Protection was on a generous scale with a main belt 80mm thick (tapering to 70mm) extending almost the whole length of the waterline while the hull was bulged to provide additional protection against torpedoes. The main deck was covered with 20–30mm armour and the upper deck was also armoured between 12 and 20mm. Barbettes were given 100mm protection while turrets and the conning tower received up to 150mm. Even the secondary turrets received 12mm armour plating. The total weight of armour was in the region of 2,000 tons, well in excess of most earlier Washington type cruisers.

As already noted, high pressure steam machinery was adopted and total installed power was 133,000 shp for a design speed of 32.5 knots. The steam plant consisted of twelve Lamont (*Hipper*) or Wagner (*Blücher*) boilers operating at 1,175/1,028 lb per square inch driving three shafts through Blohm und Voss or AG Weser geared turbines. This installation proved troublesome in service as it was difficult to maintain at high efficiency and in any case was uneconomic to run so that despite carrying 4,250 tons of oil fuel the range at a cruising speed of 18 knots was only around 6,500 miles. This placed severe limitations on possible deployments against enemy merchant shipping routes. In this context it is relevant to note that the diesel powered *Deutschland* class had a range of 10,000 miles.

As originally completed, *Admiral Hipper* featured a straight stem and little sheer to the forecastle. Although this was typical of German ships at the time, experience showed that it was less than ideal in a seaway, especially at speed. The second ship. *Blücher*, was therefore altered while building and completed with the so called Atlantic bow which featured a sharply raked stem and a noticeable sheer. A further modification was the addition of a raked smoke cowl atop the funnel. These changes were subsequently incorporated in the *Admiral Hipper* during 1939 and, although made for practical reasons, they undoubtedly much improved the appearance of these ships. Despite every pretence that these ships were within the 10,000 ton limit imposed by the Washington Treaty, they were in fact much in excess with a standard displacement of 14,250 tons. This was due to many factors including the extensive armour protection, the heavy secondary AA battery and the powerful machinery installed.

The *Admiral Hipper* had an active war including two forays into the Atlantic before being badly damaged in the Battle of the Barents Sea in December 1942. Thereafter, she spent much of her time laid up under repair and was eventually scuttled after being heavily bombed on 3 May 1945. On the other hand her sister ship, Blücher, had the shortest of careers and was sunk by Norwegian coastal defences on 9 April 1940. Consequently she was little modified before her loss but the *Admiral Hipper* saw a number of changes as the war progressed. A gunnery radar (FuMo 22) was fitted in January 1940, and a second set (FuMo 40) followed by 1942. The light AA armament was progressively increased until by 1944 it consisted of six single 40mm, four twin 37mm, and twenty eight 20mm (two quad, eight twin and four single) guns.

The third German heavy cruiser was the *Prinz Eugen* which commissioned in August 1940 and was similar to the two earlier ships, having the Atlantic bow and raked funnel cap from the start. An obvious external difference was the relocation of the catapult to a position atop the hangar and the handling cranes were moved forward to be abreast the funnel. These changes were made partly to improve the arcs of fire of the 4.1in AA guns. The same high pressure (1,012 lb/sq.in) steam plant was installed to drive Brown-Boveri geared turbines to give 32 knots on 132,000 shp. Again the light AA armament was steadily increased so that by the end of the war she carried eighteen 40mm and thirty-two 20mm guns (six quad and for twin mountings).

After working up in the Baltic, *Prinz Eugen* accompanied the *Bismarck* on her fatal sortie and was subsequently able to evade the British forces and reach Brest. From there she joined the battlecruisers *Scharnhorst* and *Gneisenaü* in forcing a passage of the English Channel in February 1942 and returning to Germany. She was torpedoed by the submarine *Trident* shortly afterwards and saw little action thereafter. When the European war ended on 8th May 1945, she was at Copenhagen where she was surrendered to allied forces and subsequently expended as a target in the Atomic bomb tests at Bikini Atol in 1946.

Her two sisters had chequered careers but were never completed. *Lützow* was sold while still under construction to Russia as part of the agreements contained in the German-Russian pact of August 1939. She was towed to Leningrad in April 1940 and at that time was complete up to the O1 deck superstructure with A and D turrets fitted, although only the forward turret carried the planned 8in guns. Subsequently, further work was carried out at the Ordzhonikidze yard with German assistance although when Operation Barbarossa (the German invasion of Russia) was launched in June 1941 she was still only 70% complete with four 8 in guns, mounted in A and D turrets, and some 37mm AA

Prinz Eugen *shortly after completion in August 1940.* WZB

guns. During the siege of Leningrad, which lasted until January 1944, she was in action against German forces on several occasions and at one point was severely damaged and settled in shallow water. She was later refloated and towed away for repairs before continuing in action. In the post-war period she remained on the active list until 1953 when she was laid up for use as a training and accommodation vessel before being scrapped in 1958.

The remaining cruiser, *Seydlitz*, was also likely to be transferred to Russia but this was stopped on the direct orders of Hitler. Construction proceeded at a very slow pace until June 1942 when it was halted, even though the ship was virtually complete. The following year it was decided to convert her to an aircraft carrier (as had been done successfully with several of the US Navy's 10,000 ton *Cleveland* class light cruisers) and to facilitate this her superstructure was stripped off but little work was done on building a flight deck. Following air raid damage she was abandoned and captured by the Russians towards the end of the war. Her subsequent fate is unclear but most accounts agree that the Russians did some further work on her which was never completed and she was eventually broken up.

CHAPTER VI

Italy

During the First World War Italy fought against Germany and, more particularly, its Austro Hungarian allies. The Italian Navy's operations were generally restricted to the Mediterranean Sea and consequently it had no particular requirement for warships of the cruiser type as needed by Britain and France with their extensive colonial dependencies. Nevertheless, it did not wish to be outclassed by other nations and when the French laid down their first heavy cruiser in 1924, Italy had little option but to compete if they wished to remain as a major naval power in the Mediterranean. The result was that two *Trento* class cruisers (*Trento* and *Trieste*) were laid down in 1925, the design conforming to the requirements of the Washington Treaty so that an armament of eight 8in guns, equally disposed fore and aft in twin turrets, was selected. Like most Italian warships, and following the French example, they were designed for speed. Although again lacking the radius of action of British and American cruisers, in the context of Mediterranean operations this was not a serious drawback. However, armour protection was more extensive than the

Trieste was the first Italian treaty cruiser to be completed, in 1928. MPL

A close up of the after section of Trieste *taken in 1933. Points of interest include the twin 3.9in mountings and the two circular apertures for the hull-mounted fixed 21in torpedo tubes.* Marius Bar

French contemporaries.It included a 50mm armoured deck stretching from the fore turret to the after magazines, and tapering further aft to 20mm horizontal and 30mm sloped sections covering the steering gear. A full height armoured 70mm main belt protected the magazines and machinery spaces which were closed off with transverse 40–60mm bulkheads fore and aft. Turret faces and the conning tower were protected by 100mm of armour with less on the turret sides and crowns. Altogether, 888 tons of protection was carried.

In order to achieve high speed, machinery delivering 150,000 shp was installed and comprised twelve Yarrow type boilers connected to Parsons SR geared turbines in a four shaft arrangement. Designed speed was 35 knots (35.6 being achieved in trials) but under wartime full-load conditions 31 knots was a more realistic speed. The machinery was configured in a unit system with two boiler rooms forward, then an engine room with the turbines for the outer shafts, followed by two further boiler rooms and the after engine room containing the turbines driving the inner shafts. This arrangement led to two widely spaced broad funnels which, together with the flush decked hull, gave the ships a balanced appearance. A prominent recognition feature was the heavy tripod foremast carrying the fire control equipment that towered over the forward superstructure.

Apart from the 8in main armament, a secondary battery consisting of sixteen 100mm/47 OTO 1924 dual purpose guns in eight twin mountings was disposed abreast the funnels at upper and shelter deck levels. The light AA armament consisted of four single Vickers 2pdr pom-poms. A total of eight 21in torpedo tubes were carried but, unusually, these were fitted in fixed twin mountings at main deck

Heavy cruiser Trento *at Taranto in 1936*. Maurizio Brescia collection

level, discharging through the hull sides. Another unusual feature of these ships was the arrangements for handling the three Piaggio P6 floatplanes which were housed in a hangar below the forecastle and launched from a fixed rail compressed air catapult installed in the bows. This unique arrangement saved the weight and complexity of a training catapult but the aircraft on its catapult would have obstructed the forward arcs of the main armament and render the aircraft susceptible to blast damage, even when firing on the beam.

Zara at anchor with awnings spread in 1933. Marius Bar

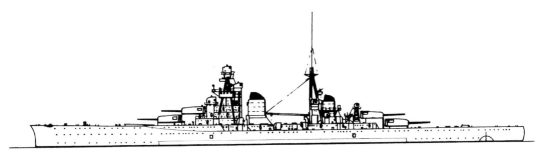

Zara, 1940 (Italy)

Both ships were laid down in 1925 with *Trieste* completing in December 1928 and *Trento* in April of the following year. Interestingly, they were named after towns which Italy had gained as a result of the defeat of Austro Hungary in 1918. In 1937 both had their close range AA guns augmented by eight 37mm/54 automatic guns in four twin mountings, although this entailed the removal of the two after 100mm mountings. Subsequently, the obsolescent Vickers 2 pdrs and some light 12.7mm machine guns were replaced by four twin 13.2mm machine guns. Both ships then received only minor modifications during the war and *Trento* was torpedoed and sunk by a British submarine on 15 June 1942. *Trieste* was also torpedoed, in November 1941, and was out of action for some time. She was eventually sunk by US bombers in April 1943.

Despite the various attempts to save weight, the greater armour protection and heavier secondary armament carried by these ships when compared to the French *Dusquense* resulted in their final

A view of the cruiser Trieste *as she sppeared at the end of 1940.* Maurizio

standard displacement being some 10,500 tons, 500 tons over the treaty limit. At the time however, it was claimed that these ships did actually conform despite reservations expressed by some observers.

At the time that the Trento class cruisers were under construction, the builders of the lead ship (OTO – Odero Terni Orlando) won a contract to build two heavy cruisers for the Argentinean Navy. The orders were placed in 1926 and the two ships, named *Almirante Brown* and *Venticinco de Mayo*, were laid down in October and November 1927. Both were completed in July 1931 and although the design was notionally based on that of the Trento class, the end products were entirely different ships. For a start the main armament comprised eight 7.5in guns in four twin turrets and standard displacement was only around 7,000 tons. Protection was limited and an installed power of 85,000 shp gave the ships a speed of 32 knots. Although Argentina was not a signatory of the Washington Treaty and the ships were well below the 10,000 ton limit, they were nevertheless the most powerful cruisers operated by any of the South American Navies. Both were laid up and scrapped in the early 1960s.

The bridge and fore funnel of the cruiser Fiume *as completed. Two of the eight twin 3.9in (100mm) gun mountings are visible and a single Vickers 40mm gun can be seen on the upper deck below the foreward director.* Marius Bar

Because the Italian Navy was inferior to that of France in terms of capital ships, it was envisaged that heavy cruisers would in some circumstances have to make up for this deficiency and at one time designs for a cruiser displacing around 15,000 tons were mooted. However, these were obviously well outside the treaty limits and consequently work on a new design was based on the existing *Trento* class but considerable efforts were made to increase armour protection. Four ships of the new *Zara* class were laid down, two in 1929, one in 1930 and another in 1931. Building times were relatively short for ships of this size and all were completed in 1931 apart from the last ship, *Pola* which was completed to a slightly revised design in December 1932.

If the main battery of eight 8in guns was to be retained then, as the French had found, some sacrifice in speed and machinery weight would have to be accepted. This was achieved by changing to a two shaft layout with a nominal output of 95,000 shp to achieve a design speed of 32 knots. On trials, with the machinery operating under forced conditions, output was raised to around 120,000 shp in some instances and speeds of up 35 knots were obtained. But these were run under entirely artificial conditions (*Zara* did not even have her main armament fitted at one stage) and in wartime the average speed was a much less spectacular 29 knots. The unit arrangement was retained resulting in two well spaced funnels although in *Pola* the forward superstructure was extended aft to merge with the fore funnel. All four ships carried the gunnery directors and searchlight platforms on a solid tripod foremast which entirely straddled the forward superstructure. As a further weight saving effort, the flush deck hull of the *Trento* was changed to a forecastle layout with the deck cut down from abreast the bridge. Also, the reduced machinery allowed the hull length to be shortened by almost 50 feet (14m). The torpedo armament was deleted and only two aircraft were carried, although the forecastle hangar and fixed bow catapult were retained.

The outcome of all this effort was a 28% reduction in hull weight and a 39% reduction in machinery weight and this allowed armour protection to be increased to around 1,500 tons, almost double that of the preceding *Trento* class. The main belt was now 150mm thick, tapering to 100mm on the lower edge and abutting the 70mm deck armour at its upper edge. Above this was a 20mm armoured deck for splinter protection while above the main belt was a strake of vertical 30mm protection extended to upper deck level. The main belt covered the magazines, were machinery spaces closed off by transverse bulkheads tapering vertically from 120mm thickness to 90 mm at the lower edges. The main armament barbettes were protected by 150mm of armour above deck and 140mm below, while the conning tower protection was also 150mm. Despite the efforts to reduce weight so that additional armour could be carried, the scale of the protection meant that standard tonnage rose to 11,471 tons (11,680 tonnes) and this was substantially in excess of the 10,000 treaty limit. *Zara*, the fourth ship was almost 200 tons heavier while all four displaced around 14,300 tons at full load including 2,400 tons of oil fuel.

Although carrying eight 8in guns, these were of a new pattern with a longer (53cal) barrel and higher muzzle velocity although, as before, the barrels in the twin mounting were close together,

Bolzano, *as completed 1933. (Italy)*

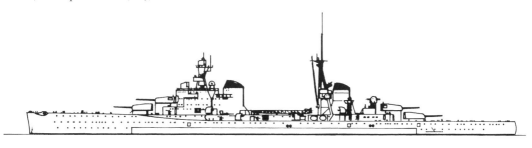

sharing a common cradle, and this affected accuracy when firing broadsides due to blast interference. The rest of the armament, comprising sixteen 3.9in (100mm) dual purpose guns in eight twin mountings and four 2 pdr pom-poms, was unchanged. By 1939 all four ships had lost two twin 3.9in mounts in order to fit four twin Breda 37mm AA mountings and two quadruple 13.2mm machine guns. After the outbreak of war all were fitted with two single 120mm/ 12 starshell guns abreast the bridge superstructure for target illumination at night. After the early loss of three of the class, the remaining ship (*Gorizia*) had these removed and eventually carried a total of twelve 37mm and fourteen 20mm AA guns, the 13.2mm machine guns having been removed.

With their heavy armour these were formidable cruisers and when the older Italian battleships were withdrawn from service in the 1930s for extensive modernisation, the *Zara* class ships were the most powerful operational ships in the fleet for some time. In fact *Zara* was flagship of the 1st Squadron from 1933 to 1937 but most of the ships were normally assigned to the 1st Cruiser squadron and took part in operations during the Spanish civil war and later, in 1939, the invasion of Albania. When war came in 1940 the whole class was in the forefront of naval actions including the inconclusive action off Calabria on 9 July 1940. Further actions followed but in March 1941 *Zara*, *Pola* and *Fiume* were sunk in the battle of Matapan leaving only *Gorizia* as the sole survivor of the class. She subsequently took part in the First and Second battles of Sirte (December 1941 and March 1942), and was also involved in actions against the various heavily escorted convoys attempting to supply the beleaguered garrison at Malta. She was eventually bombed by USAAF aircraft on 10 April 1943 and proceeded to La Spezia for repairs where she was captured by German forces on 9 September following the Italian surrender. Bizarrely, she was finally sunk by a combined British and Italian human torpedo attack on 26 June 1944.

The last of the Italian 8in treaty cruisers was the *Bolzano* which was ordered in 1929 and was completed in August 1933. She was an improved Trento design with the longer hull and four shaft machinery layout. Total power output was 150,000 shp for a design speed of 35 knots, although she carried only ten boilers of an improved design as against twelve in the *Trento* class. Electrical power was derived from steam driven turbo generators instead of the diesel generator sets in the earlier ship and this resulted in some volume savings in the machinery spaces. Despite these changes there was little saving in weight. On trials she achieved 36.81 kts although this was entirely artificial as the machinery was forced to give an extra 20,000 shp under conditions which could not be reproduced in service and no armament was fitted at the time. Such expedients were common practice at the time as great store was set by high speed, both from a prestige and contractural point of view. In service, *Bolzano*'s best speed was around 34 knots.

The main armament of eight 8in guns was retained but these were the improved 53cal model in the M1927 turrets as fitted to the *Zara* class. The secondary armament remained unchanged at eight twin 3.9in mountings although initially it had been planned to fit only four as a weight saving measure. A fixed hull-mounted torpedo armament was retained but a major change was the arrangement for handling the aircraft. A training catapult was placed between the funnels and up to three aircraft could be embarked: one on the catapult and the other two stowed on deck as there was no hangar. In the event no more than two were ever carried. The space previously occupied by the bow hangar was utilised for accommodation. As in *Pola*, the bridge superstructure was extended aft to blend in with the fore funnel, again providing more accommodation space, but having an incidental effect of giving these ships a very modern streamlined appearance.

Protection was similar to the *Trento* class with detail differences. A main belt of 70mm was complemented by a 50mm main deck running through from A to Y turret with a further 20mm deck with 30mm oblique surfaces covering over the steering gear and propeller shafts. Main armament barbettes carried 70mm armour, tapering to 60mm below decks while the turrets faces were 100mm with 80mm applied to the crown and sides. The conning tower protection was 100mm (50mm on the roof) and the main armament director was protected by 80mm and 60mm on the sides and roof respectively. Total weight of the armour was around 940 tons, slightly more than the *Trento* class, and representing 8.5% of the *Bolzano*'s standard displacement of 10,825. Once again this ship was over the treaty limit although not to the extent of the *Zara* class and this was despite a number of measures intended to keep the weight down. These included reduced ammunition stocks for the 8in guns (80 rounds per gun instead of 100) and 3.9in guns, and carrying two anchors instead of three, together with reduced cable lengths. There were corresponding reductions in stores including lubricating oils and fresh water. Fuel oil bunkerage totalled 2,240 tons, slightly more than the *Trento* class giving a range of 4,430nm at 16 knots.

Wartime modifications were limited to the removal of two 3.9in mountings so that two 37mm twin AA mountings could be fitted. The bridge structure was altered in 1939 to allow better positioning of the AA fire control equipment while in 1942 four 20mm AA replaced the ineffective quadruple 13.2mm machine gun mountings originally fitted. By the outbreak of war she formed part of the 3rd Cruiser Division together with her half sisters, *Trento* and *Trieste*. After taking part in several operations she was torpedoed by a submarine (HMS/M *Triumph*) off the Straits of Messina on 25 August, 1941 and was out of action for several months. Almost a year later she was torpedoed again (HMS/M *Unbroken*), but this time the damage was much more serious and she had to be beached to prevent her sinking. Eventually she was refloated and towed to Naples and subsequently to La Spezia but full repairs were never completed. She was captured by German forces after the Italian armistice and was sunk in the same Anglo-Italian operation which also sank the *Gorizia* on 21 June 1944.

During the Spanish Civil War, the heavy cruiser *Gorizia* was one of several Italian vessels assisting the movement of Nationalist troops from North Africa to Spain. While anchored at Tangier in August 1936, she suffered serious damage in a petrol explosion and was towed to Gibraltar for emergency repairs. Whilst in dock, British observers were able to take detailed measurements from which it was confirmed that her displacement was, as suspected, well in excess of the 10,000 ton treaty limit. Although a formal protest was considered, no action was taken as the government was still trying to encourage Italy to accede to the 1936 London Naval Treaty and did not want a straining of diplomatic relations. In the event Italy did not sign the Treaty but the matter was not pursued.

CHAPTER VII

Japan

There is no doubt that without the Washington treaties the world's navies would have embarked on a leapfrogging naval arms race in the aftermath of the First World War and the Japanese entry into building heavy cruisers clearly illustrates this point. Having noted the trend to larger cruisers such as the British *Hawkins* class and the American *Omaha* class they decided to go one better and laid down two cruisers (*Furutaka* and *Kako*) in late 1922. Armed with six 7.9in (200mm) guns and designed for high speed, they were intended as counters to the British and American ships which they outgunned. Strictly speaking, they were not treaty cruisers as all the design work had been completed before the treaty was signed. However, once it came into force they were subject to its provisions and when the later London Naval Treaty came into effect in 1930, they were counted within the total tonnage of Class A heavy cruisers.

Even before the 10,000 ton limitation was brought in by the treaty, the Japanese naval architects had been conscious of a general need to reduce displacement and had introduced a novel method of construction with the 3,000 ton light cruiser Yubari which was completed in 1923. In a conventional warship, the armour protection was additional to the ships basic structure and was attached directly to the normal plating. The naval architect Vice-Admiral Yuzuru Hiraga came up with a scheme whereby the armour protection was an integral part of the ship's structure. While the idea obviously had some technical merit, in practice it achieved little as the new heavy cruisers came out considerably over their intended displacement of around 7,000 tons, the final figure being nearer 8,000 tons. Even so, they were smaller than the subsequent treaty cruisers and more comparable with the British *York* class laid down almost a decade later. Previous Japanese cruisers were much smaller (c. 5,000 tons) and were armed with 5.5in guns. As such they were very similar to contemporary British and German light cruisers and were intended to act as leaders of destroyer flotillas as well as carrying out traditional scouting tasks. The new *Furutaka* class were intended as the first of four ships which, by virtue of their heavy armament and a greater degree of protection, could act as an homogenous division independent of the destroyer flotillas.

As completed they were armed with six single 7.9in (200mm) guns mounted on the centre line with three forward of the bridge and three right aft. In each case the middle gun was raised to superfire over the other two. The guns were protected by weatherproof gunhouses which were not true turrets. The secondary armament consisted of four single 80mm guns, two on either beam amidships, and a couple of 7.7mm machine guns. Twelve 24in torpedo tubes were fitted, but were fixed installations with three pairs on each side at main deck level to avoid problems associated with launching torpedoes from the deck of high freeboard ships. At the time of the ships' construction, no suitable catapult was available so a flying-off platform was fitted atop X turret in front of the mainmast and a hangar was sited abaft the funnels. This was not a very satisfactory arrangement and in practice the aircraft were lifted into the water by crane for a conventional take-off from the sea.

Machinery was a four shaft steam turbine layout fed by fourteen Kampon boilers paired in seven boiler rooms. The uptakes were led to two raked funnels, the fore funnel being much broader than the other. Power output was 102,000 shp which gave a maximum speed in the region of 34 knots. The machinery spaces were protected by a 3in armoured belt which extended some 7 feet above the

Furutaka was the first of the Japanese heavy cruisers to be completed, although her design pre-dated the Washington treaty. This photograph shows her original armament of six 7.9in guns in single mountings. Maritime Photo Library

waterline and 6 feet below. Originally it should have been almost 11 feet above and only 2 feet below but these proportions altered due to the ships being heavier than originally designed. Above the belt the 1in hull side plating was reinforced by 0.75in armoured steel. The main armoured deck was 1.375in and the upper totalled almost 2in in two layers. Magazines had 2in sides while the gunhouses received 1in on the front and 0.75in on the crowns.

A characteristic feature of these ships, and subsequent Japanese heavy cruisers, was the unusual run of the sheerline in a classic example of form following function. The forecastle had a marked sheer to improve seaworthiness while the midships section was straight where the machinery spaces were enclosed. Right aft the sheer dipped down towards the stern, as a weight saving measure that also reduced the freeboard so that, at high speeds, the quarterdeck was almost awash.

Both ships were completed in 1926 but were continually modified between then and the outbreak of war. In 1927 the funnels were heightened and the design of the caps altered to reduce smoke effects around the bridge. The flying-off platform was removed in 1930 and both ships underwent a major refit in the early 1930s when a catapult was at last fitted between the hangar and X turret although only one aircraft was carried. The secondary armament was upgraded to four single 4.7in guns in HA mounts. A few years later, in 1936 and 1937, a more extensive refit saw the main armament altered to six 7.9in guns in three twin turrets while the light AA armament was reinforced by four twin 25mm and two twin 13mm mountings. The fixed torpedo tubes were removed and replaced by two quadruple trainable mounts on the upper deck abreast the catapult. A more powerful catapult was fitted and aircraft complement increased to two. The machinery was overhauled and ten new oil burning boilers replaced the previous fourteen, some of which were mixed fuel so that they could also burn coal if required. These changes added extra weight and to cater for this, overall beam was increased by 3 feet by the addition of wider bulges. This also marginally improved stability which, like most Japanese warships of this period, was not very satisfactory.

Kinugasa *(shown here) and* Aoba *were designed from the outset to carry six 7.9in guns in three twin turrets.*
Maritime Photo Library

At the outbreak of war *Furutaka* and *Kako* formed part of the 6th Cruiser Squadron. Participating in the Solomons campaign, *Kako* was torpedoed by a US submarine on 10 August 1942 in the aftermath of the Battle of Savo Island and *Furutaka* was lost at the Battle of Cape Esperance on 11 October, 1942.

Back in 1922, the construction programme for that year included two more *Furutaka* class but the design of these was altered to include three twin 7.9in mountings. Provision was made for a catapult which, in this case, was sited between the mainmast and the after turret, providing a recognition feature to distinguish these two from their earlier sisters (although the catapult was not actually installed until after the ships had entered service). The secondary armament was also standardised as four 4.7in guns in single mountings. The two ships, *Aoba* and *Kinugasa*, were laid down at the start of 1924 and were both completed in September 1927. Apart from the differences outlined above, they were otherwise very similar to the earlier *Furutaka* class and subsequent modifications were along similar lines, although the machinery overhaul in 1937/38 only included upgrading the mixed fuel boilers to oil fired and the others were not replaced. However, one significant change was to the main armament in which the 7.9in (200mm) guns were replaced by true 8in (203mm) guns as fitted to all subsequent Japanese heavy cruisers. The quadruple-torpedo tubes were mounted abreast the main mast on the upper deck.

Aoba, 1945. (Japan)

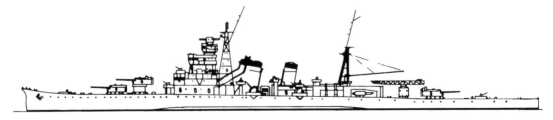

The *Furutaka* and *Aoba* class ships together formed the 6th Cruiser Squadron at the outbreak of war and this unit was heavily engaged in the fighting around the Solomon Islands, although with the loss of *Furutaka* and *Kako* it was disbanded in November 1942. *Kinugasa* was lost to an air attack by aircraft from the USS *Enterprise* on 14 November. *Aoba* had previously been severely mauled in the Battle of Cape Esperance and was out of action until the end of 1943. At that stage her light AA armament was increased to fifteen 25mm guns and an AW radar set was installed. Her machinery was not fully operational so that her maximum speed was reduced to 28 knots. In October 1944 she was torpedoed by a US submarine and returned to Japan for repairs which were never completed. During the closing stages of the war she was repeatedly bombed by US naval aircraft and finally destroyed on 28 July, 1945.

The advent of the Washington Treaty in 1922 effectively halted further Japanese development of the smaller 8in cruisers. Consequently a staff requirement was drawn up for a new design which, initially, was very similar to foreign contemporary designs with eight 8in guns, a displacement of 10,000 tons, a range of 10,000 miles and a speed of 35 knots. However, the basic design was quickly expanded to carry ten 8in guns in five twin mountings, three forward and two aft, a heavy AA armament of six 4.7in guns on HA mountings, and twelve torpedo tubes in four fixed hull-mounted triple installations. Like their US counterparts, the Imperial Japanese Navy was an enthusiastic supporter of the 10,000 ton heavy cruisers but there was an additional factor that encouraged this attitude. Under the terms of the Washington Treaty, Japan's total tonnage of capital ships (i.e. those greater than 10,000 tons) was pegged at three-fifths of the American or British tonnage. However, as there was, initially, no restriction on the numbers of ships below the 10,000 ton limit, Japan saw their construction as a way of offsetting the US Navy's superiority in other categories.

The new *Myoko* class of four ships was ordered in 1923 and the first two were laid down the following year, while all four were commissioned by August 1929. Many features of the earlier small cruisers were incorporated including the integral armour plating and the undulating hull form. The main belt was increased to 4in and covered both machinery spaces and magazines. Internally, the belt was sloped outwards at an angle of 12 degrees and the hull was bulged over a length of 305 feet to provide additional protection against torpedoes. The main belt was closed by 3 or 4in bulkheads. The main armoured deck was 1.5in and an additional 1.5in at lower deck level covered the magazines. Compared to US cruisers the protection to the main armament was lighter with 3in to the barbettes and only 1in to the turrets. The machinery installation was based on that produced for the *Amagi* class battlecruisers whose construction was cancelled under the treaty arrangements and comprised twelve oil fired boilers in eight boiler rooms forward, coupled to a four-shaft turbine installation located abaft the boiler spaces. Power output was 130,000 shp for a design speed of 35.5 kts and the long slim hull with a 10:1 length/beam ratio assisted in achieving these speeds, at least at light displacement.

Initially, the main armament consisted of ten 7.9in/50 cal guns but these were changed to 8in/50cal in all four ships by the end of 1934. The secondary armament of six single 4.7in guns was replaced by a battery of eight 5in guns in twin HA mountings with a new fire control system in. The original fixed torpedo tubes were replaced by no less than four quadruple training mounts on the upper deck at the same time. The aircraft arrangements were also improved and the single catapult on the starboard side was supplemented by a second one and aircraft complement increased from two to four, although three was a normal complement. As completed, the *Myoko* class had suffered from stability problems and the additional 680 tons added in the above alterations necessitated increasing the size of the bulges by extending their shell plating to the top of the side armour. As completed these ships were well over the displacement limit at around 11,000 tons and the changes incorporated in the 1934/35 refits took the standard displacement to around 12,000 tons. Up to the time of Pearl Harbor in 1941 further changes included augmentation of the light AA armament, although, even then, it only consisted of four twin 25mm and two twin 13mm machine gun mountings. More powerful catapults were fitted and the hull strengthened as result of experience

Ashigara *dressed overall at the Coronation Review held at Spithead in 1937.* Maritime Photo Library

with typhoons and hurricanes in 1934 when several ships were damaged and a small destroyer was lost. This experience had highlighted the limited stability of many Japanese warships and the slim lines of the *Myoko* class did not help.

During the war the usual increase in light AA armament occurred so that, finally, up to forty-eight 25mm were carried in triple, double and single mountings. Radar equipment was fitted but in general the IJN lagged a long way behind Allied developments in this field (which makes the post-war Japanese resurgence in electronic equipment all the more remarkable!). By 1941 the four *Myoko* class cruisers formed the 5th Cruiser squadron and were subsequently active in the attacks on the Dutch East Indies, and *Nachi* and *Haguro* took part in the defeat of the joint Australian, British, dutch and American (ABDA) force in the Battle of the Java Sea. Thereafter, they ranged far and wide in the Pacific and Indian Oceans and led something a charmed life, and it was not until November 1944 that *Nachi* was sunk by aircraft from the carrier USS *Lexington*, while *Myoko* and *Haguro* were damaged in the fighting around Leyte Gulf in October of that year. *Haguro* was subsequently sunk in a brilliant night attack by British destroyers off Penang in May 1945 and *Ashigara* was torpedoed by the submarine HMS *Trenchant* in the following month. The sole survivor at the end of the war was *Myoko* which, already heavily damaged by a torpedo from an American submarine in December 1944, was surrendered at Singapore and subsequently scuttled in July 1946.

By 1927 all the major Navies were building 10,000 ton heavy cruisers and the Imperial Japanese Navy was determined not to be left behind, particularly as the US Navy was slowly getting into the race. Accordingly, four new cruisers were authorised in March of that year and the first pair, *Takao* and *Atagi*, were laid down a month later. Another two, *Chokai* and *Maya*, were laid down in March and December 1928. The delay in the latter being due to the fact that the contracted yard had gone bankrupt and government intervention was necessary before the ship could be laid down. In general, these ships followed the basic layout of the preceding *Myoko* class but there was a significant change to the main armament. This remained at ten guns in five twin turrets but, from the start the 8in/50cal weapon was adopted and these were to be carried in Model E turrets capable of 70 degrees elevation to allow them to operate in the AA role. This development was obviously influenced by the British *Kent* class which had pioneered the concept of heavy calibre AA fire. However, as both navies found, the technical problems of heavy calibre AA outweighed any possible tactical benefits and consequently only *Maya* was so equipped. The remaining three ships carried their guns in Model E2 turrets in which the maximum elevation was reduced to 55 degrees. Since the 8in guns were intended to provide the main AA defence, the secondary armament was relatively light, consisting only of four single 4.7in guns in HA mountings backed up by a couple of Vickers 2pdrs and two light machine guns. Only eight 24in torpedo tubes, in four twin trainable mountings at upper deck level, were fitted but sixteen spare torpedoes were carried and a mechanical system ensured rapid reloads in action.

These ships had a particularly imposing appearance due in part to the massive and distinctive bridge structure which towered up to seven deck levels. This resulted from the fact that all ships of the class were designed to act as flagships, a role they often undertook during the Second World War. A broad raked fore funnel and smaller upright second funnel were immediately abaft the bridge, and the after superstructure and mainmast were immediately aft of the funnels so that from a distance the superstructures and funnels merged into an unmistakable mass with the turrets spaced fore and aft. The after superstructure incorporated a large hangar which opened onto an aircraft handling deck with catapults port and starboard. Three aircraft were normally carried. Machinery was the same as that in the *Myoko* class and design speed was 35.5 knots.

Armour protection was similar in principle to the earlier ships with the armour plating forming an integral part of the ship's structure. The internal inclined main belts was 5in at its thickest point but tapered downwards to 3in and 1.5in at its lower edge. The hull was bulged for anti-torpedo protection and a 1.75in armoured deck covered the magazines. Additional protection was provided to the conning tower and the total weight of protection was 2,368 tons. The design predictions for the standard displacement were wildly optimistic at 9,850 tons and the final figure was in the region of 11,400 tons although the fiction was maintained that these ships were actually within the treaty limit. All four *Takao* class cruisers were completed by mid-1928 and entered service as the 4th Cruiser squadron so that at that time the IJN had twelve heavy cruisers compared to the Royal Navy which had five (plus two for the RAN) and the US Navy which had none actually in service. These figures clearly indicate the priority that Japan accorded to the construction of this type of warship.

Initially, the *Takao* class were little altered, although some topweight was removed in 1936 to improve stability and the 2pdr AA guns were replaced by multiple 13.2mm machine guns.

Chokai, 1938. (Japan)

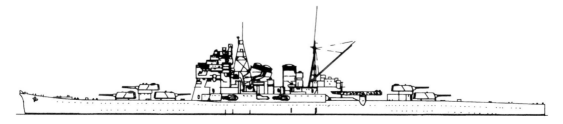

Subsequently with *Takao and Atago* were modernised by updating the main armament fire control system and replacing the machine guns six twin 25mm mountings. The torpedo armament was changed to four quadruple tubes and the bridge structure was rebuilt as part of a drive to reduce topweight. Coupled with this, the hull bulges were enlarged to assist stability. Finally, improved catapults capable of operating heavier aircraft were fitted. In 1942, after the outbreak of war, these two ships had their single 4.7in guns replaced by four twin 5in mountings to improve AA fire. Subsequently, in 1943, the light AA armament was augmented by additional twin and triple 25mm mountings, ultimately to a total of twenty-six guns, and basic radar equipment was also fitted.

The other two ships, *Chokai and Maya*, were not modernised prior to 1941 due to a lack of shipyard capacity and their subsequent alterations differed in some respects from their sisters. More powerful catapults were fitted and the torpedo tubes upgraded to handle the liquid-oxygen powered Long Lance 24in torpedoes. Light AA armament was increased to twelve 25mm in twin mountings. *Chokai* subsequently had her light AA armament supplemented by ten single 25mm guns and additional twin mountings were fitted, while a basic radar outfit was also installed. *Maya* was heavily damaged in an air raid at Rabaul in November 1943 and returned to Japan where C turret was removed along with all the 4.7in guns and the 25mm twin mountings. Her new armament comprised eight 8in guns, twelve 5in AA in six open twin mountings and thirty-five 25mm guns in triple and single mountings, later augmented by a further eighteen single 25mm guns. The torpedo armament remained at four quadruple sets of tubes but no reloads were carried. A similar refit was planned for *Chokai* but the opportunity never arose before she was lost.

The four *Atago* class ships comprised the 4th Cruiser Squadron in 1941 and, apart from *Chokai* which had sustained damage in a grounding incident, were active in the operations to capture the Dutch East Indies. Subsequently, they operated in the Aleutians and then in the Solomons. *Chokai* took part in the Japanese victory at Savo Island although she was damaged in that battle. After various

An artist's impression of the Mogami *following her conversion to a heavy cruiser with ten 8in guns in five twin mountings.* via Author

View of cruiser Mikuma *(sister to* Mogami*) following attacks by US aircraft after the battle of Midway.* US Navy Hostorical Branch

adventures the 4th Cruiser Squadron remained a cohesive unit as part of the Mobile Fleet in the Leyte Gulf battles when *Atago* and *Maya* were lost to US submarines (23 October, 1944) while *Chokai* succumbed to air attack during the Battle off Samar (25 October, 1944). The sole survivor, *Takao*, was also torpedoed but managed to make her way back to Singapore where she acted as a floating AA battery despite being seriously damaged by a Royal Navy midget submarine attack. She was finally scuttled in October 1946.

By 1930 the IJN was planning construction of a further class of "Improved *Takaos*" but the London Naval Treaty signed that year laid down a tonnage limitation on heavy cruisers and Japan's formidable fleet of twelve such ships was already at the permissible limit. The only option was to build light cruisers and even this depended on scrapping some of the older ships of this type. Some abstruse mathematics allowed Japan to build four 8,500 ton light cruisers by 1936 and another two 8,450 ton ships the following year. The four ships of the *Mogami* class were therefore designed to carry no less than fifteen 6in guns in five triple turrets, three forward and two aft, and a secondary battery of eight 5in AA in four twin mountings. Four triple 24in torpedo tubes with a full set of reloads was included and, as completed, the light AA armament comprised eight 25mm AA and four 13.2mm machine guns. In an effort to reduce topweight, aircraft hangars were deleted and the three aircraft carried were parked on the open deck abaft the mainmast with catapults mounted on either beam.

In order to achieve a design speed of 37 knots the installed machinery had a power output of 152,000 shp, the highest of any of the treaty cruisers and only approached by the Italian *Trento* and *Bolzano* classes. The first two ships, *Mogami* and *Mikuma*, had ten boilers but *Suzaya* and *Kumano* had only eight, although the power output remained the same. The boiler uptakes were joined in a unique bifurcated single funnel which gave these ships a distinctive appearance. The tall bridge lacked the mass of the *Takao* class and both these features helped to reduce topweight. Protection was on a similar scale to the *Takao* class with a 4in main belt tapering down to 1.25in at its lower edge, the whole structure inclined inwards at 20 deg. The magazines had a maximum of 5.5in tapering to 1.25in, also inclined. A 1.25in (30mm) armoured deck (40mm over the magazines) was increased to 2.4in (60mm) at the edges were it was angled downwards at 20 deg. Barbettes were protected by 3-4in armour.

The first pair were laid down in 1931 and completed in 1935. *Suzaya* and *Kumano* were laid down in late 1933 and April 1934 and their completion was delayed until late 1937 to allow for modifications. For so called light cruisers, these were exceptionally powerful ships and rumours of the characteristics were directly responsible for the US *Brooklyn* class (fifteen 6in guns, 10,000 tons) and British *Southampton* class (twelve 6in guns, 9,100 tons) light cruisers. However the Japanese ships exceeded the original design displacement of 8,500 tons by almost 1,000 tons and full load displacement was over 12,000 tons. As a result, all four ships suffered from stability problems and also poor welding which resulted in serious storm damage to *Mogami* and *Mikuma* in 1936. As a result they were laid up for a while so that the hulls could be strengthened and the bulges increased in size, these modifications being extended to the final pair whilst under construction, and these changes resulted in a further increase in displacement so that, although still fast ships, they were nowhere near capable of achieving 37 knots.

Although designed and built as 6in gunned light cruisers, the Japanese Naval Staff had always envisaged that these ships could be upgraded to 8in whenever the treaty restrictions were lifted. Accordingly, the substructure for the triple 6in turrets was designed from the start to accept a twin 8in turret. In fact, Japan gave formal notification of withdrawing from the provisions of the London Treaty in 1936 although the change to an 8in main armament did not occur until 1939/40. At this time more powerful aircraft catapults were fitted and the torpedo tubes adapted to fire the 24in Long Lance torpedoes. In this configuration they went to war, although *Mikuma* was sunk by air attack in June 1942 in the aftermath of the Battle of Midway and her sister ship, *Mogami* was heavily damaged and lucky to survive. She was subsequently rebuilt as a hybrid aircraft carrying cruiser during a long refit in which her after 8in turrets were removed and replaced by handling facilities for up to eleven floatplanes. Thirty 25mm guns in triple mountings were added and an AW radar outfit was installed. By June 1944 the light AA armament comprised no less than sixty 25mm guns in fourteen twin and eighteen single mountings. *Kumano* and *Suzaya* were less drastically altered, retaining the ten 8in guns although their light AA armament was progressively boosted and radar equipment was added.

The four ships served together as the 7th Cruiser Squadron and initially saw much successful action in the Dutch East Indies when *Mikuma* and *Mogami* sank the Allied cruiser USS *Houston* and also HMS *Perth*. As already mentioned, *Mikuma* was subsequently sunk at the Battle of Midway and the others participated in various actions in the Solomons before being involved in the Leyte Gulf battles on 25 October 1944. Mogami proved difficult to kill, absorbing gunfire from US heavy cruisers, a collision with the Japanese cruiser *Nachi*, air attacks from US carrier aircraft before being finished off by an American submarine! *Suzaya* was also lost on the same day. Initially torpedoed by a US destroyer, she also suffered damage from air attack and was eventually finished off by the Japanese destroyer *Okinami* to prevent her falling into American hands. Despite extensive damage, *Kumano* survived the day's actions and reached Manilla for emergency repairs. When these had been effected she attempted to run for Japan but was intercepted and torpedoed by the US Submarine Ray off Luzon. Again, she survived and went to Santa Cruz for repairs but was eventually finished off by US navy aircraft on 25th November. Whatever faults this class may have had, they certainly showed a remarkable ability to absorb punishment and all of them were only lost after continuous and protracted attacks.

The outcome of the London Naval Treaty allowed Japan to build up to six large light cruisers and the two following on from the Mogami class were originally intended to be of a similar design. Named Tone and Chikuma, they were laid down in December 1934 and October 1935 respectively. In March 1934 the torpedo boat Tomozuru was lost when she capsized in a heavy sea, and the subsequent inquiry highlighted stability problems with the Mogami class. Consequently the design of the Tone class was substantially altered, the most obvious difference being the reduction of the main armament by deleting one turret and the remaining four were all grouped together on a long forecastle. This arrangement permitted the after section of the ship to be given over to aircraft handling arrangements in which up to eight floatplanes could be parked on deck with a complex rail and turntable system allowing each to be positioned to one of two catapults mounted port and starboard abaft the mainmast. The machinery installation was identical to the last two Mogami class with the uptakes from the eight boilers trunked into a single funnel although greater bunkerage gave the Tone class a range of 8,000nm at 18 kts as opposed to the same distance at only 14 knots in the earlier ships. While the ships were building, the IJN's Fourth Fleet suffered severe damage during a typhoon and, in particular the welded seams aboard Mogami and Mikuma showed a tendency to come apart while main welded joints appeared to lack strength. Consequently it was decided to revert to riveted construction for Chikuma although as construction of Tone was too far advanced to fully incorporate this change both techniques were applied in her case.

Although nominally laid down as light cruisers armed with 6in guns (initially fifteen, later reduced to twelve) both were completed with eight 8in guns in four E3 twin turrets following the Japanese abrogation of the London Treaty in December 1936. In fact there seems little evidence that there was ever any serious intention to mount the lighter armament. The remaining armament included eight 5in AA guns in four twin mountings (a fifth mounting to be carried aft on the centreline was deleted to allow more space for aircraft) and six twin 25mm guns. A heavy torpedo armament of four triple 24in tubes was carried at upper deck level. Despite the effort put into the aircraft arrangements, the normal complement was only five. Armour protection comprised a 4in (100mm) internal main belt covering the machinery spaces. This was inclined inwards and was tapered at its lower edge, continuing down to the hull's lower plating, and the space between the inclined armour belt and the outer hull plating acted as an internal anti torpedo bulge. The magazines forward were protected by up to 5.5in (145mm) armour plating and a horizontal 2in (55mm) armoured deck. A 1.25in (31mm) deck covered the machinery spaces and a 2.6in (65mm) sloping surface joined these decks to the top of the side belts. Further plating 0.75in (19mm) thick provided additional protection at upper deck level.The main arament was relatively lightly protected with 1in (25mm) plating on the turrets and barbettes. The total armour weight was 1,671 tons although the various alterations had brought the overall standard displacement 11,258 tons and over 15,000 tons at full load. By the time that these ships were completed (November 1938 and May 1939) Japan had already withdrawn from the *London* and Washington treaties and the breach of the 10,000 ton limit was academic.

Due to the fact that they were relatively modern ships and already incorporated changes brought about by experience with earlier ships, they were not subject to any subsequent major modifications. Such changes as were effected mainly involved the augmentation of the light AA armament to an eventual total of around fifty eight 25mm guns in triple, twin and single mountings including several on the after aircraft parking deck. In service the two sister ships operated together as the 8th cruiser squadron until early 1944 when they were redesignated as the 7th Cruiser squadron. Up to that point they had been in the thick of many major actions and campaigns. In the fighting around Guadalcanal in 1942 Tone was damaged by air attack on 24 August while Chikuma survived hits by no less than five bombs during the Battle of Santa Cruz. Both underwent repairs before seeing further action including a unique sortie into the Indian Ocean to attack allied merchant shipping although only one merchant ship was sunk. Both ships were involved in the attack on US escort carriers off Samar on 25th October 1944 but Chikuma was sunk by the resulting air attacks. Tone survived on that occasion but was damaged by air attack in March 1945 while at Kure. Still in home waters she was attacked by over 100 carrier based aircraft on 24th July 1945 and suffered extensive damage from four hits and several near misses. She was beached in order to prevent her sinking but was subsequently salvaged and broken up after the war.

Including the two Tone class, Japan built a total of eighteen heavy cruisers between 1923 and 1939 and a further pair were approved under the 1941 programme and both were laid down in 1942. Known as the Ibuki class, these would have had a standard displacement of around 12,000 tons and were closely based on the later Mogami class with modifications incorporated to improve their strength and stability. The lead ship, Ibuki, was launched in May 1943 but construction was then suspended while plans were drawn up to complete her as an aircraft carrier. Subsequent work then proceeded slowly and the ship was finally laid up in an incomplete state in March 1945 although the flight deck was complete and some armament was fitted. Surprisingly the ship survived the depredations of roving American aircraft in the closing stages of the war in a relatively undamaged state but was eventually scrapped in 1947. Her unnamed sister ship (Job Number 301) was begun in June 1942 but little work was done before she was broken up some two months later to allow the slipway to be used for the construction of the aircraft carrier Amagi, laid down 1st October 1942.

CHAPTER VIII

United States

It is surprising to note that the United States Navy built no cruisers at all during the First world War and it was only in 1918 that a new class of ten light cruisers was laid down, and none of these were completed before 1923. Consequently, there was a desperate need for new ships as all the older cruisers were obsolete. Even so, there was little money to be made available and consequently it was not until October 1926 that the first new heavy cruiser was laid down, although design work dated back to 1919 when serious work began on a new class of so called Scout Cruisers. A variety of sketch designs were investigated for ships ranging in size from 5,000 to 10,000 tons, while all types of guns including 6in and 8in were considered. Almost inevitably, several factors conspired to push the displacement up to around 10,000 tons and to require an 8in gun armament. The size and armament were really dictated by the existence of the Royal Navy's *Hawkins* class cruisers as the US Navy was not going to equip itself with an inferior vessel, especially as at that time Britain had to be considered has a possible enemy however remote the likelihood in reality. However, the increasing power of Japan could not be ignored and they were a much more likely antagonist. A Pacific war

The USS Pensacola *(shown here) and USS* Salt Lake City *were the first US heavy cruisers. They carried ten 8in guns in two triple turrets superfiring over two twin turrets. Note the typical American tripod masts and large fighting tops.* Maritime Photo Library

An aerial view of USS Augusta. US Navy Historical Branch

would require long ranged ships capable of acting independently and this again pointed to a large, heavily armed cruiser. The Washington Treaty was signed while the cruiser design was still being considered but the outcome of the political negotiations in respect of cruiser limits was entirely satisfactory as far as the US Navy was concerned. Indeed, the 10,000 tons 8in armed cruiser was well suited to its requirements and it was eventually to build more of this type of warship than any other navy and continued to build new heavy cruisers when their construction had been abandoned by all the other treaty signatories.

The design of the new *Pensacola* class was finalised in March 1925 and two ships (CA24 *Pensacola* and CA25 *Salt Lake City*) were ordered, although they were not laid down until October 1926 and June 1927 respectively. At this stage the US programme lagged well behind that of the Royal Navy which had already completed and commissioned three *County* class cruisers by the end of 1927. The outstanding feature of the *Pensacola* class was the heavy main armament which comprised no less than ten 8in guns arranged in two twin and two triple turrets. Rather unconventionally the triple turret superfired over the twin and the reason for this was that the fine hull lines forward could not accommodate the wider barbette of the triple mounting. The requirement for a heavy main armament was well judged as the Japanese *Myoko* class ships, then under construction, were also armed with ten 8in guns, although these were arranged in five twin turrets. To keep within

USS Augusta *shown at the end of the Second World War. One of six* Northampton *class ships, she spent most of the war in the Atlantic theatre including a period in 1943 with the British Home Fleet. In August 1942 she carried President Roosevelt to a historic meeting with Churchill at Argenta Bay, Newfoundland.* Wright and Logan Collection

treaty limitations, the *Pensacola*'s secondary armament consisted only of four 5in/25cal guns in single DP mountings and, initially, there were no short range light AA weapons apart from a few machine guns. Two triple 21in torpedo tubes were carried at upper deck level abreast the after funnel. In the vast expanses of the Pacific the cruiser's scouting role was extremely important and no less than four aircraft were carried and they were launched from two catapults mounted port and starboard between the funnels. There was no hangar and the aircraft were carried on the upper deck abaft the catapults, handled by a single crane on the centreline between the funnels.

The two funnels resulted from the unit machinery arrangement which consisted of eight White-Foster boilers connected to Parsons geared turbines driving four shafts. Installed power was 107,000

USS Pensacola, *1943. (USA)*

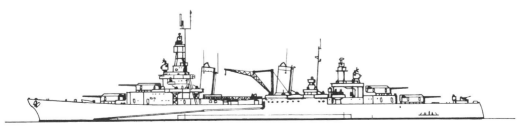

The USS Indianapolis *pictured in July 1945, shortly before she was torpedoed and sunk by a Japanese submarine. The subsequent delay in mounting a rescue mission resulted in one of the US Navy's worst disasters of the War.*
US Navy Historical Branch

shp (compared with 80,000 shp in the British *Kent* class) and this, coupled with the fine lines of the flush decked hull gave a speed of 32.5 knots. The funnels were raked, giving these ships a silhouette not unlike the contemporary French *Dusquense* class although the American ships could be readily distinguished by tall tripod masts fore and aft. The tall tripod foremast carrying the main fire control station and air defence platforms was particularly impressive.

The original sketch design incorporated 773 tons of armour protection but initial calculations indicated that the ships would be well under the 10,000 ton limit by a margin of at least 250 tons so some improvements were incorporated. The final scheme provided for a main belt of 3in protecting the machinery spaces and increasing to 4in abreast the forward magazines, although the after magazines were not so protected on the basis than any action would involve engaging a ship forward of the beam (a rather dubious premise at best!). Transverse bulkheads varied between 2 to 3.5in and a 2in armoured main deck protected vital spaces with a further 1in at lower deck level in places. Turrets and barbettes received 1.5 in of armour while the conning tower was heavily protected with 8in armour. In total, protection accounted for around 6% of the light ship displacement – less than many of the contemporary designs. Nevertheless, the final standard displacement was only 9,100 tons and was well below the treaty limit. Considering the heavy main armament, this was a remarkable achievement, although it was achieved by keeping protection to a minimum, a characteristic which was improved in later designs.

Salt Lake City was completed in December 1929 and *Pensacola* some two months later. In the decade before America's entry into the war in late 1941 there were a few modifications, mostly relating to changes in the armament. In the 1930s a general decision was made that heavy cruisers did not require torpedo tubes and they were consequently removed where already fitted. It was expected that these ships would engage at ranges beyond which effective use of torpedoes would be difficult and, in any case, supporting flotillas of destroyers (some of which carried an exceptionally heavy torpedo armament – sixteen 21in in the *Craven* class) would carry out this task. What was not envisaged were the bruising close range night actions which cost the US Navy dear in the first two years of the Pacific War. The removal of the torpedo tubes did make margins available for four additional single 5in/25 cal guns in single mountings fitted abreast the bridge at shelter deck level. In addition two quadruple 1.1in AA mountings were also shipped and *Pensacola* was an early recipient (November 1941) of a CXAM radar. During the war, both ships received improved radar outfits and the light AA armament was boosted by the addition of 20mm guns and more 1.1in guns, although from 1943 onwards the much superior 40mm Bofors began to replace the 1.1in guns which never had a very good reputation. The mainmast was struck in both ships and an additional main armament DCT installed on a pedestal in its place. In contrast to the Royal Navy, the US Navy retained aircraft aboard its cruisers, although in the case of these two ships the complement was reduced to two.

Both ships had extremely active wartime careers and *Pensacola* was hit by a torpedo at the Battle of Tassafaronga on the night of 30 November 1942 and was subsequently out of action until the following November while undergoing repairs. She subsequently saw action in support of various amphibious actions as US forces began their advance across the Pacific towards Japan in 1944/45. She was hit by shore batteries during February 1945 off Iwo Jima and in the following April returned home for repairs which lasted almost to the end of hostilities. Rather ignominiously, she met her end as a target ship in the 1946 atom bomb trials at Bikini Atoll. *Salt Lake City* was also heavily occupied in the opening rounds of the war including forming part of the task force which accompanied the carrier *Hornet* on the famous mission to launch Army B-25 bombers under Colonel Doolittle against Tokyo in April 1942. During the Guadalcanal campaign she was damaged in the Battle of Cape Esperance and was refitted at Pearl Harbor from November 1942 to March 1943. Dispatched to the northern Pacific she fought a force of Japanese cruisers in the Battle of the Kormandorski Islands and received damage which necessitated more repairs but by the end of 1943 she was back in action supporting the drive across the Pacific. Like her sister ship, she was a target at Bikini Atoll but was not sunk in these tests. She was finally expended as a conventional target off the Californian coast in May 1948.

The next group of US heavy cruisers consisted of the six ships of the *Northampton* class, all laid down in 1928 and completed in 1930-31. In many respects these were very similar to the *Pensacola* class and the main change related to the armament. Almost all foreign navies had opted for a main battery of eight 8in guns in four twin mountings so it was thought that the ten guns in the US ships could safely be reduced in order to allow for more armour protection and make more space for aircraft facilities. There was one debate over whether to follow the general trend and mount eight 8in guns but the final arrangement was nine guns in three triple mountings, an elegant arrangement which still gave some superiority in firepower. The rest of the armament was much the same, comprising four single 5in/25, guns and two triple 21in torpedo tube mountings, although the latter were later removed. The light AA armament was virtually non-existent on completion as a 37mm intended for these ships failed to materialise. A couple of obsolete 3pdrs were fitted, and a few single 0.5in machine guns were added after completion. On the other hand, aircraft facilities were considerably

USS New Orleans *in 1934. Note the starboard side 5in guns in single mounts, three at upper deck level and the forward one on a raised platform below the bridge.* Wright and Logan Collection.

improved, a large hangar occupied the space abreast and forward of the after funnel and this could accommodate four aircraft. Another two could be carried on catapults sited amidships in either beam so that the total complement could be as many as six aircraft, although in practice it was rare for more than four to be embarked. This illustrates the importance accorded to aircraft which were used mainly for scouting and reconnaissance, a vital task in the vast expanse of the Pacific, even following the later advent of radar. The hangar provided a covered space for maintenance and also protected the aircraft from blast damage when the main armament was firing.

The flush decked *Pensacola* class suffered as a result of the relatively low freeboard and the *Northampton* class featured a raised forecastle deck which in some ships (*Agusta*, *Chicago*, and *Houston*) was extended aft to the catapults to provide additional accommodation so that they could be used as flagships. With tall tripod masts and twin raked funnels, the ships otherwise retained the basic outline of their predecessors, the most obvious difference being the three turret arrangement, two forward, and the other well aft. The space between the after funnel and turret was used to position the secondary 5in battery while the ship's boats were clustered around the base of the mainmast. The machinery installation was identical to the *Pensacola* class. As completed, these ships had a tendency to roll which necessitated the fitting of deep bilge keels. Another early modification was the fitting of two HA directors, although, initially, there was no complementary strengthening of the AA armament.

Before Pearl Harbor, all six ships had their secondary armament increased by the addition of a further four single 5in/25 cal guns and, while the need for a more effective light AA firepower was accepted, the lack of suitable guns led to a lack of standardisation. Initially, most received four 3in/50 cal guns in single mountings pending the availability of quadruple 1.1in mountings. The foremast was cut down to allow the fitting of various radars and the bridge structure was enlarged. Those ships which survived the early actions subsequently received many 20mm guns while the 40mm Bofors gradually replaced the 1.1in quad. By 1945 a typical light AA outfit comprised twenty-four 40mm (four quad and four twin mountings) and twenty single 20mm guns. By then, of course, a substantial radar outfit was carried including air and surface warning sets, and gunnery ranging radars for all classes of armament. Other detailed changes including welding over the lower deck scuttles, providing forced ventilation throughout the ship and the addition of a cowl to the funnels to deflect smoke away from the bridge and gunnery control positions.

The pre-war heavy cruisers took the brunt of the fighting, particularly in the fierce surface actions around Guadalcanal from August 1942 onwards, and half of the *Northampton* class were lost in action. *Houston* was flagship of the US Navy's Asiatic Fleet at the time of Pearl Harbor and was immediately allocated to the joint Australian, British, Dutch and American (ABDA) command which attempted to halt the Japanese advance towards the Dutch East Indies and its valuable oil fields. A bomb hit put her after turret out of action on 4 February 1942 but she could not be spared and was present at the disastrous Battle of the Java Sea. Although surviving this defeat, she and the Australian cruiser HMAS *Perth* were sunk by Japanese cruisers and destroyers on 1 March while trying to escape through the Sunda Strait. *Chicago* was present at the Battle of Savo Island in August 1942, another allied disaster, and had her bows blown off by a Japanese torpedo. She returned to San Francisco for repairs but was back in action again by January 1943 when she was sunk off Rennell Island by Japanese air attack, taking no less than six torpedoes in two separate attacks. *Northampton* was another casualty – after a series of operations including the Doolittle raid, Midway and the Battle of Santa Cruz, she was torpedoed by the Japanese destroyer Oyashio during the Battle of Tassafaronga on the night of 30 November 1942 and sank a few hours later. Although the other ships survived the war, an element of luck played its part in some cases. *Chester* was torpedoed by a Japanese submarine on 20 October 1942 in the South Pacific and was fortunate to survive, having lost all power. However, she lived to fight again and was back in service by mid 1943. After the war she was laid up in June 1946 and although scheduled to be scrapped, it was not until 1959 that this actually occurred. *Louisville* seemed to bear something of a charmed life until she was hit by two kamikazes in January 1945. Repaired and back in action, she was again hit by kamikazes on 5 June while off Okinawa. After the war she was laid up in 1946 but was not scrapped until 1959. Finally, The remaining ship, *Augusta* spent virtually the entire war in the North Atlantic and Mediterranean. She was in action against French ships during Operation Torch, the invasion of North Africa in November 1942, and at one time served with the British Home Fleet based at Scapa Flow. Subsequently, she was involved in supporting the Normandy landings in June 1944. Like her surviving sister ships, she was laid up in 1946 but languished in reserve until finally being sold off for scrapping in 1959.

Based on experience of the earlier cruisers, the *Northampton* class set the standard for the remaining American Treaty cruisers which, although offering incremental improvements, retained the

A close up of USS Minneapolis *in 1934 showing her complement of Vought O3U Corsair scouting floatplanes embarked.* Maritime Photo Library

A rare view of USS Minneapolis *taken in 1943.* US Navy Historical Branch

same basic layout and armament. Long ranged and heavily armed, they can be regarded as a successful design despite the heavy losses that occurred. Originally, the successor to the *Northampton* class would have been the *New Orleans* class of which no less than fifteen were to have been ordered, five each in the Fiscal Years 1929, 1930 and 1931. This programme had its origins in a move, following the abortive 1927 Geneva Naval Limitation Conference, in which President Coolidge urged the United States Navy to aim for full parity with the Royal Navy. A plan was therefore put forward for an ambitious construction programme which included no less than 25 cruisers as well as 5 aircraft carriers and 41 other ships over the following nine years. However, the American public and many politicians were not ready for such a move. This was still the time when Isolationism reigned supreme, to say nothing of the financial implications, and consequently the programme was severely pruned to include the 15 cruisers and only one carrier. Even this was rejected by the Senate but at the end of 1928 President Coolidge pushed forward another attempt and this time the necessary legislation, known as the Cruiser Bill was passed. Even so the first two of the FY29 (CA33 *Portland*, CA 35 *Indianapolis*) programme were not laid down until early 1930 and the remaining three (CA32 *New Orleans*, CA34 *Astoria*, CA36 *Minneapolis*) spilled over into 1931. Only three of the FY30 programme (CA37 *Tuscaloosa*, CA38 *San Francisco*, and CA39 *Quincy*) were built and were laid down in 1931–33, while only two of the FY31 programme(CA44 *Vincennes*, CA45 *Wichita*) were ever built and it was 1934 and 35 respectively before work commenced on their construction. The reason, for these changes were partly financial and political, but mainly because of the outcome of the 1930 London Naval Treaty which, for the first time, laid down limits on the total tonnage of heavy cruisers which each Navy could build. This suited the British who were the moving force behind these changes, having already decided to move to the construction of smaller 6in armed cruisers. However, the US Navy was less happy and when they were eventually forced to begin building 6in gun Class B cruisers in 1935 they were 10,000 ton monsters carrying no less than fifteen 6in guns in five triple turrets.

In the meantime, work began in 1930 on two cruisers under the original batch of five authorised in the FY29 programme. Originally, all five were intended to be repeats of the *Northampton* class but by this time the fact that both they and the *Pensacola* classes were going to be well under weight was realised and it was also accepted that in consequence they were under armoured. The new cruisers would therefore have to be substantially redesigned in order to incorporate additional protection and to bring their displacement closer to the treaty 10,000 ton limit. However, as by then the contracts had been let to the shipyards, there was going to be a serious cost implication if the design was changed too much. In the end a compromise was agreed under which the two ships let to commercial yards would be built to the basic *Northampton* class design with relatively few modifications, while the other three having been awarded to government owned naval yards would incorporate a more substantial redesign. Thus, after much debate the USS *Portland* (CA33) was laid down at the Bethlehem Steel Company Yard, Quincy, on 17 February and the USS *Indianapolis* at New York Shipbuilding, Camden, on 31 March 1930.

USS New Orleans, *1945. (USA)*

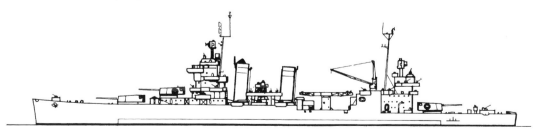

A wartime view of USS Minneapolis. *Note augmented AA armament including 20mm guns on the forecastle. The hull sides have been painted to give the ship the appearance of a destroyer when viewed from a distance.* Author's collection

The general design followed that of the *Northampton* class and the profiles were very similar. The machinery was identical except that Portland had Yarrow boilers in stead of the usual White-Foster. The main armament of nine 8in guns in three triple turrets was retained but both ships were completed with eight single 5in/25 cal guns and the torpedo tubes were omitted. The main belt armour was 4in, tapering to 3in at the ends and only covered the machinery spaces. It was 10 feet deep and reached up to lower deck level, backed by 2.25in shell plating which continued up to main deck level, and was closed off by 3in bulkheads. Both the main and lower decks had 2in armour plating covering the whole length of the ship between A and X turrets, while the turrets themselves had between 3 and 1.5in and the barbettes 1.5 to 2in armour. The control tower, as in the *Northamptons*, was well protected with 8in of armour. Compared to the earlier ships, the main improvement was the strengthening of the lower deck armour and the thicker, but less extensive main belt. Although a tripod foremast supported the fire control positions, it was noticeably shorter than on the *Northamptons*. A light tripod mainmast with no fighting top was stepped just forward of the after turret. Aircraft arrangement remained the same with the hangars abreast the after funnel and two catapults, one on either side amidships. Two aircraft could be carried in the hangars, and two on the

The USS Vincennes *had a relatively short career. The last of the New Orleans class to be completed, in 1937, she was lost at the battle of Savo Island in August 1942.* Wright and Logan Collection

The last of the American treaty cruisers, USS Wichita *(CA45). The design was based on the* Brooklyn *class of light cruisers but with an armament of nine 8in guns.*

USS Chicago, *a* Baltimore *class cruiser completed in January 1945 just in time to see action in the closing stages of the war. She was named in commemoration of the original USS* Chicago *sunk at the Battle of Savo Island in 1942.* Author's collection

catapults, with provision for two more in the well deck between the catapults. The normal complement was four aircraft.

Both ships werecommissioned in 1932 and subsequently were little altered, although at one stage Portland had her fore funnel heightened. During the war the light AA armament was considerably boosted and several radar sets were added as they became available. In 1943 both underwent major refits in which the bridge was enlarged and a new tripod mainmast stepped around the after funnel. The after superstructure was cut down to provide improved arcs of fire for additional light AA guns and distinctive funnel cowls were fitted (Portland's funnel height was reduced again at this point so that both ships now had identical funnels). The final light AA outfit included twenty-four 40mm (either six quads or four quads and four twins), and up to nineteen 20mm guns.

As might be expected, both ships saw arduous war service. *Portland* took part in the Coral Sea, Midway and the Guadalcanal battles, and in October 1942 was hit by three aircraft torpedoes in the Battle of Santa Cruz. Fortunately, these failed to explode but she was less lucky the following month when a torpedo from a Japanese destroyer hit her stern, shearing off two screws and putting X turret out of action. Repairs at Pearl Harbor kept her out of action until March 1943 and, after supporting various amphibious operations, she underwent a further refit in 1944 before taking part in the massive Leyte Gulf actions and subsequent operations around the Philippines and Okinawa. Like most of the pre-war heavy cruisers, she was laid up in 1946 and scrapped in 1959. Her sister ship *Indianapolis* spent much of her career as a flagship, noticeably carrying Admiral Raymond Spruance as commander of the US 5th Fleet in many operations including assaults on Tarawa and the Marianas. She supported the operations against Iwo Jima and Okinawa and on 31 March was hit by a kamikaze, the resulting damage necessitating a return to Pearl Harbor for repairs. When these were completed, she was detailed to convey components of the world's first operational atomic bomb to the island of Tinian where B-29 bombers were preparing for the attacks against Hiroshima and Nagasaki. Having safely discharged this task the ship sailed to rejoin the fleet at Leyte but was torpedoed and sunk by the Japanese submarine I-58 whilst on passage. Due to a breakdown in procedures and communications, her loss went unnoticed for several days so that when a search was eventually organised only 316 men out of a total complement of 1,199 were rescued. The loss of a fine ship and so many men so close to the end of hostilities was one of the great naval tragedies of the war.

As already noted, the Portland class ships were actually something of a stopgap while a more substantial revision of the basic design was undertaken. The result was the seven ships of the *New Orleans* class of which five were laid down in 1930/31 and these were all completed in 1934. Two further ships (CA39 *Quincy*, CA44 *Vincennes*) were laid down in 1933 and 34, and completed in 1936 and 1937 respectively. Externally these ships differed from the previous American heavy cruisers in that their two funnels were closely spaced abaft the bridge. This was the result of a re-arrangement of the machinery spaces in which the unit system was abandoned and the boiler spaces were all grouped together amidships, with the engine rooms aft of them. The safety margins of the unit system were lost as a single torpedo hit could bring the ship to a standstill. However, the risk was deemed acceptable and outweighed by the fact that it was now possible to reduce waterline length by 14 feet and beam by 4 feet. The shorter length of the machinery spaces meant that they could be more heavily armoured without adding extra weight. Apart from the distribution of its components, the machinery system was identical to the earlier ships and power output remained at 107,000 shp although these ships were marginally faster. Less desirable was a reduction in oil fuel bunkerage which was around 2,100–2,200 tons (figures varied between ships) compared with 3,000 tons on earlier classes.

Previous US heavy cruisers had come out well under weight (almost 1,000 tons in the case of the *Northampton*, mainly due to the fact that their designers were installing new machinery and weapons and were paranoid about keeping under the 10,000 ton limit. It was now realised that there was a considerable margin available and taking advantage of this and other weight reductions achieved, the main belt armour was increased to 5in on the upper section of the main belt, but remained at 3in on the lower section. It was closed off by 5in bulkheads and the magazines were separately protected by 3 or 4in armour. Horizontal protection comprised a 3in main deck and 2in lower deck (tapering to 1in or 0.5in outside the magazine areas). The main armament turrets were heavily protected with 5in faces and 3in sides and crowns, while the barbettes also received 5in. The Conning Tower was protected by 8in armour as in the earlier ships. In all, armour protection now accounted for 15% of the standard displacement, over double the proportion in the original US Treaty cruisers (*Salt Lake City*). The last four ships (*Tuscaloosa*, *San Francisco*, *Quincy* and *Vincennes*) were armed with a lighter version of the standard 8in gun and consequently their triple mountings were some 40 tons lighter. In the first two, this margin was utilised to increase the barbette armour to 6.5in but this was not extended to the last two as their standard displacement had risen to very near the treaty limits. Some of these changes resulted from a significant reappraisal of the method by which armour requirements were calculated. With previous cruisers the traditional approach employed empirical methods of determining the armour thickness necessary to resist hits by shells of a given calibre with little thought as to how likely was such a scenario. A more sophisticated method was carefully to asses the tactical situations which the ships were likely to face and then determine the least range at which the side armour would provide protection, while also calculating the maximum range at which the deck armour would protect against long range plunging shell fire. The difference between these two ranges was designated as the immune zone in which the ship was well protected against shellfire of the specified calibre (i.e. 8in or 6in). By introducing the concept of the immune zone, the ships designers could apply a more scientific approach to the distribution of armour protection. In this case the immune zone against 8in fire was 12,000 to 24,000 yards for the magazines and 15,000 to 24,000 yards for the machinery spaces. The New Orleans class also introduced another concept in that the magazines were positioned lower down, below the waterline. Previously, this had been thought too risky in case of a torpedo hit, but the risk was now accepted so that they could be better protected from shellfire within the 10,000 ton limit. In the end, the *New Orleans* class came out at almost exactly 10,000 tons so the various compromises adopted were at least successful from that point of view.

The standard main armament of nine 8in guns in three triple mountings was retained but the designed secondary armament was boosted to eight single 5in/25cal guns evenly distributed on either beam abreast the bridge and funnels. Eight single 0.5in machine guns provided a light AA defence. No torpedo tubes were fitted. The alterations to the machinery spaces and the adoption of two closely spaced funnels allowed a change to the aircraft arrangements. The after superstructure was dominated by a large hangar while two catapults were installed port and starboard abaft the funnels. Twin cranes atop the hangar handled aircraft and also the ship's boats stowed on the hangar roof. Instead of a tripod foremast, a more modern tower bridge was adopted with a main armament DCT mounted above, while a second DCT was carried high up aft of the light mainmast. As completed, a series of high searchlight towers occupied the spaces between the funnels although manning these must have been an uncomfortable experience in some wind conditions. It had been planned to complete at least one of the class as a flagship with extra accommodation spaces, but as the ships were so close to displacement limits this was not possible.

In 1940 it was recommended that the light AA armament be increased by the addition of four quadruple 1.1in guns and that splinter screens be provided around the open 5in gun mountings. This work was put in hand but it took until a few months after Pearl Harbor before all ships were so modified. By then other changes were in hand including a reduction in the height of the foremast so that it could carry an AW radar and more urgently needed 20mm guns were added. However, stability and weight margins required compensating alterations and over a period of time this resulted in the armoured conning tower being removed, together with one catapult and crane. Those ships which survived the war had an enhanced light AA armament which included four quadruple 40mm and up to twenty eight 20mm guns, the obsolete 1.1in guns having been removed.

Out of the seven ships completed, no less than three (*Astoria*, *Quincy*, and *Vincennes*) were lost in the Battle of Savo Island on the night of the 8 August 1942. The name ship, *New Orleans* was involved in several major actions including the Battle of Tassafaronga (November 1942), when she had her bows blown off by a torpedo hit. Repairs took until August 1943 and thereafter she was again in the thick of the action including the Philippine Sea, Leyte and Okinawa. *Minneapolis* had a very similar career, to the extent that she also lost her bows at Tassafaronga. *San Francisco* also spent her war in the Pacific and was severely mauled in a night action off Guadalcanal in November 1942 which put her out of action until the end of February 1943. After a spell in the Aleutians she joined the push against Japan in the Central Pacific. In contrast to her sisters, *Tuscaloosa* spent some time in the Atlantic, supporting the North African landings and spending time working with the British Home Fleet of Norway. She also supported the Normandy landings and subsequently the assault on the French Mediterranean coast. It was not until January 1945 that she joined Pacific operations for the final assaults on Iwo Jima and Okinawa. All four survivors were laid up in early 1947 and after years in reserve were scrapped in 1959.

The 1930 London Naval Treaty for the first time placed restrictions on the total tonnage of heavy cruisers allowed to each of the signatories. The effect of this was temporally to halt US construction and, as already related, the *New Orleans* programme was stretched out so that the last ship (CA44 *Vincennes*) was not laid down until 1934. Thereafter, there was only enough allowance to lay down one more heavy cruiser (CA45 *Wichita*) in 1935. Originally this would have been a repeat *New Orleans* class but another effect of the London Treaty had been to bring about the construction of large 10,000 tons 'light' cruisers armed with twelve or fifteen 6in guns. The US Navy had produced the *Brooklyn* class armed with fifteen 6in guns and the general design was based on the New Orleans class. However, apart from the obvious difference in armament, the hull was modified to a flush deck layout with high freeboard and the aircraft hangars, cranes and catapults were all moved right aft to the stern, a practice adopted by all subsequent US cruisers and battleships. The scale of protection and machinery installation was very similar to the *New Orleans* class.

With such a heritage, the *Brooklyn* class had obvious potential as a heavy cruiser if armed with 8in guns instead of the lighter 6in piece. Accordingly, a suitable design was drawn up and *Wichita*, the sole example, was laid down in October 1935 and completed in February 1939. The most obvious feature was the standard heavy cruiser armament of nine 8in guns in three triple mountings in place of the five triple 6in mounts of the original *Brooklyn* class. These guns were carried in a new Mk.4 turret which allowed the barrels to be more widely spaced to reduce problems associated with dispersion of shot in the earlier heavy cruisers. The secondary armament consisted of eight single 5in guns but, compared with the *New Orleans* class, they were better distributed with three on either beam and one on the centreline immediately forward of the bridge and another on the centreline aft, superfiring over X turret. More importantly they were the new 5in/38 cal weapon which was being extensively adopted throughout the fleet and had a longer range and better rate of fire than the 5in/25 cal, and was much more effective in the AA role. The centreline mountings and those immediately abreast the bridge were in enclosed turrets, but the remaining beam guns were open mounts. As completed, two of the latter were omitted due to stability concerns, but they were finally fitted in mid 1939. There were no torpedoes and the usual light AA armament of eight 0.5in machine guns was initially fitted. The aircraft arrangements on the stern allowed up to four aircraft to be carried, two on the catapults and two in a hangar below the quarterdeck.

Wartime modifications were relatively limited and mostly involved additions to the light AA armament, initially two quadruple 1.1in mountings but these were later replaced by 40mm guns and by 1945 the outfit comprised twenty 40mm (4 quadruple and two twin) and twenty single 20mm guns. Air and surface warning radars were fitted and the gunnery directors all eventually received gunnery ranging radars. The midships boat crane was removed and, in common with most of the pre-war cruisers, the lower deck scuttle openings were plated over to improve watertight integrity.

After completion in 1939 *Wichita* served with the Atlantic fleet until the end of 1942 when she transferred to the Pacific and was involved in the Aleutian campaign in the middle of 1943. Following a refit at the end of the year, she was involved in several operations in support of the Allied advance in the South and Central Pacific including the Battle of the Philippine Sea and the Leyte actions. As with the other heavy cruisers, she was laid up in 1947 and scrapped in 1959 although at one stage was considered for conversion to a missile-armed cruiser.

With the completion of the *Wichita*, the US Navy possessed a total of eighteen heavy cruisers and under the terms of the 1930 London Naval Treaty was not permitted to build any more until the oldest existing ships were at least 20 years old. However, the outbreak of the European war in 1939 effectively put an end to any necessity of conforming with any of the treaty restrictions and designs for a new class of heavy cruiser were investigated. The resulting *Baltimore* class ships were, therefore, not treaty cruisers in any sense and in fact were considerably larger than any previous heavy cruisers. However, it is relevant to follow the story of the heavy cruiser to its logical conclusion and therefore they and their successors are described below. In fact, the United States was the only country to continue building heavy cruisers in any significant numbers (Japan actually laid down two ships during the war but neither was completed) and no less than twenty-four *Baltimore* class ships were ordered although only eighteen were actually completed including four to modified designs and only six saw any significant service before the end of the war.

The design was originally based on the *Wichita* but beam was progressively increased, at first to improve stability margins and then to allow the installation of a secondary battery of twin 5in/38cal mountings. Hull length was increased in proportion so that overall length was some 65ft greater. The standard main armament of nine 8in guns in three triple turrets was retained and the secondary battery now consisted of no less than twelve 5in guns in twin mountings, one each on the centreline fore and aft, and two more on either beam. A light AA battery of four quadruple 40mm mountings was planned but by the time the first ships were completed no less than twelve such mountings were fitted together with up to twenty-eight 20mm guns. There were no torpedoes and the aircraft arrangements followed the now standard arrangement on the stern with two catapults and cranes. As standard displacement had now risen to over 14,000 tons, the machinery utilised new high pressure boilers to raise output to 120,000 shp. Boiler rooms and turbine spaces were arranged on the unit principle resulting in two well spaced funnels giving the ships a balanced appearance. From the very start, the hull was designed with no scuttles and all internal spaces were provided with forced ventilation and artificial lighting. This, of course, inevitably raised the demand for electrical power, already high due to the demands of the radar, fire control systems, and power control of the gun mountings so that a substantial generating capacity was built in. Armour protection was to the same scale as the *Wichita* although the main belt and decks were longer. Overall, protection accounted for almost 13% of the standard displacement and it was backed up by increased sub division of the hull to assist damage control.

Only *Baltimore*, *Boston*, *Canberra*, *Quincy*, *Pittsburgh* and *St. Paul* saw any wartime action. *Canberra*, named after the Australian cruiser sunk at Savo Island, was hit by a torpedo during the Leyte campaign and with several boiler rooms and turbine spaces flooded she was immobilised and had to be taken in tow by *Wichita*. This put her out of the war as repairs were not completed until October 1945.

Even while the first *Baltimore* class ships were being built, the design was reviewed in 1942 and a number of changes were incorportaed. The most obvious of these was the combination of the boiler uptakes into a single broad funnel and the bridge superstructure was rearranged into a more compact structure so that the HACS was mounted further forward. These changes had the effect of improving the arcs of fire for the AA batteries. A redesign of the stern area allowed a single crane to plumb both catapults and the hangar size was reduced. It was envisaged that all new heavy cruisers laid down from 1943 onwards would be built to this revised design, known as the *Oregon City* class after the lead ship, but in the event only three (CA122 *Oregon City*, CA123 *Albany*, and CA124 *Rochester*) were actually completed, well after the end of the war. A fourth ship, CA125 *Northampton*, was laid down in 1944 but was finally completed as a command ship in 1953 and bore no resemblance at all to the cruisers of the Second World War.

The ferocious battles around Guadalcanal in 1942 had highlighted the relatively slow rate of fire of the standard 8in gun, perhaps justifying the arguments of those who favoured light cruisers armed with more of the faster firing 6in guns. However, the US Navy was firmly attached to the concept of the heavy cruiser and sought to remedy the problem by producing an automatic 8in/55 cal gun capable of ten rounds per minute. Development of this weapon was not completed until the end of 1945 and its associated triple mounting was too heavy to install in the *Oregon City* class as originally intended and it was necessary to draw up a new design. This was based on the earlier ships but length and beam was increased in order to carry a main armament of nine 8in/55cal guns in three triple turrets, a secondary armament of twelve 5in/38cal guns in six twin turrets and an AA battery of twenty-four 3in/50cal in twin mountings. The fire control systems were upgraded and included radar equipped directors for the 3in guns. As a consequence of these improvements the standard displacement rose to around 17,000 tons and over 21,000 tons at full load. In almost every respect, apart from the weight of main armament and protection, which was similar to the standard *Baltimore* scale, these ships were the equal of or superior to the typical Second World War battleship. Initial plans called for the construction of twelve *Des Moines* class cruisers but most of these were cancelled at the end of the war and only four were laid down in 1945 and of these, only three (CA134 *Des Moines*, CA139 *Salem*, CA148 *Newport News*) were completed in 1948/49. *Des Moines* and *Salem* were laid up in 1961 and 1959 respectively but *Newport News* remained in commission until 1975, the last 8in gunned heavy cruiser in service anywhere in the world. With her passing the story of the traditional heavy cruiser, brought about originally by the Washington Treaty of 1922, finally came to an end. Although many navies still include cruisers in their fleets, these are sophisticated vessels with entirely different characteristics, armed with guided missiles and utilising modern electronic technologies. There is no comparison with the heavy cruisers of the past whose fighting power was still measured almost entirely by the number and calibre of the guns carried.

PART THREE

The Final Test (Cruisers at War)

CHAPTER IX

Atlantic, NW Europe and Trade Protection

At the outbreak of war on 3 September 1939 the Royal Navy's heavy cruisers were widely scattered around the globe. Apart from *Suffolk*, *London* and *Norfolk*, which were undergoing refits, none were based in home waters. *Devonshire*, *Shropshire* and *Sussex* formed the 1st Cruiser Squadron with the Mediterranean Fleet while *Kent*, *Cornwall* and *Dorsetshire*, along with the light cruiser *Birmingham*, formed the 5th Cruiser Squadron on the China Station. *Exeter* and *Cumberland* were in the South Atlantic while *Berwick* and *York* were attached to the America and West Indies Station. This widely scattered disposition was part of the overall forces deployed around the world to protect and represent British interests but, now that war had broken out, their prime task was the traditional role of cruisers: protection of British and Commonwealth maritime trade and also ensuring the safe passage of numerous troop convoys as Britain concentrated her military forces at strategically important points.

Although the German Navy was relatively small in 1939, and none of the new heavy cruisers had been commissioned, it did however have the three *Deutschland* class *panzerschiffe* (literally armoured ship, but more popularly known as pocket battleships). Displacing over 10,000 tons and armed with six 11in guns, these diesel powered commerce raiders posed a serious threat to British maritime interests. One of these, *Admiral Graf Spee* commanded by Kapitan zur see Hans Langsdorff, had sailed from Germany on 21 August 1939, before hostilities had opened and headed for the open spaces of the South Atlantic where she remained undetected until claiming her first victim on 30 September. In reaction to this the Admiralty organised hunting groups, comprising no less than four aircraft carriers, three battlecruisers and thirteen cruisers to reinforce the existing patrols in the South Atlantic and Indian oceans. The cruisers were organised as Force F (*Berwick*, *York*), Force G (*Cumberland*, *Exeter*), Force H (*Sussex* and *Shropshire*), Force I (*Cornwall* and *Dorsetshire* plus the carrier *Eagle*), while Force M, based at Dakar, comprised the French cruisers *Dupleix* and *Foch*. Even if the *Graf Spee* had not sunk a single ship, this diversion of effort to track her down was a major success for the Germans. As it was, the *Graf Spee* claimed several further victims in the South Atlantic and Indian Oceans. Later she headed towards the Plate estuary and on the morning of the 13 December 1939 was some 300 miles east of Montevideo. In the meantime, Allied patrols had been searching fruitlessly for the elusive pocket battleship but one of Langsdorff's victims, the 10,086 ton Doric Star, got off a distress message before being sunk. Based on this report Commodore Harwood, commander of the RN South American Division, made an inspired calculation of the *Graf Spee*'s likely actions, forecasting that she would be off the Plate estuary by the 13th December, and instructed his scattered force of three cruisers to concentrate accordingly. These comprised the 8in cruiser HMS *Exeter* and two 6in cruisers, Ajax and Achilles. This was not quite the best combination to tackle the *Graf Spee* but in the circumstances it had to suffice.

As dawn broke on the 13th, Harwood's ships were in line ahead steering north-east when smoke was sighted at 06:14 on a bearing of 324°. In accordance with his pre-planned tactics of trying to split the enemy's main armament, he ordered *Exeter* to close and identify the unknown vessel while the two light cruisers continued on their original course. *Exeter* soon signalled that she had a pocket battleship in sight and two minutes later the *Graf Spee* opened fire on her. For a while, Langsdorff continued to head south-east and chose to split his main armament, using one triple turret against *Exeter* and the other against *Ajax* and *Achilles* which were now approaching his port bow on a course of 340°. However as *Exeter* closed the range and her 8in guns began firing full salvoes, Langsdorff concentrated both 11in turrets on her and quickly scored several hits. *Exeter* was now seriously damaged with both forward turrets out of action, a fire raging amidships, most of her bridge staff killed or wounded and was being conned from an emergency steering position right aft. Her after turret was in local control. Despite this she manoeuvred to fire her port torpedoes although these missed.

Seeing *Exeter's* predicament, Harwood ordered his two light cruisers to close the range and they in turn came in for some punishment, *Achilles* suffered from a near miss while *Ajax* had her after turrets knocked out by an 11in shell. For a while, the light cruisers hauled off, but closed the range again when Langsdorff turned towards the crippled *Exeter* with the apparent intention of finishing her off. Fortunately, he turned away and after a few parting salvoes which brought down Ajax's topmast and wireless aerials, he settled onto a westerly course with the two British light cruisers trailing him but keeping out of range. From the British point of view, the action was now in the balance. The *Exeter* was too seriously damaged to continue (her after turret had now failed) and she was instructed to make for the Falkland Islands for repairs. *Ajax* and *Achilles* were both damaged and had expended over half their 6in ammunition. On the other hand, although declining action, the *Graf Spee* appeared relatively undamaged and could still be capable of sinking the British ships if the action was renewed.

Amazingly, apart from a few salvoes to keep the cruisers at bay, Langsdorff continued to retreat eastwards and eventually entered Montevideo harbour, in Uruguay just after midnight. Daylight inspection revealed that the *Graf Spee* had received around 60 hits, including several 8in shells around the bridge area. Some of the forward 11in guns and also some 5.9in secondary guns appeared to be out of action. Nevertheless, the situation was still critical. With the nearest British forces two days steaming away, the odds were still in the German's favour if the *Graf Spee* was to sortie before reinforcements could arrive. Fortunately, the heavy cruiser HMS *Cumberland* arrived at 22:00 on the 14th having steamed 1,000 miles from the Falklands in 34 hours. Ashore a diplomatic game was played to ensure that the *Graf Spee* was not permitted to depart from the neutral port until heavier reinforcements could arrive. However, at 18:15 on evening of 17 December the *Graf Spee* left Montevideo and headed south-west for only six miles before stopping and offloading her remaining crew to an accompanying German supply vessel. Within minutes the once proud ship was rent apart by demolition charges in the magazines and she burned fiercely as she settled in the shallow waters. Kapitan Langsdorff and his crew were taken to Argentina where he subsequently committed suicide. This victory was a major boost for the Royal Navy in the early stages of the war.

Nevertheless, it had been a close run affair. The *Graf Spee's* gunnery had been unerringly accurate in the early stages and the *Exeter* had been seriously damaged although, considering that she had not been designed to withstand direct hits by 11in shells, it was miracle that her machinery was unaffected and she was able to manoeuvre and steam out of range. However, she was completely disabled as a fighting unit and might well have sunk were it not for the valiant diversionary tactics of the light cruisers. On the credit side, the Germans were surprised at the effectiveness of the British 8in shells and damage caused by *Exeter's* hits was one of the major factors in causing Langsdorff to break off the action and subsequently to scuttle his ship. *Exeter* limped south to the Falklands where it was seriously considered that she was beyond economic repair and should be laid up. Churchill, however, would have none of this and insisted that the ship be brought home and she eventually arrived at her home port of Devonport on 14 February, 1940.

Despite the loss of the *Graf Spee*, the *Kriegsmarine* mounted other commerce raiding sorties by various warships and auxiliary cruisers. Combating these operations tied down significant numbers of Allied cruisers for much of the first half of the war and some of the relevant actions will be recounted. However, the next major naval operations involving the European navies were occasioned by the German invasion and occupation of Norway which began on 9 April 1940. Virtually the whole of the German Navy was thrown into this operation and although the objectives were met, the naval losses were serious, although not quite as bad as the Naval High Command had forecast. Two of the *Kriegsmarine's* heavy cruisers were involved. The *Admiral Hipper*, together with four destroyers was assigned to convey troops to occupy the port of Bergen on Norway's west coast. Early on 8 April, while en route to their objective, one of the destroyers sighted the British destroyer Glowworm and the *Admiral Hipper* turned back to assist. In a short but fierce action, *Glowworm* managed to close within yards of the heavy cruiser under cover of a smoke screen. At pointblank range she was torn apart by the *Hipper*'s 8in guns but not before she successfully rammed her larger protagonist on the starboard bow. Despite the damage, *Hipper* continued to Trondheim to land her troops before returning to Kiel for repairs which lasted until well into May. In the meantime her sister ship, the newly commissioned *Blücher*, set out in company with the *panzerschiffe Lützow*, light cruiser Emden and several smaller vessels carrying troops intended to occupy the capital, Oslo. The approach to the city was along the 50 mile stretch of Oslofiord; narrow waters which were known to be defended by forts and gun batteries. In the circumstances the attempted passage was fraught with danger and it can only be assumed that the Germans thought that the impressive show of force would reduced the Norwegian defenders to a state of passivity. In fact, the outcome was quite different. As the ships entered the Drobak Narrows the Norwegian batteries, which included 11in guns, laid down a storm of fire which engulfed the *Blücher*, setting her on fire and jamming her steering. As she drifted helplessly, she was hit by two torpedoes fired from the Kaholm Island fort. The resulting fires spread to her magazines which blew up and the battered hulk sank just over an hour later taking 125 of her crew and 195 soldiers with her. The *Lützow* was also heavily damaged and the German ships were forced to withdraw until troops could be landed to overpower the forts. This was duly done and German forces occupied Oslo on the following day.

The Norwegian campaign saw several other major actions including the two battles of Narvik where the German destroyer force was all but wiped out, but heavy cruisers were not involved. On the British side operations were covered by the Home Fleet under Admiral Forbes and this included the heavy cruisers *Berwick*, *Devonshire* and *Suffolk*. For the first time in naval operations, the use of air power had a significant influence and the Royal Navy deployed two aircraft carriers, *Glorious* and *Ark Royal*. However the land based *Luftwaffe* controlled the skies and in an effort to counter this threat the cruiser *Suffolk* was dispatched to bombard the coastal airfield at Stavanger on the night of 16 April. This operation was fraught with difficulties. The ship's two Walrus amphibians were launched to spot for the bombardment but both suffered radio failures and only visual signalling was possible. Despite this, the gunfire was very effective and considerable damage was done before the force withdrew at high speed after dawn had broken. RAF fighter cover had been arranged to cover the withdrawal but due to a misunderstanding regarding the ship's position the rendezvous was not effected. *Suffolk* now suffered a continuous series of air attacks over the next six hours until she was out of range. High level attacks were broken up by the effective high angle fire of the 4in battery and bombs which fell near the ship were evaded. However, as was so often to prove the case, the German Stuka dive bombers were an entirely different proposition and their precision attacks were much more difficult to dodge or fight off, especially as at that stage of the war the close-in light AA armament was woefully inadequate. Inevitably the *Suffolk* was hit and a heavy bomb penetrated the quarterdeck at the base of X turret, destroying the turret, setting fire to the magazine, and killing 33 officers and men and wounding another thirty-eight. The stern was flooded and the steering temporarily disabled. Speed was reduced to 18 knots as the ship struggled westwards for a further three hours before friendly aircraft finally put in an appearance. When the ship finally limped into Scapa Flow on the 18 April, it was obvious to all that naval operations were now prey to the effects of air power and that the big gun warship was no longer master of the seas. *Suffolk*'s damage was so serious that she was out of action for almost a year, only rejoining the fleet in February 1941.

Norwegian operations continued until the end of May 1940 when it was obvious that further resistance to the German advances was futile and the decision was made to withdraw all Allied forces (both French and British troops were involved, and French warships had played a significant part in support of the British effort). Of course, the disastrous events in France and Holland were also a major factor. A major evacuation was planned for the first week of June and some 24,000 troops were successfully brought off. A major reverse for the British was the loss of the carrier *Glorious* which, sailing independently, was caught and sunk by the battlecruisers *Scharnhorst* and *Gneisenaü*. Her calls for assistance were not picked up by any allied warship except the cruiser *Devonshire* which, flying the flag of Vice Admiral John Cunningham, had sailed from Tromso on 7 April carrying the King of Norway and his entourage, as well as the countries gold reserves. Assuming that the message would have been picked up by other ships, and thinking of the security of his important passengers, Cunningham maintained radio silence. This had unfortunate results as the loss of the *Glorious* was not realised for two days and consequently many of the survivors died before they could be found and rescued.

The withdrawal from Norway followed closely on the heels of the Dunkirk evacuation and with the fall of France, Britain now stood alone against the combined forces of Germany and Italy. In an attempt to ensure that some of the French African colonies remained within the allied sphere of influence, an expedition was mounted to land Free French forces at Dakar in French West Africa. Under the nominal command of General de Gaulle, it was anticipated that a British show of strength would be enough to allow the landings to be unopposed. Although the operation, code named 'Menace', was not scheduled until 22 September, the 1st Cruiser Squadron comprising *Berwick*, *Cumberland* and HMAS *Australia* was earlier involved in an abortive attempt to prevent three Vichy light cruisers from reaching Dakar as reinforcements. The landing operation itself was an embarrassing failure as the Vichy opposition was much stronger than expected. *Berwick* had been replaced by HMS *Devonshire* and the 1st Cruiser squadron was heavily engaged over the three days of fighting. *Cumberland* was hit by a 9.4in shell fired from one of the forts during the initial bombardment. *Australia* was detached to pursue an enemy destroyer which turned out to be *L'Audacieuse*, one of the French super destroyers armed with 5.5in guns. *Australia* opened fire when within range and almost immediately scored fatal hits, the French ship quickly sunk under a hail of 8in shells. Over the next two days *Devonshire* and *Australia* were engaged in gunnery duels with shore batteries as well as French warships which included the partially completed battleship *Richelieu* as well as two of the light cruisers which had previously eluded the British patrols. *Australia* was straddled and hit by two 6in shells although the damage was not serious and there were no casualties. By the 25 September, the shore defences were still resisting strongly, the battleships *Barham* and *Resolution* had both been damaged and the former also took a torpedo fired by the submarine *Bévésiers*, while the aircraft carrier *Ark Royal* had lost several aircraft. Faced with such determined resistance, Churchill ordered the operation to be abandoned and the ships withdrew.

While she rebuilt her shattered army and fought the Battle of Britain to secure the home base, Britain was even more dependent on her maritime trade routes to maintain a flow of food, armaments and raw materials so that she could continue the war. Fortunately for the Royal Navy, the U-boat fleet was still relatively small, although it was inflicting growing losses, and the Germans had no surface warships available in the immediate aftermath of the Norwegian campaign. Eventually the *Admiral Hipper* sailed from Kiel for the North Atlantic on 24 September 1940 but was forced to return with machinery defects, a recurring problem with the German heavy cruisers. She left again early in December and subsequently attacked convoy WS5A off the Spanish coast on Christmas Day. The convoy included two aircraft carriers but their decks were packed with aircraft being transported to North Africa. However, the escort included the heavy cruiser *Berwick* and light cruisers *Bonaventure* and *Dunedin*. This meeting led to the first action of the war between opposing 8in cruisers as the *Hipper* successfully engaged *Berwick* at long range and scored two hits before her captain, Kapitan sur Zee Meisel, decided to withdraw in view of the strength of the escort and also because of further machinery problems. Two of the convoy's merchantmen were damaged and, while siling for Breat, *Hipper* sank another merchantman that was sailing independently. Two of the convoy's merchantmen were damaged and while sailing for Brest *Hipper* sank another merchantman that was sailing independently. The capture of the French port was one of the factors that allowed the short ranged *Hipper* to sortie into the Atlantic and the port was also subsequently used by other major German warships. By the beginning of April 1941, as well as *Hipper*, *Lützow* and the battlecruisers *Scharnhorst* and *Gneisenaü* had made Atlantic sorties, together sinking a total of 48 ships totalling 275,000 grt. Although nowhere near the totals sunk by U-boats in the same period, the deployment of these major warships in the North Atlantic entailed an enormous counter effort on the part of the Royal Navy and most of the Home fleet heavy cruisers were constantly at sea on patrol or as part of a hunting group.

In April the *Kriegsmarine* planned its most powerful Atlantic raid of all, Operation Rheinübung, involving the new 50,000 ton battleship *Bismarck* accompanied by the newly completed heavy cruiser *Prinz Eugen*. Sailing on 18 May 1941 the two German ships passed through the Kattegat between Denmark and Sweden under the command of Admiral Gunther Lütjens before proceeding north to the Norwegian port of Bergen with the intention of breaking out into the Atlantic to attack

In preparation for the Bismarck *sortie (Operation Rheinübung),* Prinz Eugen *was given a distinctive disruptive camouflage scheme.* Bismarck *was given an identical scheme in order to confuse the enemy forces, a scheme which seems to have worked as initially the* Hood *and* Prince of Wales *aimed to engage the cruiser although the mistake was realised before fire was opened.* WZB

Allied convoys. Their passage from the Baltic was reported from Swedish sources and the two ships were located at Bergen by RAF reconnaissance aircraft on the afternoon of the 21st. At Scapa Flow Admiral Tovey, C-in-C Home Fleet, immediately planned the deployment of ships to counter any possible foray by the German force into the North Atlantic. To the north, the heavy cruisers *Norfolk* and *Suffolk* under Rear Admiral Wake Walker patrolled the Denmark Strait between Iceland and the Arctic ice field and these two ships were destined to play a critical role in what was to become one of the greatest sea chases of all time. South of Iceland, covering the Faroes Gap, were the cruisers *Manchester*, *Birmingham* and *Arethusa*. The Admiralty also placed the battlecruiser *Repulse* and aircraft carrier Victorious at the disposal of the C-in-C, these ships having previously been scheduled to accompany a Gibraltar bound convoy. Finally, the battlecruiser *Hood*, the new battleship *Prince of Wales* and escorting destroyers, were ordered northwards to assist Wake Walker's force covering the Denmark Strait. This powerful force left Scapa flow at 00:52 on the morning of the 22nd although it was not until the evening that a Fleet Air Arm aircraft finally confirmed that the *Bismarck* and *Prinz Eugen* had left Bergen. In fact they had sailed almost 24 hours earlier. Admiral Tovey immediately left Scapa Flow with the rest of the Home fleet, including HMS *Victorious*, and set course to the west where he would be in the best position to support the forces already deployed. The 23 May passed slowly with no news of the German ships until late in the evening when the cruiser *Suffolk* sighted the two German ships racing through the fogbanks of the Denmark Strait. Sighting reports were immediately dispatched and the two cruisers settled down to shadow the enemy ships until heavier forces could be brought to bear. In fact Admiral Tovey's dispositions had been remarkably effective and it was quickly apparent that Vice Admiral Holland's force (*Hood* and *Prince of Wales*) was ideally placed to intercept the *Bismarck* and *Prinz Eugen* early on the 24th to the south-west of Iceland. Accurate and effective reporting from the shadowing cruisers enabled Holland to bring his two capital ships into contact with the enemy at 05:35, just as dawn was breaking.

Not wasting any time, Holland ordered the *Hood* and *Prince of Wales* onto a north-west course to close the enemy as quickly as possible. At 05:52, Hood opened fire while *Bismarck* replied two minutes later with very accurate shooting. As the range fell to less than 20,000 yards. Holland ordered the *Hood* and *Prince of Wales* to turn to port in order to open the A arcs so that all guns could fire but, even as they did so, the *Bismarck*'s fifth salvo crashed home on the Hood. Within seconds the great battlecruiser was rent apart by a massive explosion and sank within three minutes, leaving only a pall of smoke and three survivors from a crew of over 1,400 men. It was the Royal Navy's worst ever calamity. To make matters worse, the German ships quickly concentrated their fire on the *Prince of Wales* which was hit several times. One shell landed directly on the bridge killing or wounding most of the men stationed there. With her after turret jammed, she was forced to withdraw and the two German ships made off to the south-west still doggedly shadowed by the cruisers *Norfolk* and *Suffolk*. Aboard HMS *Norfolk*, Rear Admiral Wake Walker now found himself in command of the forces in contact with the enemy. Although not immediately realised, the *Bismarck* had not escaped unscathed having been hit at least twice by heavy calibre shells. One of these had caused flooding in some of the bow compartments and ruptured vital fuel tanks, this damage subsequently restricting the ship to a maximum of 28 knots.

The loss of the Hood now made it vital for the Royal Navy to sink the *Bismarck* if pride was to be restored. With the *Prince of Wales* partially disabled and no match for the *Bismarck*, the responsibility for maintaining contact until other forces could be brought to bear fell to Wake Walker's two cruisers. Throughout the 24th more ships were ordered to join the hunt including the battleships *Rodney*, *Ramilles* and *Revenge* which had been escorting various convoys while Force H (*Ark Royal*, *Renown* and *Sheffield*) was already heading north from Gibraltar. By the end of the day, as the *Bismarck* and *Prinz Eugen* headed south still shadowed by the British cruisers, there were 5 battleships, 2 battlecruisers, two aircraft carriers and 12 cruisers, as well as many destroyers actively involved in the operation. Among these was the carrier *Victorious* which was ploughing steadily westwards in an attempt to get within range to launch an air strike. As her hangars were full of crated Hurricanes for delivery to Malta, she could only operate a small force of six Fulmars and nine Swordfish. Armed with torpedoes, the latter were launched late in the evening of the 24th and made a brave night attack through rain showers, claiming at least one hit. By now the German battleship was alone, the *Prinz Eugen* having separated undetected before the air attack and she eventually reached Brest on 1 June. In the meantime the *Bismarck* continued south, but in the early hours of the 25th the shadowing British cruisers lost radar contact with her after maintaining contact for over 30 hours. Having managed to shake off the cruisers the *Bismarck* altered course to the south-east, heading towards Brest. The two cruisers, with the damaged *Prince of Wales* still in company, fanned out to the south-west on the assumption that Lütjens was still heading out into the Atlantic to attack the vulnerable convoys, but in so doing, they began to draw away from their prey. The next 24 hours were critical for the British forces as all resources were concentrated on relocating the *Bismarck* but, as the hours dragged by, there was a very real prospect that she would escape. Unaware that contact had been lost, the *Bismarck* transmitted several long messages back to Germany which were picked up by British D/F stations. Unfortunately, these were incorrectly plotted and gave a false impression that she had reversed course and was heading back towards Norway. Eventually, contact was regained at 10:30 on the morning of the 26th by a Catalina flying boat of 209 squadron, but by then the *Bismarck* was far ahead of the Home Fleet Battleship *King George V* and there was little chance of catching her. The only hope lay in the Swordfish torpedo aircraft aboard the carrier *Ark Royal* which was ideally placed ahead of the *Bismarck*'s track. The first strike of 14 aircraft was flown off at 14:50 and, sighting a ship through the broken cloud, they dived to the attack and launched 11 torpedoes. Unfortunately their target was not the *Bismarck*, but the cruiser *Sheffield* which had been detached to shadow the German battleship. Luckily, the torpedoes missed although some exploded prematurely. A second strike was hastily arranged and, benefiting from experience, the torpedo's duplex pistols were replaced by contact pistols. This time there was no mistake and at 20:53 fifteen Swordfish began their gallant attacks through heavy anti-aircraft fire, coming in close before dropping their torpedoes. At least two of these hit, but initially it was difficult to ascertain what damage had been caused. In fact, one of the torpedoes had struck the starboard quarter damaging the steering gear and jamming the rudders so that the ship began circling uncontrollably before eventually settling on a meandering course to the north-west.

The way was now clear for the *King George V*, with the battleship *Rodney* now in company, to close and engage the *Bismarck* but Tovey decided to hold off until dawn. In the meantime the 4th Destroyer Flotilla harrased the enemy through the night and possibly scored a couple of torpedo hits. Thereafter, they continued to shadow the *Bismarck* until the morning when the *King George V* and *Rodney*, supported by the cruisers *Norfolk* and *Dorsetshire*, finally gained contact at 08:53 on the morning of the 27th. *Rodney* opened fire at 08:47, the *King George V* following almost immediately, while, coincidentally, the *Bismarck* replied, initially firing at *Rodney*. For once the British gunnery was as accurate as the Germans and *Rodney* scored a hit with her third salvo and further hits put the *Bismarck*'s fore turrets out of action. As the range closed to 12,000 yards, the combatants passed on reciprocal courses so at 09:16 the British ships turned northwards and further closed the range as the *Bismarck*'s fire slackened under the punishment she was receiving. Finally, at around 10:05, the two battleships closed to within 3,000 yards, *Rodney* scoring a hit with one of her 24.5in torpedoes at this point. The *Bismarck* was now a blazing wreck and was obviously finished so, desperately short of fuel, the British battleships broke off the action and set course to the north-west, leaving the *Norfolk* and *Dorsetshire* to finish her off with torpedoes. *Norfolk*, the only ship to see the whole pursuit from start to finish, fired four torpedos and *Dorsetshire* another three which eventually caused the *Bismarck* to roll over and sink at 10:40. The remaining British ships closed in to pick up survivors but only 110 were eventually rescued before it was necessary to withdraw under threat of possible aircraft and U-boat attacks. The *Hood* had been avenged and one of the greatest and most dramatic sea chases was at an end.

An interesting sidelight to this action was that the Spanish heavy cruiser, *Canaris*, was one of the ships which subsequently searched for survivors although she found none. *Canaris*, it will be recalled, was a modified version of the British *County* class cruisers.

The German cruiser *Prinz Eugen* had reached Brest on 1 June where it joined the battlecruisers *Scharnhorst* and *Gneisenaü*. The three ships were subjected to continuous attacks by British bombers and if they remained at Brest it was almost inevitable that they would eventually be sunk by bombing and, at Hitler's instigation, an audacious and detailed plan was drawn up to get them back to Germany. The chosen route was not through the vast expanses of the Atlantic Ocean, but through the narrow waters of the English Channel, right under the noses of the Royal Navy and the RAF. On paper it was an extremely risky operation and one which would almost certainly result in the loss of some of the ships attempting the passage. In fact, by a combination of planning, skill, determination and luck the German ships were to score a major tactical success and severely embarrass the British at a critical time in the war.

In the forenoon of 12 February 1942, as the ships raced up Channel at 28 knots, they were masked from air reconnaissance by low cloud and rain and were joined by torpedo boat flotillas from Le Havre and, later, from Dunkirk, while a continuous escort of 16 aircraft was stationed over the ships at all times. Thus, it was not until 10:42 that the ships were spotted already past Le Havre by a lone Spitfire whose pilot did not make a sighting report until after landing back at his base at 11:09. The first force to react were five MTBs based at Dover Making contact at 12:23, they were unable to penetrate the close escort of E-boats and torpedo boats. No hits were made but as they withdrew six Swordfish of 825 Squadron led by Lt.Cdr. Eugene Esmonde swept in to attack. An expected escort of Spitfires had missed the rendezvous and the slow moving biplanes were shot out of the sky by the German fighters or the intense AA fire of the ships. Shore batteries at Dover had briefly opened fire at 12:15 but by then the German ships were rapidly moving out of range and no damage was done. The German force continued to head north-east for another two hours without further attacks until 14:30 when *Scharnhorst* hit a mine but was not badly damaged and was soon under way again. From about 14:45 onwards, over a period of two and half hours, the German ships were subject to a series of uncoordinated air attacks by aircraft of Bomber and Coastal Commands. However, the low cloud frustrated most of these attack and no hits were scored.

The only other British forces able to intercept were the Harwich based destroyers which eventually made contact with the German ships off the Hook of Holland at 15:17. Two attacked one of the battlecruisers while the other pair pressed on and launched torpedoes at a ship which turned out to be the *Prinz Eugen*. No hits were scored and the destroyer *Worcester* was seriously damaged although she eventually made it back to Harwich. Nothing further could be done to stop the German ships although the *Gneisenaü* hit a mine at 19:55 while north of Vlieland, although damage was slight and she was soon underway again. Almost two hours later, the *Scharnhorst* struck a second mine which caused more serious damage than the first. Eventually, she got underway again and limped into Wilhelmshaven the next morning. Nevertheless, the outcome was an undoubted tactical victory for the German Navy although in strategic terms little was actually gained. The *Gneisenaü* was seriously damaged in a bombing raid only two weeks later and she was never again fit for service. The *Scharnhorst* went on to join German naval forces in Norway but at least the Royal Navy could now concentrate its own forces to meet this threat without also having to guard against a breakout by other ships based on the French ports. The cruiser *Prinz Eugen* was the only major vessel to reach Germany undamaged and she was almost immediately dispatched to Norway in order to threaten the British supply convoys to Russia. However, whilst on passage she was torpedoed by the British submarine *Trident* on 23 February 1942 and after temporary repairs at Trondheim she returned to Kiel on 18 May and was out of action until the following October. Thereafter, she was retained in the Baltic as a training ship, and from mid 1944 was engaged in support of retreating German forces on the Eastern Front. When the European War ended on 8 May 1945, she was alongside at Copenhagen where she was surrendered intact. Subsequently, she was expended as a target on the American atomic bomb trials at Bikini Atoll in December 1946.

The loss of the *Bismarck* and the return of other ships to Germany effectively ended North Atlantic operations by German surface warships. However, from the outbreak of war until the end of 1941, a number of auxiliary cruisers variously disguised as Allied or neutral merchant ships had taken a small but steady toll of Allied ships. During that period they had sunk 618,108 tons of merchant shipping as well as one armed merchant cruiser and the light cruiser HMAS *Sydney*. The latter action occurred when the *Sydney* intercepted the raider *Komoran* off the West coast of Australia on 19 November 1941. Unsure of the identity of the strange ship, *Sydney*'s Captain closed to within one mile at which point the *Komoran* dropped her disguise and opened fire with her 5.9in guns and launched torpedoes, one of which hit the *Sydney*. A short but fierce action ensued and both ships eventually sank after drifting apart.

The tracking down of the other raiders fell to the Navy's cruiser force and several *County* class cruisers were involved. On 8 May, 1941, whilst on patrol in the Indian Ocean HMS *Cornwall* picked up a signal from the SS *British Emperor* that she was being attacked by a raider. Although the position given was some 500 miles away, *Cornwall* set course at high speed and launched her aircraft late in the afternoon to search ahead. Nothing was found but early the next day one of the aircraft sighted a ship which identified itself as the Norwegian SS *Tamerlane*. However, it was not until 4 o'clock in the afternoon that the cruiser came within visual range of the ship which refused to stop when challenged. An hour later, and having fired two warning shots, the *Cornwall* had closed to 12,000 yards when the enemy ship (Raider 33, *Pinguin*) realised the game was up and decided to stand and fight. With an armament of six 5.9in guns and four 21in torpedo tubes, she was capable of giving a good account of herself and, indeed quickly straddled and hit *Cornwall*. The British cruiser, in the meantime, was in all sorts of trouble. The range had closed to 10,500 yards and at this critical moment the electrical turret training circuits failed. As she turned away a shell damaged the forward steering gear and the ship was out of control for a short while. However, within minutes the steering was restored and the main armament was back in action. *Cornwall* had taken herself outside effective range of the enemy 5.9in guns and thereafter the contest was one sided as 8in shells smashed into the *Pinguin* which blew up 11 minutes after the action had begun.

However, *Cornwall*'s misfortunes were not at and end. As she manoeuvred to recover her aircraft she suffered a total electrical failure. This caused the ventilation fans to stop and as result the engine room temperature rose to almost 95° C and had to be abandoned after one engineer officer was fatally overcome. It was nearly an hour before power was restored and only at 9:40pm was she able to set course for the Seychelles.

The next success by the British heavy cruisers occurred in the South Atlantic near Ascension Island when *Devonshire* intercepted an unidentified merchant ship on 22 November 1941. A Walrus aircraft was launched and from information obtained from the aircrew *Devonshire*'s commander, Captain R.D.Oliver DSC RN, was immediately suspicious and thought that the ship was probably Raider 16 (*Atlantis*). This was sister ship to the *Pinguin* which *Cornwall* had previously sunk. In this case Captain Oliver kept his ship at a range of 12 to 18,000 yards while he exchanged signals with the C-in-C South Atlantic to positively identify the suspicious vessel. Eventually, fire was opened at 9:35am at a range of 17,500 yards, well outside that at which any effective response could be forthcoming from the *Atlantis*. The German ship did not reply and attempted to run to south-east under cover of smoke. As the concussion of *Devonshire*'s 8in guns had put her radar out of action, the cruiser was obliged to turn east to get regain visual contact. After a break of almost 20 minutes she reopened fire and following two on board heavy explosions the *Atlantis* sank at 10:16. Captain Oliver had noted that the Atlantis had persisted with a south-easterly course and was concerned that this might have been an attempt to lead him towards a U-boat. Consequently, no search was made for survivors and he withdrew in the opposite direction. *Atlantis* had been one of the most successful raiders and, under the command of Kapitan Bernhardt Rogge, had sunk no less than 21 allied merchant ships. In fact Captain Oliver's suspicions had been all to well founded as the *Atlantis* had been in the course of refuelling a U-boat when the *Devonshire*'s aircraft was first spotted and this had immediately cast off and submerged. Thanks to the *Devonshire*'s manoeuvring and speed, the U-boat was unable to get into a firing position although it subsequently assisted in recovering survivors and handed some on to the supply ship *Python* which later came to the scene of the action.

Another success involved HMS *Dorsetshire*, commanded by Captain A.W.S.Agar VC RN, which sighted an unknown vessel some 700 miles south-west of St. Helena in the South Atlantic during the afternoon of 9 December 1941. While closing to investigate, several small boats towed by a power boat were sighted on the port bow and patches of oil were observed on the water. This led Agar to assume that a U-boat was in the area and he, therefore, kept up a high speed zigzag and remained well clear of the surface vessel which had stopped after two warning shots were fired. It was observed that the boats were being lowered and subsequently the ship blew up and sank, having been deliberately scuttled. It transpired that the ship was the *Python* which had been acting as a supply ship to U-boats in the South Atlantic and her loss effectively ended the U-boat campaign in this area for almost a year. Altogether, there were some 500 survivors including some British survivors who had been prisoners aboard the *Atlantis*. An investigation by *Cornwall*'s aircraft showed that the first spotted boats contained stores and crates and had probably been involved in transferring them to a U-boat. Consequently, Agar decided that he could not endanger his ship by remaining in the area and withdrew. After an epic voyage, Python's survivors eventually made land in Namibia.

Although the protection of convoys and the hunting down of surface raiders was almost entirely carried out by ships of the British and Commonwealth navies in the first two years of the war, throughout 1941 the US Navy was gradually drawn into the conflict although not formally at war. The seriousness of such action was dramatically illustrated when the US destroyer *Reuben James* was sunk by a U-boat in October 1941. By the end of the year the US Navy provided a powerful escort for an important troop convoy (WS-12X) from Canada to South Africa and the Far East consisting of the aircraft carrier USS *Ranger*, two heavy cruisers (*Quincy* and *Vincennes*) and eight destroyers. The two cruisers were at Capetown on the morning of 8th December 1941 when news of the Japanese attack on Pearl Harbour came through. America was now truly at war.

In European waters, the Home Fleet was based at Scapa Flow from where it could sortie to support the Arctic convoys sailing around the north coast of Norway to the Russian ports of Murmansk and Archangel. Most of the surviving German capital ships were based in Norway from where their very existence was a contiuing and potent threat to the convoys. Indeed, as the tragic events of Convoy PQ17 demonstrated in July 1942, it was not even necessary for the German ships to put to sea. On that occasion, convinced that the battleship *Tirpitz* was about to fall on the helpless convoy, it was ordered to scatter with disastrous results, the individual ships being picked off by aircraft and U-boats while the *Tirpitz* remained safely anchored in Alten fiord. Interestingly, the covering forces for PQ17 included the American cruisers *Wichita* and *Tuscaloosa* which had been attached to the British Home Fleet. On the British side the cruisers *Cumberland*, *London* and *Norfolk* were also part of the distant covering forces.

After the PQ17 disaster, the next convoy (PQ18) did not sail until 2 September and was the most heavily protected to date, its covering forces including cruisers *Norfolk*, *London* and *Suffolk*. Despite this, it had one of the hardest passages of any Russian convoy and ultimately lost no less than thirteen ships out of a total of forty, most to air attack. A return convoy, QP14 was run at the same time and lost three out of fifteen merchant ships. Given this scale of losses, the next convoy (JW51)was not scheduled until mid December when the longer nights and winter weather would afford additional protection. Thirty merchant ships were assembled but it was decided to split them into two smaller and more manageable convoys designated JW51A and JW51B. The convoy escort was reinforced by two light cruisers, *Sheffield* and *Jamaica*, under Rear Admiral R.L.Burnett, and these were ordered to

A camouflaged Admiral *Hipper as she appeared at the Battle of Barents Sea in 1942 when she suffered major damage at the hands of the British light cruisers* Sheffield *and* Jamaica. WZB

remain in the vicinity of the convoy east of Bear Island and all the way to the Kola Inlet. Distant support was provided by units of the Home Fleet under the C-in-C, Admiral Tovey. On the German side there were numerous U-boats as well as the pocket battleship *Lützow* and heavy cruiser *Admiral Hipper* based at Altenfiord from where they could sortie at short notice. The stage was now set for a fascinating cruiser engagement in which the British 6in armed light cruisers would be pitted against the more heavily armed heavy cruiser *Hipper*, not to mention the 11in guns of the *Lützow*. In the 1930s there had been considerable debate over the relative merits of a light cruiser armed with twelve or fifteen 6in guns against a heavy cruiser with eight or nine 8in guns. Although firing a lighter shell, the 6in gun fired at a faster rate and given the greater number of guns the light cruiser could put up a similar, or greater, weight of shell over a given period when compared with the slower firing 8in gun, although the latter had the advantage of greater range. It was therefore thought that at night, or in conditions of low visibility, when actions might be fought at short range, the heavy cruiser would have no great advantage. This was about to tested in spectacular style.

JW51A sailed from Loch Ewe on 15 December 1942, and JW51B followed seven days later. The former had an unexpectedly quiet passage and reached the Kola Inlet safely on Christmas Day. JW51B also made good progress initially with its close destroyer escort under the command of Captain R.St V. Sherbrooke. On 28 December the convoy was hit by a storm which caused some of the merchantmen to become detached. By New Year's Eve, the storm had blown itself out although being mid-winter, full daylight was never attained and visibility varied between four and ten miles, reducing in frequent snow showers. Following a U-boat sighting report, the *Lützow* and *Hipper* together with six destroyers, had left Altenfiord on the evening of the 30th. Admiral Kummetz, in command of the German ships, planned to deploy *Hipper* and three destroyers to the north of the convoy to engage and draw off the escorting destroyers. The Lü tzow and three more destroyers would then come at the convoy from the south and sink the merchant ships while the escort was otherwise engaged. Initially, everything went well with the *Hipper* passing astern of the convoy at around 07:15 on the morning of the 31st. Sighting some ships in the distance, *Eckholt* and two other destroyers were sent to investigate. These in turn were later sighted from the destroyer HMS *Obdurate* which was ordered to close and report, although it was not until 09:30 that she was close enough to confirm their identity, at which point the German destroyers opened fire. Aboard the *Onslow*, Captain Sherbrooke immediately ordered *Orwell* and *Obedient* to join him and set off towards the sound of the guns. In the meantime, Kummetz ordered the *Hipper* to turn towards the convoy but for a while Sherbrooke successfully held the *Hipper* at bay and, with some intuition of the German plan, ordered *Obedient* and *Obdurate* to return cover the convoy. In the half light and intermittent visibility, a cat and mouse game continued for a while until the *Hipper* eventually turned on the two remaining British destroyers and scored four hits on Onslow, causing severe damage and seriously wounding Sherbrooke. Meanwhile Rear Admiral Burnett's two cruisers were to the north of the convoy although, due to radio silence being maintained, Burnett was not sure of its exact position. When he received Sherbrooke's sighting report, he also had radar contact with some unidentified ships to the north-east and initially headed towards them until it was realised that they were probably stragglers from the convoy. At the same time, the sight and sound of gunfire to the south increased and he therefore turned in that direction, working up to 31 knots. At around 10:30 some radar contacts were picked up and shortly afterwards more gunfire erupted to the south. Sheffield had a brief visual contact with the *Hipper* which was then lost from sight as she headed south and then east, aiming again for the convoy. As she did so, the destroyer *Achates* suddenly emerged from the drifting smokescreen and was hammered at point blank range by the 8in guns of the *Hipper*. The gallant destroyer drifted away, to capsize and sink after the action, although eighty-one of her crew were later rescued. The *Hipper* now turned north-west and engaged the other British destroyers, but this turn took her straight into the path of the *Sheffield* and *Jamaica* coming down from the north. With the advantage of the light they were able to open rapid fire and got off several salvoes before the German cruiser was able to reply. The *Hipper* was hit several times and one boiler room was put out action, reducing her speed. As the cruisers slugged it out at ranges down to four miles, two German destroyers suddenly appeared out of the gloom heading for the Sheffield, which they had mistakenly thought to be the *Hipper*. *Sheffield*'s captain immediately sized up the situation and turned towards the destroyers, pouring a withering fire into the *Eckholt*, and this was followed up by more of the same from the *Jamaica*, turning into a blazing wreck. However, this distraction enabled the *Hipper* to turn away and eventually make good her escape to the west. At 11:37 Kummetz ordered the remaining German forces to break off the battle and withdraw. During all this time the *Lützow* had been hovering to the south-east of the convoy but her captain lacked the resolution to take advantage of the situation and quickly withdrew when ordered. As the *Lützow* headed west she was briefly engaged by the British cruisers but the German ships continued to withdraw and the action was over by 12:36. JW51B was now safe and eventually reached the Kola Inlet without further loss.

When Hitler received the reports of the battle he was furious and the resulting restrictions under which German warships subsequently operated were almost enough to ensure that they would never again have such a good opportunity to destroy one of the British convoys. For the British it was a confidence boosting victory after the fiasco of PQ17 and Captain Sherbrooke was awarded the VC for his courageous leadership of the destroyers. The *Admiral Hipper* was seriously damaged and by February 1943 she was in Kiel dockyard for repairs although these were never fully completed and the ship saw no further action. She was seriously damaged by air attack on 3 May 1945 and was scuttled at Kiel, her hulk being broken up after the war.

The last serious attempt to attack the Russian convoys with a strong surface force occurred at the end of 1943 when the battlecruiser *Scharnhorst* sortied with six destroyers to attack convoy JW55B which had been located and shadowed by U-boats and aircraft from the 22 December. By 04:00 on the morning of the 26th JW55B was some 50 miles South of Bear Island, heading east with a close escort under the command of Captain McCoy (D17) of no less than fourteen destroyers, two frigates and a minesweeper. Vice Admiral Burnett's cruiser covering force consisting of the light cruisers *Belfast* and *Sheffield* supported by the veteran heavy cruiser HMS *Norfolk*, was closing from some 150 miles to the east. The C-in-C with the battleship *Duke of York* was some 350 miles to the south-west but on a parallel course to the convoy. News that the battlecruiser *Scharnhorst* was at sea was confirmed by an ULTRA report on receipt of which Fraser had begun deploying his ships in an attempt to intercept the German ships. By 08:00 the *Scharnhorst* had turned back onto a south-westerly course and was still attempting to locate the convoy when forty-five minutes later she was detected by Burnett's cruisers approaching from the south-east. The British cruisers manoeuvred to close the range and *Norfolk* opened fire with her 8in guns on the *Scharnhorst*, obtaining two hits, one of which damaged the German ship's radar. As the *Scharnhorst* turned to escape this attack, her destroyers became detached and played no further part in the action. Weather conditions were very rough (wind force 7-8) and the *Scharnhorst* was better able to maintain speed than the cruisers, drawing away to the north-east in an attempt to get around them and attack the convoy. Contact was lost for a while but Admiral Fraser ordered four destroyers to leave the convoy and reinforce the cruisers as they took up station ten miles ahead of JW55B, ready for any further attack. There was now a lull of almost two hours before the *Scharnhorst* was again detected on radar approaching from the east. At 12:21 she was within range and the British cruisers again opened fire, the *Scharnhorst* replying with her 11in guns. However, the combined firepower of the three cruisers, supported by the destroyers was enough to frustrate the *Scharnhorst*'s efforts to get at the convoy and she therefore turned away to the south with the intention of returning to Altenfiord, 200 miles away. During this exchange, *Norfolk* took two hits from the *Scharnhorst*'s 11in guns, one of which put X turret out of action, and all her radar, except the Type 284, was put out of action. One officer and six ratings were killed and several were injured. As the battlecruiser made off at high speed the cruisers including *Norfolk*, which was able to maintain speed despite her damage, followed astern and reported her movements to the C-in-C who, approaching in the *Duke of York* with light cruiser *Jamaica* and four destroyers in company from the south-west, was now ideally placed to intercept. At 16:17 radar contact was gained and as the range steadily closed, the destroyers were deployed ahead of the battleship in preparation for a torpedo attack. It was not until the range had closed to 12,000 yards that the *Duke of York*'s 14in guns opened fire on the *Scharnhorst* which until that moment had been totally unaware of her dangerous situation. She immediately altered course to the east and a stern chase developed with the range slowly increasing as the German ship made the most of her speed advantage over the British battleship. The *Duke of York* obtained several hits on the *Scharnhorst*, one of which disabled the forward 11in gun turret but her speed was unaffected and the two ships continued to fight it out. It was not until 18:20 when the *Scharnhorst* suddenly appeared to slow down, probably as the result of a 14in hit, that the pursuing British destroyers able close the range and launch their torpedoes. At least four hits were obtained and the *Scharnhorst*'s fate was sealed although she continued to fight against the increasingly overwhelming odds. The *Duke of York* and *Jamaica* now closed the range and pounded the burning battlecruiser with numerous salvoes, while *Norfolk* and Belfast approaching from the north-west were also able to join in. By now the *Scharnhorst* had slowed to less than five knots and was a sitting target for further torpedo attacks by destroyers. *Jamaica* also fired torpedoes and scored another two hits. The *Scharnhorst*, obscured by smoke and flames, was clearly finished and the British ships stood off as she eventually sank at around 19:45. Despite an intensive search, only thirty-six survivors were rescued from a crew of almost 2,000 men, including forty cadets who had been embarked for training. It was fitting that the *County* class cruiser HMS *Norfolk* was present at the conclusion of this action, as she had been over two years earlier when the *Bismarck* had also been finished off by superior British forces.

The loss of the *Scharnhorst* effectively ended the surface threat to the Russian convoys. Although the *Tirpitz* was still in being, she was disabled by midget submarines in September 1943 and when repaired was again hit by a concentrated series of carrier based air attacks in April 1944. She was subsequently finished off by RAF Lancaster bombers dropping 12,000 lb Tallboy bombs. After the *Scharnhorst* action, HMS *Norfolk*, was paid off for repairs and refit and did not rejoin the Home Fleet until November 1944. However, the destruction of the German heavy units meant that ships could now be transferred to the Far East where they were sorely needed for the advance against Japan. Most of the active *County* class cruisers were therefore operating in the Indian or Pacific Oceans by mid 1944 where some of the greatest naval actions of the war were now being fought.

The crowning naval event in European waters was Operation Overlord, the great invasion of Normandy on 6 June 1944. In common with established practice, fire support during the landings was provided by a mixture of battleships and cruisers. American forces landing on the western beaches, Utah and Omaha, were supported by the Western Naval Task Force commanded by Rear Admiral Kirk USN flying his flag aboard the heavy cruiser *Augusta*. Amongst the ships supporting the landings on Omaha were the cruisers *Tuscaloosa* and *Quincy*, while British and French light cruisers were also part of the forces covering both Omaha and Utah. *Quincy* was one of the new *Baltimore* class heavy cruisers having commissioned only at the end of 1943 and was the only one of the class to be assigned to the Atlantic Fleet. On the eastern flank the British and Canadian landings on Gold, Sword and Juno beaches were supported by the Eastern Naval Task Force which did not include any heavy cruisers in its bombardment line up. Once the landings had been consolidated, the great invasion fleet was disbanded, many units proceeding to the Mediterranean for Operation Dragoon while others, following refits and repairs, joined the steady progression to the Far East.

CHAPTER X

The Mediterranean

The outbreak of war in September 1939 initially produced little naval action in the Mediterranean and many units of the Royal Navy's Mediterranean Fleet were withdrawn to support operations in the Atlantic and off Norway. It was not until 10 June, 1940 that Italy finally entered the war as Germany's ally and at that time the Royal Navy had no heavy cruisers in the Mediterranean. However, a force of French ships was based at Alexandria and operated in conjunction with the British in the Eastern Mediterranean. This included the heavy cruisers *Dusquense*, *Tourville* and *Suffren* and an offensive sweep was made into the Aegean Sea while British ships operated off Tobruk. The Italian fleet, including the heavy cruisers *Zara*, *Fiume* and *Gorizia* sortied to attack these forces but no contact was made and both sides returned to harbour. However, there was more activity in the Western Mediterranean when a French force made up of the heavy cruisers *Algérie*, *Foch*, *Dupleix* and *Colbert*, escorted by eleven large destroyers set out from Toulon on 14 June to bombard Italian positions on the Ligurian coast including the port of Genoa. This was successfully accomplished and the French force returned without loss, although one of the destroyers had been hit by shore battery fire. A week later, British and French forces based at Alexandria participated in a joint sortie along the North African coast but on the 22 June all co-operation ceased as France capitulated to the German advance and an armistice was signed. Technically, the French ships overnight became non-belligerent neutrals and those at Alexandria remained uneasily at anchor while events unfolded elsewhere.

Apart from ships at the main French ports of Brest and Toulon, the greatest concentration of French ships, including battleships and battlecruisers was at Oran on the Algerian Coast. Following unsuccessful negotiations for these ships either to join the Allied cause or be interned in a neutral port, Churchill reluctantly ordered their destruction and Operation Catapult was initiated on 3 July. Several of the French ships were destroyed or damaged, although the modern battlecruiser *Strasbourg* and five destroyers escaped to Toulon. Although perhaps necessary, this action weighed heavily on French minds for many years afterwards. At Alexandria events fortunately took a different turn. Following personal negotiations between Admiral Cunningham and Vice-Admiral Godfrey (commanding French forces) it was agreed that the French ships there would be deactivated and interned. This included the three heavy cruisers (*Dusquense*, *Tourville*, and *Suffren*) which remained immobilised

Algérie, 1942. (France)

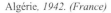
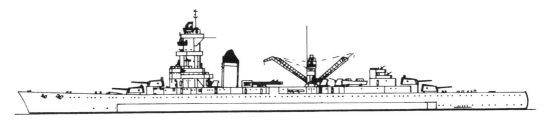

All four Zara *class cruisers, together with other ships, make stirring sight as they steam of to intercept the British fleet off Calabria, 9th July 1940.* Erminio Bagasco collection via Maurizio Brescia

The heavy cruiser Pola *under air attack just after the action off Calabria on 9 July 1940. Fortunately for all concerned, the ship was not damaged as this attack was made by high level Italian bombers as a result of a misidentification.* Erminio Bagasco collection via Maurizio Brescia

until May 1943 when Admiral Godfrey committed his ships to the Allied cause and after refitting they assisted in the final actions in the liberation of France. The remaining French heavy cruisers (*Foch, Dupleix, Colbert, Algerie*) were all at Toulon when German forces occupied Vichy France and, in accordance with previously laid plans, were scuttled along with almost seventy other vessels in order to prevent them falling into German hands. It was a sad ending for many fine ships.

From the time of the entry of Italy into the war until the end of 1942 the Royal Navy fought some of its most significant actions of the Second World War in the Mediterranean in an attempt to support allied forces fighting in North Africa and Greece, and to keep open essential supply routes while attempting to prevent passage of Axis forces and supplies. With a few exceptions the British forces allocated did not include any heavy cruisers, greater reliance being placed on the more modern light cruisers. On the other hand, the seven Italian heavy cruisers were involved in several actions, although their overall record was disappointing. The first major fleet action occurred early in July 1940 when both sides had large forces at sea in order to cover respective convoys. Led by two battleships, the Italian force included the 1st Division with cruisers *Zara, Fiume*, and *Gorizia*, and the 3rd Division with heavy cruisers *Trento* and *Bolzano*. They were accompanied by several light cruisers and numerous destroyers. British forces included the battleships *Warspite, Malaya*, and *Royal Sovereign* supported by five light cruisers and a number of destroyers as well as the venerable aircraft carrier, HMS *Eagle*. The forces clashed off the toe of Italy (Cape Calabria) on the afternoon of the 9th after two days of manoeuvring but the action was short lived as the Italian forces withdrew under cover of a smoke screen after some amazingly accurate long-range shooting by *Warspite* resulted in hits on the Italian battleship *Cesare*. A brief encounter between the opposing cruisers resulted in three 6in hits on the *Bolzano* which put her steering temporarily out of action, although she was able to effect repairs and withdrew with the other Italian ships.

On the night of 11 November, the Royal Navy scored a major success when Swordfish aircraft from the carrier *Illustrious* struck at the Italian port of Taranto and sank or damaged three battleships as well as damaging the heavy cruiser *Trento*. Among the force escorting the carrier were the heavy cruisers *York* and *Berwick*. The latter had been sent as a reinforcement to the Gibraltar based Force H. Although she spent only a few weeks in the Mediterranean, she was involved in a further action on 27 November when an attempt to pass two convoys to Malta resulted in a large scale sortie by the Italian fleet. including the 3rd Division comprising the cruisers *Trieste, Trento*, and *Bolzano*. The British forces included the battlecruiser Renown and battleship Ramilles and the heavy cruiser *Berwick* accompanied by three light cruisers and several destroyers. With a top speed of only 20 knots, the elderly *Ramilles* was not able to join in the action as, again, the Italians decided to withdraw when their promised air cover had not materialised. Nevertheless, the opposing cruisers exchanged some fire resulting in a hit on the *Berwick*. This was the only occasion in which British and Italian heavy cruisers were in action against each other.

In October 1940 Italian forces had invaded Greece. Subsequently British troops were withdrawn from the Western Desert to reinforce the position in Greece and these were sent in convoys from Alexandria. The lack of Italian success in this theatre, coupled with the build-up of British forces, caused Hitler to demand more positive action from the Italian Fleet in advance of his own plans to commit German forces to the area. In response to this prompting, Admiral Ianchino planned a powerful sortie against the British convoys in the area west of Crete and this was to lead to one of the major naval engagements of the war in which the Italian heavy cruiser force was to suffer badly. On 26 March 1941 he sailed from Naples aboard the modern battleship *Vittorio Veneto* accompanied by four destroyers. His movements were co-ordinated with a force of three heavy cruisers (1st Div. *Pola, Zara*, and *Fiume*) from Taranto, two light cruisers from Brindisi and three more heavy cruisers (3rd Div. *Trieste, Trento*, and Bolzano) from Messina, each group accompanied by escorting destroyers. Making rendezvous south of the Straits of Messina on the morning of the 27th, the Italian fleet then set course towards Crete. Later that day an RAF Sunderland flying boat located and reported one of

The cruiser HMS York *lies beached at Suda Bay, Crete, after having been attacked by Italian explosive motorboats. Despite desperate efforts to refloat her, she had to be abandoned when German Parachute forces attacked the island at the end of May 1941.* Author's collection

the cruiser divisions some eighty miles east of Sicily giving Admiral Cunningham his first positive information that the Italians were at sea.

Forewarned by ULTRA decodes, the Mediterranean Fleet prepared to sail from Alexandria on the evening of the 27th and a force of four light cruisers (*Orion*, *Ajax*, *Perth* and *Gloucester*) and four destroyers under the command of Vice Admiral Pridham-Whippel was ordered from the Aegean Sea to rendezvous with Cunningham to the south of Crete at dawn.

The stage was now set for the largest fleet action to be fought by the Royal Navy in the Second World War. Its battlefleet of one carrier, three battleships, four light cruisers and thirteen destroyers was heading towards the Italian force of one battleship, six heavy and two light cruisers, and also thirteen destroyers. Although the British had superiority in battleships, they were all elderly ships of First World War vintage and the fastest (*Valiant*) was only capable of just over 24 knots while the Italian *Vittorio Veneto* was one of the new breed of heavily armoured fast battleships capable of a speed in excess of 30 knots. Also the Italian force included the six heavily armed 8in cruisers against which the smaller British cruisers with their 6in guns were poorly matched. Thus, on paper the fleets were very evenly matched but the British had two priceless advantages of which they made full use.

This view of Trieste *shows the ship's appearance in April 1942 following her return to service after being torpedoed in November 1941.* Aldo Fracarroli collection via Maurizio Brescia

This shot shows Gorizia *in action during the second battle of Sirte, 22nd March 1942. Note the main armament trained forward.* Aldo Fracarroli collection via Maurizio Brescia

One was an aircraft carrier (Formidable), although its complement of only twenty-seven aircraft severely limited its offensive capability. The other was radar, which was to prove invaluable, especially in the night actions.

Early on the morning of the 28, one of *Formidable*'s aircraft reported sighting four cruisers and four destroyers heading south-west off Gavdo Island and, shortly afterwards, a second aircraft reported another sighting of cruisers and destroyers miles away. These reports were difficult to interpret as it was not clear whether all the ships sighted were Italian or whether some were, in fact, Pridham-Whippel's cruisers hurrying to the rendezvous position. This uncertainty was only removed at 08:24 when HMS *Orion* reported enemy ships in sight, by which time Pridham-Whippel had ordered his force onto a south-easterly course in order to lead the enemy vessels towards the approaching British battleships. As the faster Italian cruisers (*Trieste*, *Trento*, and *Bolzano*) closed the range, they opened fire at 08:12 but their gunnery was generally inaccurate and when *Gloucester* started returning fire when within range, they stood off and eventually reversed course to the north-east. The tables were now turned as the Italians attempted to lead the British cruisers back towards the *Vittorio Veneto* which was now pushing forward at 30 knots in the hope of joining the engagement. Up to this point, neither commanding admiral was aware of the other side's battleships but shortly after 09:00, Ianchino received a report indicating that the British fleet, consisting of an aircraft carrier and at least two battleships as well as cruisers and destroyers was approaching from the south. However, he was reluctant to believe the aircraft report and placed greater credence on D/F bearings which put them 170 miles away.

As Cunningham's battleships continued towards the scene of the action at a stately 22 knots (the best speed of the slowest ship, *Barham*), he ordered a strike by land-based Swordfish from Maleme airfield on Crete and subsequently a strike of six Albacores and two Fulmar fighters was flown off *Formidable* at 09:52. An hour later HMS *Orion*, the leading British cruiser, suddenly sighted the *Vittorio Veneto* at 10:58 and although Pridham-Whippel immediately ordered his force to turn back to the south-east, they came under heavy and accurate fire from the battleship and the *Trieste* group of cruisers which now conformed with their flagship. With Cunningham's battleships still 80 miles away, the British cruisers were in a critical situation when *Formidable*'s strike force arrived on the scene. Although their attack was pressed home with great determination, they did not score any hits, and three Swordfish of 815 squadron which arrived shortly afterwards from Crete were also unsuccessful. However, these attacks did prompt Ianchino to break off the surface action and alter course to the north-west, his main aim now being to return home and escape further air attack. The British cruisers, no longer threatened, continued their south-easterly course with the intention of joining with Cunningham's main force.

Now that the *Vittorio Veneto* was drawing away, Cunningham ordered another carrier strike to be launched, but this again comprised a pitifully small number of aircraft (three Albacores and two Swordfish) and it did not catch up with the Italian battleship until 15:19. However, they were assisted by the fact that as they manoeuvred to start their attack a formation of RAF Blenheims were also making a high level bombing attack which distracted the attention of the Italian gunners. Consequently, the low level torpedo bombers were not spotted until the last minute and were able to drop their torpedoes at close range. One aircaft managed to score a hit, although it was shot down even as the torpedo was launched. It struck below the stern, damaging the rudders and propellers and bringing the battleship to a temporary halt. As the news reached Cunningham, there was now every prospect that his battleships would be able to catch the damaged Italian battleship and finish her off but, instead, the Italian crew through heroic damage control efforts succeeded in getting their ship underway and eventually she was making off at over 16 knots.

There was no rest for the aircrews aboard *Formidable* who were now ordered to make a third strike and six Albacores and two Swordfish were launched, these later being reinforced by two more Swordfish from Maleme (Crete). By now Ianchino had drawn his cruisers and destroyers around the *Vittorio Veneto* in a protective screen and consequently the air attack beginning at 19:25 was met by a wall of AA fire which caused the formations to split up. Although no further hits were obtained on the battleship, one torpedo hit the heavy cruiser *Pola* which came to a dead stop in the water with her engine rooms flooded. Ianchino continued to withdraw but ordered the remaining ships of the 1st Cruiser Division (*Zara* and *Fiume*) together with four destroyers to remain with the damaged cruiser. It was now night and the pursuing British battleships were still relentlessly closing when Admiral Cunningham ordered his destroyers ahead in order to catch and attack the *Vittorio Veneto* but she managed to evade them in the darkness and eventually regained the relative safety of Taranto.

In the meantime Cunningham's battleships were finally joining the battle and, following a report of a radar contact from the cruiser *Achilles*, he was able to bring his ships within range of an unidentified stationary target off the port bow. At almost the same time (22:20), one of the British destroyers reported a group of Italian cruisers and destroyers passing in line ahead across the path of the British ships. These were the *Zara* and *Fiume* with their accompanying destroyers sailing to the assistance of their damaged sister ship, totally unaware that they had strayed into the path of the British battlefleet. Cunningham calmly manoeuvred his ships into an ideal firing position on a parallel course using radar information until visual contact was achieved. At 22:27, the battleships opened fire on their unsuspecting targets at almost point blank range. Within minutes the *Zara* and *Fiume* were blazing wrecks while the destroyers *Griffin*, *Greyhound*, *Stuart* and *Havock* slogged it out with the Italian destroyers, sinking the *Carducci* and finishing off the *Alfieri* which was already mortally damaged by 15in gunfire from the *Barham*. The other destroyers that had been sent ahead in the unsuccessful attempt to catch the *Vittorio Veneto*, eventually rejoined after 02:00 and the flotilla leader, HMS *Jervis*, finished off the *Zara* with torpedoes before going alongside the lifeless *Pola* to take off some 257 survivors. She in turn was subsequently sunk by torpedoes from both *Jervis* and *Nubian*.

The destroyers then made off to join up with the battleships and the fleet entered Alexandria in the late afternoon on 30 March. It was an outstanding victory for the Mediterranean fleet under Admiral Cunningham. They had sunk three heavy cruisers and two destroyers for the loss of a single aircraft while Formidable's fighters had shot down several Ju.88s attacking the fleet.

Although there were no British heavy cruisers present at Matapan, HMS *York* had been attached to the Mediterranean Fleet from October 1940 as part of the 3rd Cruiser Squadron based at Alexandria and, as already noted, took part in the Taranto action. Subsequently, she was engaged in escorting convoys to Malta and also troop convoys to Greece and Crete. While involved in the latter she was anchored in Suda Bay on the night of 26 March 1941 when she was attacked by units of the Italian 10th Light Flotilla using radio controlled explosive motor boats (EMBs). This was a bold and imaginative coup which deservedly achieved success although, in fact, *York* did not sink immediately and her crew were able to beach her despite the serious damage. Using local facilities, work went on round the clock to effect temporary repairs so that she could sail to Alexandria. Despite constant interruptions by German air attack, she was almost ready to sail when German parachute forces launched the airborne invasion of the island on 20 May. In order to prevent the ship falling into enemy hands, the decision was reluctantly taken to scuttle ship and this was done with explosive charges on 22 May.

Following the evacuation of Crete at the end of May, the Royal Navy was forced onto the defensive, its operations severely restricted by Axis air-power based on Crete, Sicily and North Africa. For the next eighteen months the highest priority was given to sustaining and supplying the island of Malta so that it could survive as a base for air and submarine attacks against the Axis shipping routes. Although there were no British heavy cruisers available, the surviving Italian heavy cruisers were often in action against the convoy covering forces although they achieved little. A typical action occured at the end of August 1941 when the British launched Operation Mincemeat in which the fast minelayer *Manxman* would make a dash to Malta under cover of a carrier based air attack on Sardinia. This drew a response from the Italian fleet which put to sea in strength, including the 3rd Division comprising the heavy cruisers *Trieste Trento*, *Bolzano* and *Gorizia*. However, the Italians were not able to intercept the British force which successfully carried out all its objectives and, to make matters worse, the *Bolzano* was torpedoed by the submarine HMS *Triumph* off the northern entrance to the Messina Straits. She had to be taken under tow and was sent to Messina for repairs where she lay for three months. During this time she was hit during an air raid and suffered several casualties.

While the *Bolzano* was out of action, the remaining cruisers of the 3rd Division were engaged in an operation to support the passage of a troop convoy through the Messina Straits to Benghazi. On the night of 21 November the convoy and its escorting cruisers, were sighted and attacked by the submarine HMS *Utmost* which succeeded in torpedoing the heavy cruiser Trieste. The ship was badly damaged but eventually managed to limp into Messina where she was out of action for over six months. Although eventually repaired and in action against later Malta convoys, the Trieste was eventually sunk by USAAF B-24 Liberators while at La Maddalena, Sardinia.

By the end of 1941, Malta was increasingly isolated and it became ever more difficult to run supplies through to the island. In December a major naval effort was mounted in order to get a single oil tanker (*Breconshire*) through and this happened to coincide with an attempt by the Italian Navy to run a convoy to Tripoli. This convoy was escorted by a strong force including three battleships and two heavy cruisers (*Gorizia*, and *Trento*) which ran into a British force of cruisers and destroyers escorting the *Breconshire* at nightfall on 17 December. Under the command of Rear Admiral Vian, the outnumbered British destroyers and cruisers acted aggressively and the Italian force withdrew under the threat of a night torpedo attack. This skirmish became known as the First Battle of Sirte but was followed by my a much more complex engagement a few months later when another convoy (MW10) of four fast ships including the tanker *Breconshire* was preparing to sail from Alexandria to Malta. A simultaneous operation by Force H in the western Mediterranean would attempt to fly Spitfires into the beleaguered island. MW10 sailed on 20 March 1942 with a close escort consisting of the AA cruiser *Carlisle* and six destroyers and a covering force of three light cruisers and four destroyers with Rear Admiral Vian again in command. The convoy and its escorts were sighted by Italian aircraft and submarines on the following day and in response Admiral Iachino sailed from Taranto aboard the battleship *Littorio*, accompanied by *Gorizia* and *Trento*, as well as a light cruiser and several destroyers. On 22nd, the convoy escort was reinforced by the light cruiser *Penelope* and a destroyer from Malta and the stage was set for a major fleet action.

Vian was aware of the approaching Italian force thanks to ULTRA and C38m intercepts but pressed on as planned although subjected to air attacks by Italian bombers. At 14:27 *Euryalus* sighted four enemy ships approaching from the north-east. The convoy and its close escort immediately turned away to the south-west while Vian's cruisers and destroyers steamed between the fleeing convoy and the approaching Italian cruisers, laying a thick smoke screen. There was a strong south-easterly wind which rapidly spread the smoke but was also whipping up the sea, causing the ships of both sides to pitch heavily and making accurate gunnery difficult. Vian's movement's caused the Italian ships to break off to the north-west and he therefore led his own ships back towards the convoy which was now under heavy attack from Luftwaffe Ju88s. Initially, he thought that the Italians had withdrawn but, in fact, the cruisers had joined up with the *Littorio* and the whole force was sighted again approaching from the north-east at 16:40. Vian, flying his flag aboard *Cleopatra*, ordered his cruisers and destroyers out towards the Italian ships. The weather conditions hampered the Italian fire although *Cleopatra* was struck by a 6in shell and *Euryalus* suffered damage from a 15in shell exploding alongside. However, Iachino was reluctant to approach too close in case he should suffer a torpedo attack from destroyers emerging from the swirling smoke screen. He therefore turned to the west in an attempt to get around the smoke and then attack the convoy. This proved to be, literally, a long winded affair as the smoke was drifting to the north-west and it was not until after 18:00 that he eventually turned south and ran down on the convoy. Unfortunately for Iachino, Vian had anticipated that Iachino would actually try to pass round to the east of the smoke screen and had stationed some of his cruisers there in anticipation. Thus it fell on the available destroyers to meet the advancing Italians which they did with great bravery, pressing home to fire torpedoes at ranges of less than 6,000 yards. No hits were scored and both *Havock* and *Kingston* were severely damaged by near misses from 15in shells. Attacks by the Italian destroyers were equally unsuccessful and, with darkness falling, Iachino called off his ships and turned away to north having achieved nothing despite his overwhelming superiority. In fact, there was worse to come as the destroyers Lanciere and Scirocco foundered in the storm which was increasing in severity through the night.

Meanwhile, Vian ordered the now scattered merchant ships to head independently at their best speed for Malta, each accompanied by a destroyer escort. The freighters *Talabot* and *Pampas* reached Grand Harbour but were then sunk by air attack before their cargo had been unloaded, although some was later salvaged. The *Clan Campbell* was sunk some 20 miles out and the brave *Breconshire* was disabled with only 8 miles to go. Although towed to the south shore along with the damaged destroyer *Legion*, both ships were finished off a few days later. In the end, only some 5,000 tons of supplies was landed out of a total of 26,000 tons aboard the four ships when they had set out from Alexandria. Overall, a sad outcome after the brilliance of the British cruiser action.

By May 1942 Malta's situation was again extremely critical and preparations therefore began for a major convoy operation to take place in mid June. Five fast freighters were to sail from Gibraltar escorted by a force which included a battleship and two aircraft carriers, under the code name Operation Harpoon. Simultaneously, a larger convoy of eleven merchant ships would sail from Alexandria in the east (Operation Vigorous). Although the Mediterranean Fleet at that time had no carriers or battleships, an escort of no less than eight light cruisers and twenty-six destroyers was assembled. Neither force included any heavy cruisers but the Italian reaction would include the 3rd Division with the cruisers *Gorizia* and *Trento*. The western convoy and close escort passed Gibraltar on 12th and was joined by the its heavy cover, Force W, later that day. The passage of the Harpoon convoy was vigorously contested and at one point it was intercepted by a force of Italian light cruisers while outside the range of Malta's fighters. What should have been a massacre was prevented by the brave actions of the escorting destroyers and the AA light cruiser HMS *Cairo*. Eventually, only two of the six mercahant ships that had set out from Gibralatar suceeded in reaching Gibralatar.

Although Harpoon could be regarded as having been reasonably successful, given the scale of the opposition, the Vigorous convoy in the eastern Mediterranean was a total failure. During 14 June, the convoy of eleven ships escorted by cruisers and destroyers under Rear Admiral Vian had fought off no less than seven separate air attacks and had lost only one freighter, but others had been damaged or detached for various reasons so that only eight were left. As night fell, the convoy was subjected to probing attacks by German E-boats and he was also aware, from ULTRA intercepts, that a major portion of the Italian fleet, including the battleships *Littorio* and *Vittorio Veneto*, together with the cruisers *Trento* and *Gorizia* was at sea and in a position to engage him in the morning. It was therefore decided that the convoy would reverse course at 02:00 but executing this complicated manoeuvre gave the E-boats the chance they were looking for. The destroyer *Hasty* was sunk and the cruiser *Newcastle* damaged by a torpedo. However at dawn on the 15th RAF Beaufort torpedo bombers attacked the Italian fleet and put a torpedo into the heavy cruiser *Trento*. She was hit squarely amidships in one of the boiler rooms and as result was brought to standstill. For several hours the crew struggled to restore some power but their efforts were unsuccessful and four hours after the original hit she was torpedoed again, this time by the submarine HMS *Umbra*. The torpedo struck a magazine which exploded and the ship then quickly sank. At a later stage in the action, the battleship *Littorio* damaged by a torpedo dropped from an RAF Wellington as she was withdrawing.

In the meantime, the convoy was ordered to turn back towards Malta in the hope that further air and submarine attacks would cause the Italians to break off their sortie. When it became apparent that this was not happening, Vian was again ordered to reverse course to the east but later in the morning another destroyer was sunk by air attack and the cruiser *Birmingham* put out of action by near misses. On the way back to Alexandria the cruiser *Hermione* was torpedoed and sunk by a U-boat and the destroyer *Nestor* sank as result of earlier damage sustained in an air attack. Of the 16 transports

Bolzano in early 1942 at La Spezia showing her distinctive camouflage pattern. Erminio Bagasco collection via Maurizio Brescia

A dramatic view of Bolzano *shortly after being torpedoed by the submarine* Unbroken *on 13th august 1942 after failing to intercept the important Pedestal convoy to Malto. The ship had to be beached to avoid sinking and full repairs were never completed.* Erminio Bagasco collection via Maurizio Brescia

originally destined for Malta in the two convoys, only two got through and several warships had been sunk or damaged. Despite the loss of the *Trento*, the Italian Navy claimed a victory but the two ships which did get through were just enough to keep the island going while a further relief effort was organised. In the event the 15,000 tons of supplies made the vital difference that kept Malta going for another few weeks in its darkest hour.

In May and June 1942 the British 8th Army was forced to retreat all the way back to El Alamein. A holding battle early in July finally stopped Rommel in his tracks and gave the 8th Army time to start re-equipping and building up its strength to retake the offensive. At the same time, Malta began to build up its fighter strength and by the end of July Royal Navy submarines were again based at Valetta, striking at Rommel's supply routes. Nevertheless, Malta was desperately short of food and fuel and unless more supplies could be got through this brief resurgence would end and the possibility of a successful offensive by the 8th Army would inevitably have to be delayed. A further relief convoy was therefore planned for early August, but it was decided to concentrate all efforts into the western Mediterranean. The lessons of the Harpoon operation were taken to heart and the most powerful Royal Navy carrier force ever assembled up to that time formed part of Force H, the covering force. The old faithful, *Eagle*, was reinforced by the modern armoured carriers *Victorious* and *Indomitable*, while the older *Furious* was attached to ferry thirty-eight Spitfires destined for Malta. Force H also included the battleships *Nelson* and *Rodney*, as well as cruisers and destroyers. The convoy close escort included the AA cruiser *Cairo*, veteran of Harpoon and other Malta convoys, but she was now backed up by the modern 6in cruisers *Nigeria*, *Kenya* and *Manchester* to counter any attack by Italian cruisers as had previously occurred. The convoy itself consisted of thirteen modern fast merchant ships (two American, the rest British) as well as the American owned, but British manned, tanker *Ohio*. Passing through the Straits of Gibraltar early on 10 August, the convoy joined up with its escorting forces and set off towards Malta. The stage was set for one of the fiercest convoy battles of the war.

The convoy was located by Axis aircraft at 10:10 on 11 August. Later that day, *Furious* flew off her Spitfires before turning back to Gibraltar with a destroyer escort. Almost at the same time, the German U-73 put a full salvo of four torpedoes in HMS *Eagle* and the carrier rolled over and sank within eight minutes, 260 of her crew perishing as she went down. Despite subsequent heavy air attacks, only one merchant ship had been lost as the convoy approached the entrance to the Sicilian Channel although the destroyer *Forester* was lost at this point. However, the convoy was now disrupted by both submarine and air attacks, to be followed by night attacks by fast Italian MAS boats which disabled and sank the cruiser *Manchester* as well as several mercahnt ships. The convoy subsequently lost all cohesion and was broken up into ad hoc groups, all struggling eastwards to Malta the next morning.

It was at this stage in the previous Harpoon convoy that the Italian cruiser squadron had appeared and, as such a force had been spotted the previous day heading south, there was no reason to expect that events would be any different on this August day. In fact, an Italian force of three heavy cruisers (*Gorizia*, *Bolzano*, and *Trieste*) and three light cruisers which should easily have finished off the convoy given the depleted state of the escort, had turned back due to lack of air cover. To make matters worse for the Italians, the submarine *Unbroken* (Lt. Alastair Mars VC) succeeded in torpedoing the Bolzano and light cruiser *Attendolo* with one salvo of four torpedoes when they were north of the straits of Messina. Although the threat of surface attack had now faded, the remaining ships faced several hours of intense air attack before coming under the umbrella of Malta-based fighter cover. Several more merchant ships were sunk but eventually by the end of the day the *Port Chalmers*, *Rochester Castle* and *Melbourne Star* had reached the safety of Valetta harbour to a frenzied welcome from the island's populace and servicemen. On the following day, and only by the superhuman efforts and exemplary seamanship of all concerned was the floating wreck of the *Ohio*, and her precious cargo of 10,000 tons of oil fuel, finally brought safely into Valetta. Including her, and the *Brisbane Star*, which also arrived on the 14th, a total of five ships had reached Malta, bringing with them enough supplies to ensure that the Island would not only survive, but thrive as an offensive base until the end of the year.

The Italian heavy cruiser *Bolzano*, as already noted, had been torpedoed off the Aeolian Islands, north-east of Sicily on the 13th. There was extensive damage and fires broke out which threatened the magazines so that these had to be flooded as a preventative measure. The ship was beached off the island of Panarea and it was over a month before she was refloated and towed to Naples for initial repairs and then to La Spezia for a full refit. However, this proved to be a long drawn out affair and the ship was still at La Spezia at the time of the Italian surrender in September 1943, over a year later. The Bolzano was taken over by German forces although no further work was carried out and, ironically, the ship was sunk by a joint Anglo-Italian underwater chariot attack on 21 June 1944. The ship settled in shallow water and lay there until broken up after the war.

By 1943 the overwhelming Allied air power in the Mediterranean meant that the Italian Navy had virtually no chance of carrying out major operations and most of its ships were withdrawn from Sicily and Taranto to northern ports. The cruiser *Gorizia*, one of the most active of the Italian heavy cruisers, was withdrawn to the port of La Maddalena in northern Sardinia where she was heavily damaged by three bombs on 10 April, 1943, in the same raid which sank the *Trieste*. Three days later she was able to get underway and proceeded to La Spezia for repairs, although these were never completed. Following the Italian surrender in early September 1943, the ship was scuttled on the 8th to prevent her use by German forces which took over the port on the following day. They eventually raised the hull but the *Gorizia* was finally sunk by a combined Anglo-Italian chariot attack on 26 June 1944, a few days after a similar attack had sunk the *Bolzano*. The sinking of the *Gorizia* spelt the end of the Italian heavy cruisers of which four (*Pola, Zara, Fiume, Trento*) had been lost in action, another (*Trieste*) bombed in harbour and the last two (*Bolzano*, and *Gorizia*) finally destroyed by human torpedo attacks.

Once Malta had been secured, the emphasis in the Mediterranean changed to the mounting of major amphibious operations as the Axis forces were eventually thrown out of North Africa and then pursued through Sicily to the Italian mainland. These were joint operations carried out in partnership with American forces and the US Navy committed substantial resources to these operations. Like the British, they employed few heavy cruisers in this theatre, preferring to deploy the majority to the Pacific where they were sorely needed. Nevertheless, the cruisers *Wichita*, *Augusta* and *Tuscaloosa* were assigned to the Western Task Force which landed on the Moroccan coast on 8 November 1942 as part Operation Torch, the invasion of North Africa. Initially, there was significant opposition from Vichy French forces and the USS *Augusta* was in action against the light cruiser *Primauget*, both sides supported by destroyers. The French cruiser was hit several times by *Augusta*'s gunfire and had to be beached. In the meantime, *Tuscaloosa* supported the battleship USS *Massachusetts* as she bombarded the port of Casablanca where various French ships, including the incomplete battleship *Jean Bart*, attempted to repel the American forces. During this action the French submarine *Antiope* made an unsuccessful torpedo attack on the *Tuscaloosa* which was able to avoid the torpedoes.

After a few days, resistance from Vichy forces ceased and following the successful completion of Torch, as well as the advance of the British 8th Army from El Alamein, Axis forces in North Africa eventually surrendered on 13 May 1943. Preparations now began for Operation Husky, the invasion of Sicily, which began on 10 July. A vast armada was assembled but both British and American navies deployed only light cruisers as surface opposition in any strength was deemed unlikely. Subsequently, heavy cruisers were not part of the forces which carried out landings at Salerno in September 1943 and Anzio in January 1944. Indeed, the last significant occasion when heavy cruisers were deployed in the Mediterranean was in support of Operation Dragoon, the landing of Allied forces on the French coast between Cannes and Toulon. The American cruisers *Augusta* and *Tuscaloosa* were among the many allied cruisers and battleships which provided fire support for the landings. On completion of this operation the two cruisers were reassigned to the Pacific Fleet and the scale of naval operations in the Mediterranean was scaled down considerably.

CHAPTER XI

The Pacific and Indian Oceans

The war in the Pacific started violently on 7 December 1941 when the Japanese fleet launched a surprise attack on the American naval base at Pearl Harbor. Their strike force of six carriers included the heavy cruisers *Chikuma* and *Tone* amongst its escort, and it was aircraft from these ships which carried out the final reconnaissance over Pearl Harbor before the main attack force was launched. The attack was a crippling blow as far as the Americans were concerned as no less than five battleships were sunk and another three seriously damaged. In addition, several light cruisers, destroyers and other vessels were damaged and shore installations including fuel storage tanks and airfields were heavily hit. The only positive outcome from the American point of view was that no aircraft carriers were present and consequently it escaped any damage. Had these been put out of action the outcome of the Pacific War might well have taken a totally different course. The heavy cruisers *New Orleans* and *San Francisco* were present at Pearl Harbor on the fateful day but emerged unscathed. Most of the other heavy cruisers were at sea. *Astoria*, *Chicago* and *Portland* were with the carrier *Lexington* taking aircraft reinforcements to Midway, while *Chester*, *Northampton* and *Salt Lake City* were escorting the carrier *Enterprise* returning from a similar mission to Wake Island.

The attack on Pearl Harbor was synchronised with attacks throughout the Pacific and South-East Asia. Off Malaya the British capital ships *Prince of Wales* and *Repulse* were lost to an overwhelming air attack off the coast of Malay on 10th and the whole Peninsula and the fortress of Singapore had fallen to the Japanese by February 1942. The Americans suffered a similar experience in the Philippines which were overrun and completely occupied by the following April. The US Navy's Asiatic Fleet consisting of the heavy cruiser *Houston*, two light cruisers and thirteen destroyers was no match for the overwhelming assault. Japanese plans also called for the occupation of Borneo and the capture of the Dutch East Indies with its vital oil fields. The Dutch forces included two light cruisers and several destroyers and several of the surviving American ships, including the heavy cruiser *Houston* and light cruiser *Marblehead*, joined this force which was under the command of Rear Admiral Karel Doorman of the Netherlands Navy. On 2 February the ships under his command moved to intercept a Japanese force reported to be heading south through the Makassar Strait between Borneo and the Celebes but on the following day they were caught by Japanese aircraft. Singling out the American ships, the *Marblehead* was hit several times and almost sank, although she eventually made it back to the States for repairs. *Houston* avoided most of the attacks but eventually was hit aft in the fourth and final attack. The bomb exploded just forward of the after 8in gun turret, putting it out of action. In all, her casualties amounted to fifty-four killed and over fifty seriously injured. However, the ship could not be spared and remained in the Dutch East Indies as part of the joint American, British, Dutch and Australian (ABDA) command set up to block the Japanese advance. A not insubstantial naval force consisting of two heavy and three light cruisers, together with nine destroyers, was now assembled. This included the British heavy cruiser HMS *Exeter*, now fully repaired and refitted following her famous action against the *Graf Spee*, as well as the Australian light cruiser, HMAS *Perth*. After an abortive sortie on the 26 February, the ABDA force sailed again from Surabaya on 27 February in an attempt to intercept and destroy a Japanese troop convoy approaching from the north. The Japanese commander, Rear Admiral Takagi, was aware of these movements from aircraft reports and sailed to intercept the Allied force, instructing the troop convoy to turn away to the west. A major engagement was now only hours away and one of the crucial factors was to be the relative capabilities of the opposing heavy cruisers.

Doorman led his ships out of Surabaya and onto a north-westerly course towards the reported position of the troop convoy. At first glance his force appeared to be well balanced and, apart from destroyer numbers, at least equal to the Japanese. However the *Houston* had only her two forward 8in turrets available, the after turret having been disabled by the bomb hit a few days earlier. Thrown together in the heat of the moment, the ships had not had time to train as a team and communication between the four navies was difficult so that only the simplest messages could be passed. To make the best of his assets, Doorman placed his cruisers in line ahead with his flagship *De Ruyter* leading, followed in order by *Exeter*, *Houston*, *Perth* and *Java*. Three modern Royal Navy destroyers were in the van with the Dutch destroyer on the port flank and the fragile American four stackers following in the rear. At 16:12 the Japanese ships were sighted, they had two destroyer divisions each led by a light cruiser, followed by the heavy cruisers *Nachi* and *Haguro* each mounting ten 8in guns against the six similar weapons available aboard *Exeter* and *Houston*. At the extreme range of 28,000 yards the heavy cruisers began exchanging salvoes and as the range closed Doorman ordered his ships onto a westerly course to run parallel to the Japanese force. This gave Admiral Takagi's destroyers an opportunity to launch torpedoes and some forty-three were fired over a period of 25 minutes. Fortunately for the Allied force, no hits were scored and the gunnery duel continued unabated, all the time edging towards the vulnerable troop convoy. At around 17:00 Rear Admiral Tanaka led one of the Japanese destroyer divisions across the path of Doorman's cruisers and loosed off over sixty torpedoes. As their targets were head on, the chances of a hit were minimal but suddenly fate took a hand in the proceedings. After almost an hour of ineffectual gunnery on both sides, an 8in shell hit the *Exeter* amidships at 17:07. It penetrated to the boiler room, putting most of them out of action so that the ship's speed dropped off quickly and she was forced to turn out of the line. The following cruisers, unable to see the flagship because of the clouds of smoke which drifted across the battle and initially unaware of the damage to *Exeter*, followed her turn to port and the flanking destroyers were forced to comply. Doorman was forced to order the *De Ruyter* to follow suit and the whole of the Allied force was now broadside on the Tanaka's approaching torpedoes. One slammed into the Dutch destroyer *Kortenaer* which sank almost immediately. The Allied ships reformed around the *Exeter* which was now making only 15 knots and the British destroyers were ordered to make a counter attack on Tanaka's flotilla to the north-west. Advancing out of the smoke, *Electra* was hit and overwhelmed, subsequently sinking at around 18:00 while the others scored no hits before turning back to the south. In the meantime Doorman had ordered the damaged *Exeter*, escorted by the *Witte de With*, to return to Surabaya. Gathering the remaining cruisers, and escorted by the American four stackers, he survived another torpedo attack by the second Japanese destroyer division and, in the gathering darkness, an attack by the US destroyers was unsuccessful. Running low on fuel and ammunition, they were later sent back to Surabaya. At around 19:30 there was a brief gunnery engagement between the opposing cruisers but Doorman sheered away to the south and then westwards following the north Java coast, still trying to get at the troop convoy. At 21:25 HMS *Jupiter* hit a mine and later sank and subsequently the destroyer *Encounter* was detached to pick up survivors from the *Kortenaer*. This left only the *De Ruyter* leading *Perth*, *Houston* and *Java* and Doorman now turned north, still hoping to get at the convoy. Instead he met Takagi's cruisers which also turned onto a northerly heading and a running fight began as the range gradually reduced to 8,000 yards. Eventually it was the Japanese torpedoes which finally decided the issue. Both *De Ruyter* and *Java* were hit, the latter sinking within 15 minutes while Doorman's flagship only succumbed after several hours. On Doorman's orders, the *Houston* and *Perth* made good their escape in the darkness, heading for Tanjong Priok at the western end of Java. The battle was over.

Apart one damaged destroyer, the Japanese force was intact and the troop convoy now proceeded to land forces all along the Java coast.

Many of the surviving Allied ships were lost over the next few days. On the night of the 28 February, *Houston* and *Perth* attacked Japanese transports in Banten Bay on the shore of the Sunda Strait. They succeeded in sinking or damaging several ships before the heavy cruisers *Mogami* and *Mikuma* engaged them with gunfire and torpedoes at almost point blank range. First *Perth* and then the gallant *Houston* were quickly overwhelmed and sunk. On the morning of 1st March, the *Exeter* and destroyers HMS *Encounter* and USS *Pope* set off from Surabaya but were intercepted by the *Nachi* and *Haguro*, together with two more heavy cruisers, *Ashigara* and *Myoko*, and the result was a foregone conclusion. All three Allied ships were sunk, the last to go being the USS *Pope* which put up a tremendous fight and was only sunk eventually by a combination of air attack and gunfire from the cruisers. The last surviving Dutch destroyer, *Evertsen*, was sunk on the morning of 1 March as she attempted to escape through the Sunda Strait. The Imperial Japanese Navy was now master of all the waters around the East Indies and their heavy cruisers had played a decisive role, brushing aside the weak Allied forces with little trouble.

The occupation of Java and Sumatra now continued apace and on 19 February the Japanese 5th Carrier Division under Admiral Nagumo launched a series of raids on the Australian mainland at Darwin. Although only one warship, the American destroyer *Peary*, was sunk, several merchants ships were also destroyed and considerable damage was done to shore installations. The attack, in two waves, triggered fears of a Japanese invasion which caused considerable apprehension for some time afterwards. However, Nagumo's carriers now moved away to the north to support the conquest of the Dutch East Indies before withdrawing for a period of rest and recuperation. By the end of March they were ready for further operations and attention was turned towards the Indian Ocean where the British were trying to build the newly constituted Eastern Fleet based on Trincomalee, Ceylon (or Sri Lanka as it is known today). It was commanded by Admiral James Somerville and by the end of March it comprised five battleships, two heavy cruisers (*Dorsetshire* and *Cornwall*), five light cruisers and seven destroyers. More significantly, he had three aircraft carriers although one of these was the old *Hermes* which only carried a dozen Swordfish for patrol duties. The other two were *Indomitable* and *Formidable*, modern carriers but sorely lacking in adequate numbers of modern aircraft. Their total air complement consisted of 33 fighters (Fulmars, Wildcats and Sea Hurricanes) and 45 Albacore biplane torpedo bombers. The Japanese carriers had sortied from Staring Bay in the Celebes on 26 March and were heading into the Indian Ocean with the purpose of meeting and destroying the British Eastern Fleet. The five carriers could muster 250 aircraft, all of higher performance and flown by experienced aircrew fresh from their successes at Pearl Harbor and in the East Indies, so any pitched battle between the two carrier forces was almost certain to end in victory for the Japanese. Somerville was well aware of the relative strengths and his prime purpose was to preserve the British force in being so that it could eventually go onto the offensive when more ships were available. In this he was aided by the Allied code breakers who were able to read the Japanese naval code and give an accurate assessment of Nagumo's force composition and intentions. Consequently, Somerville concentrated his fleet to the south of Ceylon where they were unlikely to be located by Nagumo's scouting aircraft and from where it might be possible to launch a surprise night attack, the only option which held out any chance of success. However, by 2 April, Nagumo's force had not been sighted and thinking that his attack may have been called off, Somerville decided to withdraw to Addu Atoll but detached a number of ships to Colombo and Trincomalee on the Ceylon mainland. Amongst these were the cruisers *Dorsetshire* and *Cornwall*, the former to resume an interrupted refit and the latter to join the escort of an Australian troop convoy. The carrier *Hermes* went to Trincomalee where she was to continue preparations to take part in the projected invasion of Madagascar.

Thus, when an RAF Catalina spotted Nagumo's carriers approaching Ceylon from the east on the afternoon of 4 April, the British fleet was completely wrong footed. At least the warning from the

Catalina gave time for shipping to be cleared from the harbours. The cruisers *Dorsetshire* and *Cornwall* were ordered to rendezvous with the faster ships of the British Eastern Fleet, including the two carriers, which were racing north eastwards from Addu Atoll. On the morning of the 5th Nagumo launched his carrier strikes made up of ninety-one bombers and thirty-six fighters. These were opposed by some forty-two Hurricanes and Fulmars of which nineteen were shot down having destroyed only seven Japanese aircraft. The bombers attacked Colombo and sank several ships as well as causing widespread damage ashore. While the attack was in progress, a scout plane from the cruiser Tone spotted the two British cruisers heading south from Colombo towards Somerville's ships. On receipt of this report, Nagumo ordered a strike of eighty dive bombers under the command of Lt.Cdr. Egusa to intercept them. In the clear weather conditions, Egusa's pilots had no difficulty in locating the two ships and at 13:40 they were overhead and preparing to attack. Ignoring the AA fire, the aircraft dived with great precision and obtained numerous hits. *Dorsetshire* was hit hard and within five minutes the ship had lost power and steering and all armament was out of action apart from a few machine guns, and numerous fires were raging as the ship listed heavily to port. Captain Agar had no option but to order "Abandon Ship". Even as the crew took to the water, the ship rolled over and sank, less than seven minutes after the attack began. *Cornwall* fared no better and suffered a similar quick dispatch. Even by their normal standards, the accuracy of the Japanese dive bombing pilots was absolutely remarkable. Captain Agar estimated that his ship took at least ten direct hits as well as many near misses. Although the main body of the fleet was less than 70 miles away, Somerville was reluctant to close the survivors as he manoeuvred to keep his distance from Nagumo's carriers. Consequently, it was not until almost 48 hours later that 1,129 survivors were picked up while 424 men had been lost from the two ships.

After manoeuvring east and north, Nagumo launched a second series of attack, this time against Trincomalee. There was little opposition and great destruction was wrought. The carrier *Hermes* with the Australian destroyer *Vampire* were sunk while they tried to escape, the carrier succumbing after being hit by over forty bombs. Other victims included the destroyer *Tenodos*, corvette *Hollyhock* and fleet auxiliary *Athelstone*. To make matters worse, a second carrier division under Vice Admiral Ozawa and including the heavy cruisers *Chokai*, *Kumano*, *Suzaya*, *Mogami*, and *Mikuma*, forayed into the Bay of Bengal and sank over twenty merchant ships in an operation which was every bit as calamitous as the better known Convoy PQ17 debacle. This period represented the absolute low tide of British fortunes in South East Asia. India and Ceylon lay open to invasion and little could have been done to prevent it. Fortunately, Nagumo was content with his achievements, as well he might have been, and withdrew all the way back to Japan where preparations were being made for a major expedition against New Guinea and the Solomons. It would be a long time before the Royal Navy would assert itself in these waters.

Meanwhile, back in the Pacific and in the aftermath of Pearl Harbor, the US Navy had no option but to centre its operations around carrier task forces. Although the Navy was very air minded, many admirals still thought in terms of conventional fleet actions in which lines of battleships engaged each other, Jutland style with carrier aviation acting only in support. For better or for worse, the carriers now represented the core of US Navy strength. The loss of the battleships placed a heavy burden on the heavy cruisers which were now the major surface element in the fleet and, in any case, were the only major warships capable of operating with the fast carriers. The battleships sunk or damaged at Pearl Harbor were all of First World War vintage with a top speed of around 22 knots as opposed to the 30 knots of which the carriers were capable. It was not until the new fast battleships began to join the fleet from late 1942 onwards that the cruisers were assisted in protecting the vital carriers.

In the face of Japanese advances across the whole of the Pacific and South East Asia, the carriers were employed in operations to build up defensive forces on islands still held and to carry out some morale boosting offensive missions. The most spectacular of these was the famous Tokyo raid launched from the USS *Hornet* 18 April 1942. Anxious to make a spectacular gesture against Japan, the Navy agreed to a proposal by Lt. Col Doolittle of the USAAC to fly B-25 Mitchell medium bombers off a carrier for a one way mission to Japan, flying on to land in China after the raid. Despite the immense problems involved, the raid was a complete success even if the results were insignificant in pure military terms. In carrying out this operation a substantial task force was built around the carriers *Hornet* and *Enterprise* and the heavy cruisers *Vincennes*, *Northampton* and *Salt Lake City* were part of the escort.

The Tokyo raid was, by its very nature, a sideshow and by the spring of 1942 the Japanese advance in the Pacific and Indian Oceans seemed unstoppable. To the south they launched an invasion of New Guinea as part of an ambitious plan to isolate and possibly invade Australia. For once, the allied forces were not easily defeated and Japanese landings on the north coast of New Guinea met heavy resistance. Faced with this unexpected opposition, Admiral Yamamoto, C-in-C of the Japanese Combined Fleet, approved a plan, code named Operation MO, which involved a seaborne attack to capture Port Moresby. This operation would be supported by a Striking Force consisting of two aircraft carriers, *Shokaku* and *Zuikaku*, escorted by cruisers and destroyers. On the American side, the importance of defending Port Moresby was clearly recognised and a scratch force made up of the only available carriers, *Lexington* and *Yorktown*, together with a few cruisers (*Chester*, *New Orleans*, *Portland*, *Astoria*, and *Minneapolis*) and destroyers was hastily formed as Task Force 17 under Rear Admiral Fletcher USN. These ships rendezvoused 250 miles south-east of the New Hebrides on 1 May and set course northwards towards the island of Tulagi, one of the Japanese objectives. Fletcher was also allocated the cruisers and destroyers of Task Force 44 commanded by a Royal Navy officer, Rear Admiral Crace, who was on secondment to the Australian Navy. He flew his flag aboard the *County* class cruiser HMAS *Australia* and the task force included the American heavy cruiser USS *Chicago*.

The Battle of the Coral Sea was the first major naval engagement in which the respective surface fleets never sighted each other and all sinkings were achieved solely by air attack. Consequently, it was a long drawn out affair, partly because of the complex nature of the Japanese plans and partly because of the need for extensive air searches to locate enemy forces. After mounting air strikes against Tulagi on the morning of the 4 May, *Yorktown* and her escorts headed south again to join up with the rest of the Task Force on the 5 May. During that day and the next the American ships completed refuelling and headed north-west in order to be in a position to intercept the expected passage of the Japanese invasion force through the Jomard Passage to the south-east of New Guinea. This had been spotted by land based aircraft which had also carried out an abortive attack on the carrier *Shoho*. However Fletcher was unable to locate the two large Japanese carriers although at one point the two forces had passed within 70 miles of each other and American carrier based aircraft had actually flown over the enemy ships which had been obscured by cloud. On the morning of the 7 May, a Japanese search patrol reported a carrier and cruiser well to the east and a strike consisting of seventy-nine aircraft in three waves was quickly launched from the *Shokaku* and *Zuikaku*. The reported ships turned out to be the US tanker *Neosho* escorted by the destroyer Sims which were quickly overwhelmed and sunk. While this attack was taking place, Fletcher had decided to detach Crace's TF44 to the west in order to bar the route through the Jombard Passage. This force was spotted and attacked by heavy concentrations of Japanese aircraft which were successfully fought off by some very spirited gunnery and ship handling. In addition, this action this had drawn Japanese attention away from Fletcher's carriers. In the meantime American aircraft had reported two carriers and four cruisers 225 miles north-west of TF17 and ninety-three aircraft were launched by 10:30. Although the original report subsequently turned out to be inaccurate, a flight of Dauntless dive bombers from the *Lexington* spotted the carrier *Shoho* while en route and called in the other aircraft. The 12,000 ton Japanese carrier was quickly dispatched, leaving only 100 survivors to be picked up by the escorting destroyer. News of this action now caused the invasion convoy to reverse course and alerted Rear Admiral Takagi to the fact that there were US carriers in the vicinity.

Events were now approaching a climax. Both sides knew that the enemy was close by and prepared to launch powerful air strikes on the morning of the 8th. In fact, the forces were remarkably even, the Japanese having 121 aircraft while the Americans had only one more. The subsequent exchange of air strikes had mixed results for both sides. Unable to locate the *Zuikaku* due to poor weather conditions, the American aircaft concentrated on the *Shokakau*, scoring three bomb hits which put her flight deck out of action. The Japanese attack managed only one hit on The *Yorktown* which was quickly back in action but achieved more success against the *Lexington* which was hit by two bombs and two torpedoes. Nevertheless, as the Japanese attackers withdrew there appeared every prospect of fighting the fires which had broken out. However at 14:27 a massive explosion wracked the ship, this being caused by the ignition of aviation fuel leaking from fractured feed lines. Despite heroic efforts by the crew, the resultant fires eventually spread and further explosions shook the ship. In the early evening the reluctant order was given to abandon ship and the cruisers *Minneapolis* and *New Orleans* together with a number of destroyers edged in to pick up survivors. This was a remarkably successful operation with 2,735 officers and men were picked up, virtually the entire crew with the exception of 200 already killed in the earlier stages of that action. No sooner was this operation completed when the *Lexington* was shaken by further explosions although she was eventually sunk by torpedoes from the destroyer USS *Phelps*.

On the face of it the Japanese had won a tactical victory, having sunk the 33,000 ton *Lexington* against the loss of their own, much smaller, *Shoho*. However, it was the Americans who gained the most from the battle. The invasion of Port Moresby had been prevented and, although not realised at the time, the damage to the *Shokaku* and the aircraft losses aboard the *Zuikaku* were such that neither ship would be available for the forthcoming Midway operation. In contrast, the damage to the *Yorktown* was repaired thanks to Herculean efforts at the Pearl Harbor Navy Yard just in time for her to keep an appointment with destiny.

Midway Island lay some 1,200 miles WNW of Honolulu and Pearl Harbor and is aptly named, lying just to the east of the international date line and roughly halfway between Los Angeles and Tokyo. It is formed from a large atoll 5 miles across, although its strategic importance was out of all proportion to its small size. The Japanese attack on Midway, Operation M1, was only part of a complicated plan of the type much favoured by the Japanese in which feints and diversions were expected to split up and confuse the enemy, making it easier to achieve the objectives and defeat them in detail. The main landing force was to approach Midway from the south-west carrying over 5,000 troops in twelve transports. Its close escort consisted of a light cruiser and ten destroyers, while to the south would be a covering force which included two battleships, a small aircraft carrier, four heavy cruisers (*Atago*, *Chokai*, *Haguro*, and *Myoko*)) and several destroyers. Another force including four more heavy cruisers (*Kumano*, *Suzuya*, *Mikuma*, and *Mogami*), sailed from Guam with a tanker and two destroyers. Further support included a minesweeper group and also three seaplane tenders which would set up a base at Kure Island 60 miles north-west of Midway. It was confidently expected that the seizure of Midway would bring the US carriers out in reaction and waiting for was Vice Admiral Nagumo's First Carrier Strike force comprising four large carriers with a battleship, cruisers (*Chikuma* and *Tone*) and destroyer escort. Three hundred miles to the north-west was Yamamoto himself, flying his flag aboard the new 64,000 ton battleship *Yamato* accompanied by two other battleships and more cruisers and destroyers, as well as a further light carrier. As a diversion, intended to draw US forces away while Midway was occupied, a substantial force would also attack the Aleutian islands Kiska, Adak and Attu. The covering force here included two more carriers, four battleships, three heavy (*Nachi*, *Maya*, and *Takao*) and five light cruisers and numerous destroyers. Finally a submarine patrol line was to be established to the west of Hawaii in order to intercept US ships heading out towards Midway. This operation employed virtually every active major ship, including most of the heavy cruisers of the Imperial Japanese Navy and gave them overwhelming numerical superiority over the Americans. However, it contained two basic flaws which sowed the seeds of defeat even before they sailed at the end of May.

The plan assumed complete surprise being achieved so that the Midway occupation could be completed before US forces were able to intervene, and the splitting up of the fleet into individual groups spread over thousands of miles of ocean was contrary to the basic military principle of concentration of force. Unknown to the Japanese, the element of surprise was lost even before the operation was mounted as US and British codebreakers had succeeded in building up a fairly detailed picture of the enemies intentions. This enabled the American Task Forces to be stationed 300 miles to the north-east of Midway as the Japanese approached in early June. Command had devolved on Rear Admiral Fletcher, fresh from the Coral Sea and aboard the carrier *Yorktown* whose battle damage had been repaired at Pearl Harbor in a miraculously short time. The other two carriers, *Enterprise* and *Hornet*, formed Task Force 16 under Rear Admiral Spruance. Fletcher's TF17 included the heavy cruisers Astoria and Chester, while Spruance's TF16 was accompanied by no less than five heavy cruisers (*New Orleans, Minneapolis, Vincennes, Northampton,* and *Pensacola*).

It was a Midway based Catalina which made the first sighting of the enemy invasion force some 600 miles away on the morning of 3 June. A high-level bombing attack by B-17s was carried out in the afternoon with no result. Overnight, torpedo armed Catalinas made several attacks but only succeeded in damaging a tanker. In the meantime, Fletcher ordered his carriers to proceed south towards a position 200 miles north of Midway from where he hoped to launch air strikes against Nagumo's striking force when it was located. As dawn broke, the Japanese carriers began launching aircraft for a bombing attack against Midway although, as a precaution, another ninety-three armed with torpedoes and bombs were held at readiness aboard the carriers in case the American carriers made an unexpected appearance. A major air battle soon developed over the island in which the American fighters were outclassed by the nimble Japanese Zeros so that the accompanying bombers had a virtually free run over their targets. However, few aircraft were destroyed on the ground and the strike leader, radioed that a second strike would be necessary. Nagumo needed little convincing of this as by now his ships were under heavy attack by Midway based aircraft. Nevertheless, the Japanese ships were unscathed and fighters and AA fire took a dreadful toll of the attackers. The cruisers *Chikuma* and *Tone* had earlier launched floatplanes to search east and north in order to locate any American carrier forces but so far had reported no sightings. In fact the American carriers lay in a sector due to be searched by one of *Tone*'s aircraft but its launch was delayed for 30 minutes by a catapult fault. This was to have fateful results. With no sightings reported, Nagumo decided (at 07:15) that his reserve aircraft should be rearmed for a second attack on Midway. A report was then received from one of the scouting floatplanes that American ships had been spotted some 240 miles north of Midway, although the composition of this force was not immediately clear. As a result Nagumo ordered that the rearming of the aircraft should cease and that a torpedo strike should be prepared. By 08:20, when the presence of American carriers to the north was finally confirmed, his own first strike was returning from Midway and preparing to land aboard. He therefore decided to recover these aircraft before launching a powerful force against the enemy ships to the north, confident that he had enough time to do this before any American carrier based aircraft could reach him.

News of the first Japanese strike against Midway had been passed to Fletcher and Spruance as their three carriers raced south. Spruance did some nimble calculations and worked out that if he launched a strike immediately, he could hit the Japanese carriers at a vulnerable moment as they were recovering the aircraft from the first Midway strike. *Enterprise* and *Hornet* quickly got away virtually everything that could fly although it took almost an hour for the squadrons to form up and set course. The combined strike force consisted of 116 aircraft which were later followed by another thirty-five from *Yorktown*. As these formations set off and headed towards the reported position of the Japanese carriers, Nagumo's ships recovered the returning Midway strike and began to range a rearmed strike force on deck. However, even as Nagumo's ships were finally preparing to launch their strike, the first American attack came in just before 09:30. However, these were total failures and most of the attacking aircraft were lost without a single hit being obtained. Throughout these attacks, Nagumo's carriers manoeuvred frantically to avoid some of the torpedoes but continued preparing their own aircraft to launch against the Americans at 10:30. As the last of the attacking American torpedo bombers had gone and the carriers began turning into wind ready to launch, Nagumo and his crews had every reason to think that things were going their way. They had fought off everything the American's had thrown at them and their own retaliation was about to be unleashed. However, the brave American attacks at wave top level had brought all the covering Zero fighters down to low altitude and the ship's AA crew's attention was naturally engaged fighting off the attackers. In the confusion the arrival overhead of forty-nine dive bombers from *Enterprise* and *Yorktown* was not observed until 10:27 when the first Dauntlesses came screaming down out of the clear sky and planted four bombs on the *Kaga's* flightdeck. Other dive bombers singled out the *Akagi* which was hit twice and quickly turned into a blazing wreck. In the meantime, *Yorktown's* aircraft hit the *Soryu* with three bombs. The damage caused by the bombs falling on the Japanese carriers was multiplied by the fact that other ordnance was loosely stowed on the open decks because of the haste to rearm the aircraft, and those aircraft which were on deck were fully armed and fuelled. The result was that each of the three carriers were shattered by secondary explosions and fires. *Akagi* was quickly abandoned although she did not sink until the following day, *Soryu* and *Kaga* both sank early in the evening, around 19:20. The one remaining carrier, *Hiryu*, launched a strike of twenty-four aircraft at 10:40 that managed to hit the *Yorktown* although several were shot down. Admiral Fletcher decided to shift his flag to the cruiser *Astoria* which had closed to pick up some of *Yorktown's* crew, and subsequently a second strike of ten torpedo bombers achieved two hits which caused the already damaged *Yorktown* to list alarmingly to port. Although an attempt was later made to tow the carrier to Pearl Harbor, she was later torpedoed by a Japanese submarine on 6 June and finally sank the following day. Even as *Yorktown* was fighting for survival, Spraunce organised a strike against the *Hiryu* using aircraft which had survived the morning's attack against the other carriers. This succeeded in placing three or four 500 lb bombs into the flightdeck with predictable results. The ship was completely disabled and sank in the early hours of the following day. As he recovered this last strike of the day, Spruance made a tactically wise decision to withdraw his ships to the east in order to avoid a night action with potentially powerful Japanese surface forces and the carrier battle was over. The next morning Midway based aircraft did locate and attack some of the withdrawing support force and damaged the cruisers *Mogami* and *Mikuma*. The latter was finished off later in the day by dive bombers from the *Hornet*, the first of the Japanese heavy cruisers to be sunk and the final act in one of the most dramatic sea battles ever fought. It was a decisive victory for the outnumbered American carriers and represented the most significant turning point in the Pacific War.

CHAPTER XII

South-West Pacific

After their defeat at Midway, the Japanese turned again to the south-west Pacific and New Guinea where their earlier attempt to capture Port Moresby had been repulsed at the Battle of the Coral Sea. They now planned a further attempt to land troops on the north side of New Guinea and advance to Port Moresby over the Owen Stanley mountains. Rabaul in New Britain was to act as the logistic base and the island of Guadalcanal in the southern Solomon Islands was selected as the site for an airfield on which to base bombers to support the advance. Work began at the end of June and was detected by an allied reconnaissance aircraft on 5 July, 1942. At the same time, Admiral King, the US Chief of Naval Operations was also planning a limited offensive to capture and set up bases on the islands of Tulagi and Guadalcanal. Code named Operation Watchtower, this action was intended to provide a stepping stone for later advances to recapture and liberate the Philippines. Over the next seven months the island of Guadalcanal became the centre of some of the fiercest and bloody battles on both land and sea experienced in the Second World War.

News of Japanese activity on Guadalcanal resulted in the Watchtower timetable being advanced and the Marines were hastily embarked in a force of 19 transports under the command of Rear Admiral Kelly Turner. Overall command rested with Vice Admiral Jack Fletcher who provided a supporting force including the carriers *Enterprise*, *Saratoga* and *Wasp*. The landings went ahead at dawn on 7 August and for the next two days the transports remained in the sound between Tulagi and Guadalcanal (later to be named Ironbottom Sound) unloading supplies. The main approach to the sound was from the west where the conical volcanic mass of Savo Island divided the channel. On the evening of the 8th Turner detached some of his cruisers and destroyers under the command of Rear Admiral Victor Crutchley to guard the approaches to the sound. Crutchley deployed his own ship, *Australia*, the cruisers HMAS *Canberra* and USS *Chicago*, and two destroyers to guard the southern channel. The northern channel was covered by the three American heavy cruisers *Vincennes*, *Quincy* and *Astoria* as well as two more destroyers. The radar equipped destroyers *Ralph Talbot* and *Blue* were sent to patrol a few miles to the west of Savo Island. Meanwhile Admiral Turner had just been informed that Fletcher was withdrawing his carriers to reduce their exposure to counter attack and this meant that the vulnerable transports would have no air cover the next day. He therefore summoned Crutchley to a conference aboard his flagship anchored off Guadalcanal in order to decide whether the still partly loaded transports should be withdrawn that night. This had the effect of taking one heavy cruiser, *Australia*, away from the forces guarding the approaches around Savo Island and also of removing the officer in command at what was to be a critical moment.

The Japanese reaction to news of the American landings on the 7th was prompt and positive. Vice Admiral Mikawa, commanding 8th Fleet at Rabaul, immediately gathered a scratch force of cruisers and set off at high speed down the channel through the middle of the chain of the Solomon Islands (universally known as the Slot) towards Guadalcanal. Although his force was sighted during the day, the report did not reach Turner until later that evening. In the meantime, aircraft catapulted from Mikawa's cruisers carried out reconnaissance flights over Savo and Guadalcanal and were able to report accurately the disposition of the ships guarding the approaches to Savo Island. He therefore planned to tackle the southern cruiser force before turning east and then north to attack the northern

HMAS Canberra *leaving Wellington in July 1942 en route to join the task force assembling to support operations against Guadalcanal.* US Navy Historical Branch

patrol. His flagship, *Chokai*, was in the lead and was followed by the other heavy cruisers *Aoba*, *Kako*, *Kinugasa*,and *Furutaka* in that order. Behind them came the light cruisers *Tenryu* and *Yubari*, with the destroyer *Yunagi* bringing up the rear.

At 00:43 Savo Island was in sight dead ahead of Mikawa's flagship and just at that moment the patrolling destroyer USS *Blue* was also spotted. The Japanese ships slowed down and passed behind the unsuspecting destroyer which, although radar equipped, did not see any of the passing enemy. This incident alone highlighted the greatly superior night fighting skills of the Japanese Navy. Mikawa's ships continued silently past Savo Island until the bulk of two cruisers and two destroyers loomed ahead. At 01:36 Mikawa turned his ships to port and ordered torpedoes to be launched. These were the famous Long Lance torpedoes carrying a 1,000 lb warhead at ranges up to 20 miles. It took the torpedoes almost 10 minutes to reach their intended targets and in the meantime the Japanese ships crept onwards until at last they were spotted by the destroyer *Patterson* which immediately broadcast in clear, "Warning, Warning, Strange Ships Entering Harbour". It was too late. Even as the warning went out, HMAS *Canberra* was hit by two torpedoes and was then smothered by numerous 8in shells as the Japanese cruisers opened up at almost point blank range. Within seconds the ship was a blazing wreck and out of the battle, although she did not actually sink until the following day. Next in line was the USS *Chicago* which took a torpedo in the bow and was pounded with close range 8in fire. In return she loosed off some salvoes at the Japanese destroyer Yunagi before limping out of the battle to the west.

A dramatic shot of USS Quincy *illuminated by searchlights during the Battle of Savo Island.* US Navy Historical Branch

10 August, 1942. US Navy destroyers go alongside the stricken Canberra *the morning after the disaster at Savo Island.* US Navy Historical Branch

A view of USS Quincy *taken only a few days before her loss at Savo Island.* US Navy Historical Branch

Mikawa wasted no time on her and swept round behind Savo Island to come upon the other group of cruisers patrolling to the north. Surprisingly, these had not been alerted by the sounds of battle to the south of them, and had received no warnings of the presence of the Japanese ships. This was partly because of the frequent rain squalls which covered the battle area. Leading the three Allied heavy cruisers was *Vincennes*, followed by *Quincy* and *Astoria*, and at 01:48 more Japanese torpedoes were launched towards them. At the last moment the *Astoria* spotted the enemy ships and opened fire but this reaction was too late. She was quickly smothered by 8in shells and came to a dead stop, blazing furiously, and sank later the next day. Ahead of her was the Quincy which had no warning until she was suddenly illuminated by a searchlight from the *Aoba* and came under heavy fire. Nevertheless, she quickly trained her main battery and got off a couple of salvoes at the *Chokai*, scoring a hit on the bridge, but was forced to alter course to avoid the *Vincennes* ahead of her and

126

suddenly found herself surrounded by Japanese ships. Taking a fearful pounding, she burnt fiercely and rolled over and sank at 02:35. The leading ship, *Vincennes* was also illuminated by searchlights and her Captain initially thought that this was the *Chicago* and ordered her to switch it off. The mistake was quickly realised as 8in shells started arriving and *Vincennes* replied, scoring a hit on the *Kinugasa*, but as the Japanese ships swept by they pounded her with gunfire and put three torpedoes into her boiler rooms. The damage was mortal and she sank a few minutes after the *Quincy*.

Mikawa now ordered his scattered force to regroup north-west of Savo Island. He briefly considered then re-entering the anchorage to sink the transports. Had he done so, then the entire history of the Guadalcanal campaign might have been quite different. However, fearful of air attack on the following day, he decide to withdraw and set course back towards Rabaul. In just over half an hour he had sunk four heavy cruisers and damaged another for only minor damage to his own ships. Allied casualties amounted to 1,023 killed and another 709 injured. There was some consolation for the Americans when submarine S-44 torpedoed and sank the cruiser *Kako* on the morning of 10 August as it approached its base at Kavieng. Despite this the US Navy had suffered a humiliating defeat, the effects of which would linger on for some time.

Despite their success at Savo, it soon became apparent to the Japanese that they could only retake Guadalcanal by landing a substantial force backed up by strong naval forces and Operation KA was therefore set in motion. Reinforcements would by carried down the Slot at night aboard destroyers and transports under the command of Rear Admiral Tanaka. To cover this operation a strong force including three carriers, three battleships, several cruisers (including *Kumano*, *Suzuya*, *Chikuma*, *Atago*, *Takao*, *Maya*, *Myoko*, and *Tone*) and numerous destroyers would be deployed in order to engage and destroy any US forces which might intervene. Through a combination of intelligence from intercepted messages and aircraft sighting reports, Admiral Ghormley (Comsopac) was aware of the Japanese intentions and ordered a carrier Task Force (TF61) under Rear Admiral Fletcher to a position north-east of the Solomon chain and 150 miles from Guadalcanal. Fletcher's command included the carriers *Enterprise*, *Saratoga* and *Wasp* but the latter was sent south to refuel on 23rd August when it appeared that it would be a few days before the Japanese carriers arrived in the area. In fact, they made a much faster passage than expected so that Fletcher only had the two remaining carriers to fight the battle which brewed up the following day. Amongst his escorting forces were the heavy cruisers *Australia*, *Minneapolis*, *New Orleans* and *Portland*.

Although the Japanese reinforcements under Rear Admiral Tanaka had been spotted and attacked by aircraft on the 23rd, it was not until early the following day that an American aircraft located Rear Admiral Hara's force which included the 10,500 ton carrier *Ryujo*. By early afternoon, with no sign of any other carriers, Fletcher decided to launch a strike from *Saratoga* against the *Ryujo* and this began launching at 13:45. After they had formed up and set course towards their target, Fletcher had received new sighting reports of the *Shokaku* and *Zuikaku* some 60 miles further north. However, he was unable to contact the strike group which pressed on and sank the *Ryujo*. Even while these events were being played out, Admiral Nagumo launched two strikes towards the American carriers which had now been located less than 150 miles away to the south-east. The Japanese aircraft suceeded in hitting the *Enterprise* with several bombs despite strong opposition from American fighters. Fortunately, the damage was not fatal and the *Enterprise* was evenatually able to operate aircaft. *Saratoga* escaped any attack, as did the Japanese carriers which were not located by the American bombers. With all aircraft recoved, Fletcher decided to withdraw, not wishing his carriers to be caught at night by the strong Japanese surface forces. This was effectively the end of the battle although Tanaka's force managed to land its troops successfully and his destroyers gave the US Marines ashore on Guadalcanal a sleepless night, keeping up a heavy bombardment on their positions. An unfortunate aftermath to the battle occurred on 31 August when the *Saratoga* was torpedoed approximately 250 miles south-east of Guadalcanal. Although she did not sink, the damage was enough to put her out of action for the rest of the year.

The Battle of the Eastern Solomons was a disappointment for both sides. The Americans had sunk the small carrier *Ryujo* but had not even damaged the more important *Shokaku* and *Zuikaku*. Also, they had not been able to prevent the Japanese reinforcements landing on Guadalcanal and the *Enterprise* had been damaged. On the Japanese side, Nagumo would live to regret that his aircraft had not been more successful in their attacks against the American carriers.

After the indecisive Battle of the Eastern Solomons both sides concentrated on sending more reinforcements to Guadalcanal. This caused a distinctive pattern to emerge whereby the Americans could land troops by day under the cover of aircraft from Henderson Field on Guadalcanal, while the Japanese reigned supreme at night. Their troops were brought down the Slot at night aboard destroyers and transports, these regular movements quickly being termed the Tokyo Express by the Americans. For good measure they would be backed up by destroyers, cruisers and even battleships which would then bombard the US positions before withdrawing. A major US convoy carrying the 164th Infantry Regiment left Noumé a for Guadalcanal on 9 October 1942. Distant cover included a task force based around the only available carrier, USS Hornet, and to intercept any forces which the Japanese might run down the Slot while this operation was in progress, Admiral Ghormley had formed Task Force 64 consisting of cruisers and destroyers commanded by Rear Admiral Norman Scott. Co-incidently, as the Americans were preparing to send reinforcements, the Japanese had the same intention and planned a major troop landing of their own. The transport force, commanded by Rear Admiral Joshima, comprised two seaplane carriers and six destroyers carrying 728 men as well as heavy artillery and tanks. The covering force commanded by Rear Admiral Goto consisted of the cruisers *Aoba*, *Furutaka* and *Kinugasa* with two destroyers which would bombard Henderson Field once the troops and supplies had been landed. It was this group which was spotted by patrolling B-17s on the afternoon of the 11th as they headed down the Slot towards Guadalcanal. Scott immediately set course to intercept them.

At 23:00, Scott's cruisers and destroyers were heading north-east in line ahead just off the northern tip of Guadalcanal. In the lead were the destroyers *Farenholt*, *Duncan* and *Laffey*. Then came the cruisers *San Francisco*, *Boise*, *Salt Lake City* and *Helena*, with destroyers *Buchanan* and *McCalla* bring-up the rear. Shortly afterwards, he received radar-based reports that the Japanese ships were approaching from the north-west. He continued to the north-east for another half an hour before bringing his line of ships round through 180° onto a south-westerly track and was then ideally placed to execute the classic naval manoeuvre of crossing the T. The Japanese cruisers were in line ahead with *Aoba* leading *Furutaka* and *Kinugasa*, while a destroyer was stationed on either beam. By 23:46 Scott was in an ideal position and achieved complete surprise when he ordered "Open Fire!" The range to *Aoba*, the leading Japanese cruiser was only 4,800 yards and the American fire was deadly and accurate. Within minutes both *Aoba* and *Furutaka* were ablaze and Goto ordered his ships to turn away to the right although, initially, he thought Joshima's destroyers were firing at him in some ghastly mistake. Scott also momentarily ordered a cease fire (which was fortunately ignored) as he thought that some of his ships were mistakenly firing at one of their own destroyers. This was not the case and, as the Japanese ships turned away, he ordered a turn onto a north-westerly heading to parallel the enemy ships.

The destroyer *Fubuki*, on the starboard side of the Japanese force was quickly overwhelmed as she tried to turn away and sank almost immediately. The cruiser *Furutaka* was hit several times and was mortally damaged when she took a torpedo from the destroyer *Duncan*. She subsequently sank within an hour of the start of the action. The *Aoba* was badly damaged and Admiral Goto was killed when a shell exploded next to the bridge but the ship managed to escape into the night along with her sister, *Kinugasa* which was undamaged. The other destroyer, *Hatsuyuki* was also hit but managed to escape. However, the American force was not unscathed. Despite her damage, the *Furutaka* put several 8in shells into the *Duncan* which was also engaged by the *Hatsuyuki*. She drifted away to the north east and sank later that night, although the survivors were rescued in the morning. The *Farenholt* was damaged but stayed afloat while the light cruiser *Boise* received most of the fire from the Japanese cruisers as they turned away and suffered a forward magazine explosion, although the ship was saved to fight another day. Scott's flagship, San Francisco received some minor damage but her fighting efficiency was unimpaired.

Elsewhere that night, Joshima's force completed their mission and landed all the troops with their equipment although two of his destroyers, *Murakumo* and *Natsugomo* were sunk by air attack the next day (12th). On the 13th the American reinforcements were landed safely but that night a bumper Tokyo Express included a bombardment of Henderson Field by the battleships *Kongo* and *Haruna*, and in the nights following there were more bombardments by cruisers. Although Scott had won a tactical victory at Cape Esperance, it had made little difference to the overall position and the American soldiers and Marines on Guadalcanal were still in a perilous position.

In fact, a major Japanese army offensive was planned for mid-October 1942, with the objective of capturing Henderson Field on 22nd of that month – Y Day. To support this operation virtually the entire Combined Fleet put to sea on the 11 October. Yamamoto was able to field no less than five aircraft carriers, four battleships, fourteen cruisers and almost four dozen destroyers. As far as he could see, the Americans had only one carrier fit for action (USS *Hornet*) and he was confident that his forces would this time prevail. Initially, he was right but the stubborn resistance of the GIs and Marines on Guadalcanal caused Y-Day to be postponed by at least a week. This gave time for repairs on the *Enterprise* (damaged at the Eastern Solomons) to be completed at Pearl Harbor and with her Task Group she was able to rendezvous with the *Hornet* group on 24 October 275 miles north-east of Espiritu Santu in the New Hebrides. By dawn on the 26 Admiral Kinkaid, who was in overall command of the American carriers, was aware of the presence of the Japanese carriers 200 miles north-west.

Even before first light, *Enterprise* opened the Battle of Santa Cruz by launching SBDs to scout ahead and pinpoint the enemy force. Each was armed with a 500 lb bomb and two of these aircraft came across the light carrier *Zuiho*. Without hesitation they zoomed in for the attack and planted two bombs on her flight deck, rendering her unable to operate aircraft and effectively out of the battle. With *Junyo* already detached to launch softening up attacks against Guadalcanal, the opposing carrier forces were now very evenly matched. The Japanese had already located the *Enterprise* and *Hornet* and launched a strike of 109 aircraft in two waves shortly after 07:00. At about the same time, the American carriers also launched a strike in three waves totalling seventy-three aircraft.

The American carriers were operating in two groups 10 miles apart, and the first Japanese wave concentrated on the *Hornet* which was escorted by the heavy cruisers *Northampton* and *Pensacola*, as well as two light cruisers and seven destroyers. The carrier was hit by four bombs and two torpedoes despite heavy AA fire and the efforts of the fighters overhead. At least two aircraft crashed into the stricken carrier which was now well ablaze and mortally wounded. Hidden by a passing rain squall, the *Enterprise* had initially escaped attack but the second wave of aircraft found her and launched a furious bomb and torpedo attack. Dodging the torpedoes, she was hit by two bombs but these did not materially affect her operational capacity and she continued in action. Instrumental in fighting off many of the attackers was the new battleship *South Dakota* whose intense and accurate AA fire accounted for several enemy aircraft and others were deflected from hitting the carrier. The example set by the *South Dakota* was subsequently to be emulated in future task groups where battleships found a niche role in protecting the vulnerable carriers and provided welcome relief to the hard worked cruisers.

While all this was going on, at around 09:30 the Japanese carriers were also coming under attack from *Hornet*'s dive bombers who succeeded in putting three bombs into *Shokaku*, ripping up the flight deck, penetrating the hangar and causing major fires. The crippled carrier, a veteran of Pearl Harbor, would be out of action for nine months. A second group of *Hornet* aircraft, together with others from *Enterprise* failed to find the Japanese carriers and instead attacked Admiral Abe's

Vanguard Force, seriously damaging the heavy cruiser *Chikuma* which was hit by no less than five bombs. This was small consolation for missing the carriers.

While the first early morning strikes were being launched, Admiral Kondo had ordered the carrier *Junyo* to close with Nagumo's force and to launch a further strike. These arrived overhead the *Enterprise* at 11:00, achieving surprise as they attacked out of a layer of low cloud. Fortunately, they missed the carrier, although one bomb was planted on *South Dakota*'s forward 16in turret and another went right through the AA cruiser *San Juan* before exploding beneath her keel. The destroyer *Porter* had a lucky escape, being hit by no less than three torpedoes, all of which failed to explode! More aircraft went for the crippled *Hornet*, then under tow by the cruiser *Northampton*. She was hit three more times and was then abandoned in a sinking condition as the cruiser picked up survivors.

As soon as *Enterprise* had landed on the returning aircraft, Kinkaid wisely decided to withdraw to the south-east in the face of the superior Japanese forces. This was effectively the end of the action as the carrier groups were now too far apart to attack each other. From the naval point of view, it was clear cut victory for the Japanese who had virtually eliminated US aircraft carriers from the Pacific as both the surviving ships (*Enterprise* and *Saratoga*) needed substantial repairs. Nevertheless, the picture was not all one sided. Nagumo's once powerful carrier force had only around 100 aircraft remaining and had lost many of its most experienced pilots. And on Guadalcanal, the focus of all this action, US forces were still holding out and the Americans were subsequently able to land more supplies and reinforcements.

In the first two weeks of November the Japanese continued to pour reinforcements into Guadalcanal. By 12 November Japanese forces on the island outnumbered the Americans for the first time and a major offensive was being planned in preparation for which heavy bombardments by battleships and cruisers would take place on the 13 and 14 November. These would form part of a massive deployment of naval forces by Yamamoto and would involve virtually every available ship of the 2nd and 8th Fleets based at Truk and Rabaul. Coincidentally, the Americans were also planning a substantial reinforcement and two troop convoys sailed from Noumé a and Espiritu Santu on the 8th and 9th respectively escorted by cruisers and destroyers. In support, Admiral Halsey ordered the carrier *Enterprise* to sea as part of Task Force 16 under Rear Admiral Kinkaid although she was still undergoing repairs to damage received at Santa Cruz. Task Force 64 which included the modern battleships *South Dakota* and *Washington* was initially attached to the carrier force. The stage was now set for the decisive naval battle of the Guadalcanal campaign.

The first American convoy successfully landed its troops on the 11 November and the transports then withdrew. The second and larger convoy arrived on the 12 and was subjected to heavy air attacks during the day. These were fought off by fighters from Henderson Field and by heavy AA fire from the ships but that evening Turner decided to withdraw the transports as he had received news of a strong Japanese force coming down the Slot. This was part of the 2nd fleet and comprised the battleships *Kirishima* and *Hiei*, a light cruiser and no less than fourteen destroyers, all under the command of Vice Admiral Abe. Their intention was to enter Ironbottom Sound and carry out a sustained bombardment of Henderson Field. The only US forces available to stop them were the cruisers (including *San Francisco* and *Portland*) and destroyers of TF67.4 under Rear Admiral Callaghan, re-inforced by the cruiser *Atlanta* and a couple of destroyers from TF62.4 under Rear Admiral Scott. After escorting the transports clear of the island, Callaghan led his ships back into Ironbottom Sound from the east and headed towards Savo Island. Once again, threading through narrow waters, the American ships were deployed in line ahead with the destroyers *Cushing*, *Laffey*, *Sterett* and *O'Bannon* leading. Next came his flagship, *San Francisco*, followed by the other cruisers and then the remaining destroyers with Fletcher last in line. As the two forces raced towards each other, radar contact with the advancing Japanese battleships was established at 01:24 but it was not until 01:41 that the leading American destroyer, *Cushing*, spotted two enemy destroyers almost right ahead. Almost instinctively, her commander brought her hard to port in order to fire torpedoes but his unexpected manoeuvre caused confusion in the following ships and Callaghan was reluctant to open fire in case he engaged friendly ships. Any element of surprise was now lost and at 01:50, as the light cruiser *Atlanta* finally opened fire she was immediately engaged by several Japanese destroyers and the two battleships. She was quickly overwhelmed. Rear Admiral Scott was killed when a shell hit the bridge and although she did not sink immediately she was eventually beached and abandoned the next day. There was now a wild mêlée as the American ships found themselves in the middle of the Japanese formation and both sides engaged targets of opportunity. The *Cushing* got off six torpedoes at the *Hiei* but these all missed and the destroyer was then taken apart by heavy fire from the battleship. *Laffey*, second in line-passed so close to the *Hiei* that the battleship's main armament could not bear but she was then torpedoed by a Japanese destroyer and sank. *Sterett*, the third in line managed to torpedo the destroyer *Yudichi* but was then hit herself and put out of action. The battleships turned their attention on the cruisers and the *San Francisco* was hit and seriously damaged. Rear Admiral Callaghan and most of the senior staff were killed as 14in shells battered the unfortunate cruiser. *Portland*, coming up behind was hit by a torpedo which damaged the rudders and left her steering helplessly in circles although she continued firing and scored several hits on the Hiei which had also been torpedoed and was badly damaged. *Helena*, the third cruiser, led a charmed life that night and emerged unscathed but the *Juneau* took a torpedo in the forward boiler room and was effectively put out of action although she was still under control. As the last four destroyers came into the action, the *Barton* was torpedoed and sank within minutes while *Monssen* was overwhelmed by gunfire and became a blazing wreck, blowing up and sinking later in the night. At 02:26 the surviving senior officer (Captain Hoover, *USS Helena*) ordered all American ships to join up with him and retire to the east. The only ships able to comply were the badly damaged *San Francisco* and *Juneau*, and three destroyers. In the meantime, Admiral Abe had ordered his battleships to retire to the north-west as he did not want to risk them any further in the unpredictable night action. Most of his destroyers went with them although *Akatsuki* had been sunk in the action and the damaged *Yudichi* was finished off by the *Portland* at daybreak. A more serious casualty was the Hiei which was in a bad way and at daylight was within easy reach of aircraft from Henderson Field, including some flown in from the *Enterprise*, still well to the south-east. As a result of attacks by these and other aircraft including a B-17 from Espiritu Santu, the Japanese battleship was eventually brought to a stop and sank at around 18:00 on the 13th. The other postscript to this fierce night action was the loss of the *Juneau*, torpedoed by a Japanese submarine late the following morning.

Despite the grievous loss of ships and men, Callaghan's sacrifice had not been entirely in vain. *Hiei* was the first Japanese battleship to be sunk by US forces but the most important effect had been to prevent Abe's battleships carrying out their planned bombardment that night. This ensured that Henderson Field remained operational and as well as finishing off the *Hiei*, other aircraft successfully attacked and sank Japanese transports attempting to land more reinforcements. This activity prompted another bombardment on the night of 13th–14th November by the heavy cruisers *Suzuya* and *Maya* acting as part of a larger force under Vice Admiral Mikawa. However, they did relatively little damage and at dawn on 14th US aircraft were airborne to pursue Mikawa's force as it withdrew. They succeeded in sinking the heavy cruiser *Kinugasa* and also damaged three other cruisers and a destroyer. On the same day, another Japanese force under Rear Admiral Tanaka comprising eleven transports and eleven destroyers was located by reconnaissance aircraft as they raced down the Slot towards Guadalcanal. Despite air cover from the carriers *Hiyo* and *Junyo*, American aircraft from the *Enterprise* and Henderson Field mounted continuous attacks and sank six of the transports. Nevertheless, Tanaka pressed on and succeeded in getting four transports to their destination, along with 5,000 soldiers rescued from the sunken transports. To add to the pressure on Guadalcanal, a substantial force drawn from Admiral Kondo's 2nd Fleet was detailed to enter Ironbottom Sound and carry out a further bombardment. Led by the battleship *Kirishima*, the force included two heavy cruisers (*Atago*, *Takao*) and two divisions of destroyers, each led by a light cruiser.

In an attempt to frustrate the Japanese moves, Halsey decided to commit his battleships to a night action. TF64 with the battleships *Washington* and *South Dakota* was detached from the *Enterprise* task group under the command of Rear Admiral "Ching" Lee. An hour before midnight Lee's ships picked up a radar contact near Savo Island. The battleships opened fire on this target which turned out to be the light cruiser *Sendai* and she promptly reversed course and made off. Shortly afterwards, four American destroyers, scouting ahead of the battleships, ran into a pack of Japanese destroyers and two were sunk immediately while a third foundered the next day. Lee's problems were compounded when the *South Dakota* suffered an electrical power failure which put her radar and fire control out of action. She was therefore in no fit state to take on the combined fire of the battleship *Kirishima* and cruisers *Atago* and *Takao* who between them scored over forty hits on the superstructure. On the other hand, the destroyer *Ayanami* was sunk as she attempted a torpedo attack on the American battleships.

While *South Dakota* was forming the centre of a lot of unwelcome attention, Lee continued steadily ahead in the *Washington* and right on midnight he surprised the Japanese battleship *Kirishima* with several well aimed radar directed salvoes at a range of 8,400 yards. In only 7 minutes, nine 16in and forty 5in shells crashed into the *Kirishima*, starting countless uncontrollable fires and turning her into a helpless wreck. After checking fire, Lee ordered the *Washington* to continue to the north-west in a successful attempt to draw off the ships engaging the *South Dakota*. By 00:25 Admiral Kondo had decided to abandon the bombardment mission and ordered his ships to withdraw. Lee turned back to the south, racing to rejoin the *South Dakota* south of Guadalcanal later in the morning. Despite the loss of three destroyers, Lee could be pleased with the results of the nights work. Once again Henderson Field had been saved from a major bombardment and a second battleship had been sunk. Both sides now retired to lick their wounds but in three days continuous action the Japanese had lost two battleships, a heavy cruiser (*Kinugasa*) and at least three destroyers. American losses stood at two light cruisers and seven destroyers while both sides had several ships seriously damaged and out of action for some time (*San Francisco* and *Portland* were out of action until February and March 1943). Neither side could claim a decisive victory but from this point onwards the initiative began to pass to the US Navy, although events were to show that it had some way to go before it could match the Japanese in destroyer night-fighting skills.

Despite the Japanese naval losses in mid November, the Army continued to insist that Guadalcanal should be held and so the Tokyo Express still ran regularly at night, bringing in supplies and more troops. In an attempt to stop this traffic, Admiral Halsey set up a striking force (TF67) of cruisers and destroyers which would be exhaustively trained in night-fighting tactics. Unfortunately, Rear Admiral Wright had to lead the still partially trained force into action only two days after taking over. On 30 November a Tokyo Express consisting of eight destroyers came pounding down the slot with the intention, leaving supplies and troops floating offshore to be recovered by small craft while they turned and made good their escape. In command was Rear Admiral Tanaka, veteran of many Guadalcanal night engagements. Alerted by Magic intercepts and other sources, Wright's force of cruisers (*Minneapolis*, *Pensacola*, *New Orleans*, and *Northampton* together with the light cruiser *Honolulu*) and destroyers was deployed into Ironbottom Sound to await the arrival of Tanaka's destroyers. The night was calm and Wright's leading destroyer, *Fletcher*, picked up the Japanese ships on her radar at 23:16 as they closed the shore and prepared to offload their supplies. Despite having a clear tactical advantage, Wright crucially delayed allowing his destroyers to launch their torpedoes until the enemy ships had passed so that when they were fired the range was opening and no hits were obtained. As the torpedoes hit the water, he ordered his cruisers to open fire and the Japanese destroyers, their decks cluttered with troops and supplies, were completely surprised. It should have been a massacre but, almost immediately, the skill and discipline of the Japanese destroyer crews not only saved them but allowed them to turn the tables on the Americans. Although the leading destroyer, *Takanami*, was overwhelmed and was later abandoned, Tanaka split his force and directed some to continue with the supply mission while he took the remainder off towards the American cruisers. Although he had no radar, the position of the American ships was clearly pinpointed by the flashes of their gunfire. Within minutes of being surprised his destroyers had cleared for action and got off around two dozen torpedoes. Set for high speed running at almost point blank range they quickly found their targets. *Minneapolis* took two and sheared out of line. *New Orleans* had the whole of her bow, including No.1 turret, blown away as the forward magazine ignited. Pensacola turned to avoid the two damaged cruisers and was herself hit amidships, a major blaze breaking out due to a ruptured fuel tank. After firing several salvoes the cruiser *Northampton* was hit by two torpedoes fired from the destroyer *Oyashio*. Despite the untiring efforts of her damage control teams she sank a little over three hours later. The only cruiser to emerge unscathed was *Honolulu*, saved by the quick thinking of her bridge team. In the meantime, Tanaka's destroyers completed their supply drop and, apart from the drifting Takanami, made their way out of the sound in good order and at high speed. They had inflicted a staggering defeat on the superior American force which had held every advantage including complete surprise. Apart from the loss of the *Northampton*, the three surviving casualties were all out of action for several months, requiring extensive dockyard repairs before they could return to service.

Although it was not realised at the time, this was the last major surface engagement of the Guadalcanal campaign as by early January the Japanese had decided to evacuate their forces. At the end of the month, mistaking an assembly of transports intended for the evacuation as further Japanese reinforcements, Admiral Halsey ordered a cruiser force escorted by destroyers and accompanied by two of the new escort carriers northwards to intercept. Due to poor tactical handling, this force was caught in daylight without air cover on 29 January and the heavy cruiser *Chicago* (the only survivor of Savo Island) was sunk by air attack. This engagement, known as the Battle of Rennell Island was the last of the Guadalcanal campaign. By the end of the first week in February 1943, American ground forces had advanced to the north of the island and were surprised to find that the Japanese had gone. The whole campaign was one of the bloodiest and hardest fought of the war but its successful conclusion marked a major turning point in the Pacific campaign. From now on, all roads led to Tokyo.

With Guadalcanal cleared, American forces began to advance up the chain of the Solomon Islands towards the major Japanese base at Rabaul. Japanese resistance was still strong and several major actions occurred, although none on the scale of the bloody battles around Guadalcanal. On 30 June US troops landed on Rendova Island in preparation for an assault on New Georgia and the capture of the Japanese airbase at Munda. On the night of 4 July another major landing of US troops took place on the northern shore of New Georgia and this clashed with Japanese moves to land 1,200 troops at Vila on the other side of the Kula Gulf. In a brief encounter the Japanese sank the destroyer *Strong* with a Long Lance torpedo fired at extreme range. The next night, Rear Admiral Ainsworth led three cruisers and four destroyers against the ten strong Japanese force engaged in landing a further 2,800 troops at Vila. In the ensuing Battle of Kula Gulf, the light cruiser *Helena* was torpedoed and sunk, set against the loss of two Japanese destroyers. On 12 July the Americans gained intelligence of a further Tokyo Express bringing 1,200 troops aboard four destroyer transports with another four destroyers and a cruiser in support. Halsey directed Rear Admiral Ainsworth to take TF36.1 up the Slot to intercept this force and the stage was set for another fierce night encounter. In a confused action the Japanese again demonstrated their superiority in night fighting and although the light cruiser *Jintsu* was overpowered and sunk, their destroyers succeeded in disabling all three allied light cruisers (USS *Honolulu*, USS *St. Louis*, and HMNZS *Leander*) with torpedoes as well as sinking the destroyer *Gwin*.

The USS Minneapolis *was struck by two torpedoes during the Battle of Tassafaronga on the night of 30 November 1942, resulting in the loss of the whole bow section. After temporary repairs the ship made it back to the States under her own steam for repairs but was out of action for almost a year.* US Navy Historical Branch

This last action again demonstrated the Japanese superiority in night engagements. However, painful lessons were slowly being absorbed and some subsequent actions produced better results for the Americans. As American forces slowly fought their way up the chain of the Solomon Islands, the next target was Bougainville. Empress Augusta bay, on the western side of the island was selected as the landing point for 14,000 men of the I Marine Amphibious Corps on 1 November. Carried in twelve transports escorted by destroyers and minesweeper, the landing operation went ahead smoothly against only light opposition. However, Japanese aircraft from Rabaul were quickly on the scene with raids of up 100 aircraft continuing throughout the day. Although none were sunk, the transports were forced to withdraw that evening after unloading almost all the troops and supplies. The Japanese Navy was also quick to react and a scratch force of four cruisers (including heavy cruisers *Myoko*, *Haguro*) and six destroyers set out from Rabaul with the intention of disrupting the landings before the marines could properly establish themselves ashore. The task of guarding against this expected reaction fell to Rear Admiral "Tip" Merrill with a force of four light cruisers and eight destroyers, the latter organised into two divisions led by Captain Arleigh Burke and Commander B.L. Austin.

Merrill deployed his ships to the west of the landing beaches and at 02:00 he was patrolling on a north-south axis. As they turned onto a northerly course, the Japanese force was detected on radar approaching from the north-west. Rear Admiral Omori had his ships deployed in three columns with his two heavy cruisers (*Myoko*, and *Haguro*) in the centre. The port column consisted of three destroyers led by the light cruiser *Sendai* (Rear Admiral Ijuin) and three more destroyers led by the light cruiser *Agano* (Rear Admiral Osugi) to starboard. Being now aware of the potentialities of the Long Lance torpedo, Merrill planned to push his destroyers ahead to attack while keeping his cruisers at long range to avoid torpedoes. Both destroyer divisions accordingly attacked but their torpedoes all missed so Merrill now ordered the cruisers to open fire. These were all brand new *Cleveland* class cruisers, each armed with twelve 6 in guns and were capable of a high rate of fire. Throughout the engagement they manoeuvred as a single, well drilled team despite running at 30 knots and their concentrated fire was too much for the *Sendai* which took several hits and was left with her steering disabled. In manoeuvring to avoid the American gunfire the destroyers *Samidare* and *Shiratsuyu* collided although damage was light. On the other hand, the heavy cruiser *Myoko* sliced into the unfortunate *Hatsukaze* and the destroyer was barely able to make her way off to the north-west. Eventually *Omori* got his heavy cruisers back into line and they began to return fire but, although their fire was accurate, they achieved little against the fast moving American cruisers. Only *Denver* was hit and fortunately the shells did not explode. Merrill kept the range open by tracing a figure of eight pattern through the calm waters and was not bothered by torpedoes fired by *Myoko* and *Haguro* at 03:18. At one stage the battle area was starkly illuminated by flares dropped from Japanese aircraft but these did not greatly assist Omori who, convinced that he had sunk two of the American cruisers, ceased firing at 03:29 and turned away to the west with the *Agano* and two destroyers in company.

Although the American destroyer divisions were keen to give chase, they were recalled as Merrill was concerned that they would be caught well within range of Japanese airbases at dawn if they continued on that course. As they turned back, they came across the damaged *Hatsukaze* which was finished off and sunk. Merrill's caution was well justified. As TF39 headed south in the early morning, they were attacked by over 100 aircraft from Rabaul but these only managed to put two bombs into *Montpelier*, causing relatively little damage.

In a good night's work, Merrill's ships had sunk a light cruiser and two destroyers while only *Foote* had sustained serious damage and she was successfully towed to safety. In stark contrast to many earlier night actions, Merrill had kept his cruisers under tight control and dictated the course of the battle, his tactics preventing effective torpedo attacks by the Japanese. He had also demonstrated that in close range night actions the 8in armed heavy cruisers held no advantage over the more lightly armed but faster firing light cruisers. He had, of course, fully achieved his objective of keeping the Japanese ships away from the landing force. As it transpired, this was the last major naval action in the Solomons campaign. From this point on the Japanese Navy suffered a steady attrition through the constant air attacks from both land based and carrier based aircraft. Early in November 1943 the Japanese 2nd Fleet dispatched a large force to reinforce Rabual and this included the heavy cruisers of the 4th Cruiser Squadron (*Atago*, *Takao*, Maya, and *Chokai*), the 7th Cruiser Squadron (*Suzuya*, *Kumano*, *Mogami*) and the 8th Cruiser Squadron (*Chikuma*, and *Tone*). This concentration of virtually all of the IJN's remaining heavy cruisers proved irrisistible to the

Americans who launched strikes from the carrier *Saratoga* and B24 Liberator bombers of the 5th Air Force based in New Guinea. *Atago*, *Takao* and *Maya* were all seriously damaged and had to return to Japan for repairs. The opportunity was taken at this stage to convert *Maya* to a dedicated AA cruiser, a process which involved the removal of one twin 8in turret and the addition of numerous medium and light calibre AA guns. Consequently, she did not enter service until April 1944. The heavy cruiser *Mogami* was also damaged in the November air raids and was out of action for three months.

CHAPTER XIII

Victory in the Pacific

While Allied forces gradually took the offensive in the south-west Pacific the problem now facing strategists was how best to complete the final defeat of Japan. Eventually, a two pronged offensive was adopted in which the South-West Pacific forces under General MacArthur would continue northwards and liberate the Philippines while an advance across the central Pacific supported by the new fast carrier task forces was also planned. One objective of this thrust was the occupation of the Mariana Islands on which air bases for launching bomber attacks directly against Japan could be built. However, before this advance across the Central Pacific began, an interesting cruiser action was fought in the colder climate of the North Pacific. The windswept and fogbound Aleutian Islands, to the south-west of Alaska, had been occupied by Japanese forces in June 1942 as diversion forming part of the Midway campaign. Resources which could have been better employed elsewhere were eventually diverted to their recapture in August 1943. Until that could happen, the US Navy concentrated in trying to prevent reinforcements reaching the islands and this activity led to a fleet engagement in March 1943. A force consisting of the heavy cruiser *Salt Lake City*, accompanied by the elderly light cruiser *Richmond* and four destroyers under the command of Rear Admiral McMorris was patrolling to the west of Attu with the intention of intercepting a Japanese convoy believed to be approaching from the south. At 08:00 on the 26 March, just after the dawn of a cold and clear day, the American force was heading north in open scouting order when the slower convoy was spotted almost dead ahead on a similar course.

McMorris immediately ordered his ships to form up in line ahead with the destroyers *Bailey* and *Coghlan* leading, then his own flagship *Richmond* ahead of his only 8in cruiser, *Salt Lake City*, and the destroyers *Dale* and *Monaghan* bringing up the rear. He was outgunned by the Japanese escorting force which comprised two 8in cruisers (*Nachi* and *Maya*), two light cruisers and four destroyers. Directing the freighters to turn away to the north-west at best speed, Vice Admiral Hosogaya brought his ships round to the south-east to cross ahead of the advancing Americans. As he did so his heavy cruisers opened fire at 08:40 at a range of 20,000 yards, initially at the *Richmond* but then at the larger *Salt Lake City* which subsequently became the prime target for the rest of the battle. *Salt Lake City* replied two minutes later, quickly hitting *Nachi* twice although no serious damage was caused. The Japanese ships began to launch torpedoes causing McMorris to turn away to the south-west and the Japanese ships turned to follow. All the while the big cruisers were exchanging salvoes and over the next 30 minutes *Salt Lake City* took a couple hits which did not impair her fighting ability and in return landed a few shells on the *Maya*. McMorris then started to lead round to the north in an attempt to get at the Japanese transports. However, Hosogaya also turned so as to head off the Americans whose fortunes took a turn for the worse when the *Salt Lake City* developed a problem with her steering and received another 8in hit. McMorris decided that discretion was the better part of valour and, with the cruiser's steering repaired, he headed off to the west under cover of a smoke screen which was all the more effective as none of the Japanese ships carried radar. At 11:00, worried that he was getting too close to a Japanese base at Paramushiro, McMorris turned south with the intention of withdrawing and ending the engagement.

USS Baltimore *(CA68), the first of the new heavy cruisers which played an important role in escorting Fast Carrier Task Forces in the later stages of the Pacific war.* US Navy Historical Branch

The turn gave an opportunity for the cruisers *Nachi*, *Maya* and *Abukuma* to fire torpedoes at the fleeing Americans, although they all missed. At 11:03, just as *Salt Lake City* steadied on the southerly heading, she took an 8in shell which caused the after engine room to flood. Thereafter, over the next hour, she slowly lost way and eventually came to a dead stop. Nevertheless, her main battery continued in action and she scored at least one more hit on *Nachi*. Despite this, the outlook for the American ships was not good. McMorris took his flagship, *Richmond*, close to the crippled *Salt Lake City* to lay a protective smokescreen and ordered the destroyers *Bailey*, *Coghlan* and *Monaghan* to close the approaching enemy and attack them with torpedoes. In the meantime the crew of the *Salt Lake City* worked desperately to restore power to their ship, but it appeared that only a miracle could save them. From their point of view, this was exactly what then occurred. Just after midday, Hosogaya called off his forces and turned away to the west heading for home. The only American destroyer to get within range, *Bailey*, managed to loose her torpedoes which all missed although she did manage a sprinkling of hits on the cruiser *Nachi* with her 5in guns before she was recalled. It subsequently transpired that the Japanese Admiral had not realised how badly damaged was *Salt Lake City* due to the smokescreen and he was concerned that an air attack by American aircraft based at Dutch Harbour was imminent (they were at least 3 hours away at that moment). Even as the Japanese withdrew, *Salt Lake City* got under way again and by 12:12 she was working up to full speed. Cease fire was ordered as she pulled out of range.

The Battle of the Komandorski islands was over. From a technical point of view it was perhaps the last classic fleet gunnery action to be fought without the intervention of aircraft or submarines, and even radar played only a small part.

The advance across the Central Pacific began in earnest with the assault on the Gilbert Islands (Operation Galvanic) commencing on 19 November 1943. The forces assembled were out of all proportion to what had gone before and provided a clear indication of American industrial might and shipbuilding capacity. There were no less than four carrier task forces which included four of the new *Essex* class carriers, each capable of carrying over 80 aircraft. In two of the task groups (TG.50.1 and TG.50.2) AA defence of the vital carriers was vested in the new fast battleships but heavy cruisers *Chester*, *Pensacola* and *Salt Lake City* performed that task with TG.50.3. The fourth task group was protected by *Atlanta* class light AA cruisers. Fire support for the landings on the island of Makin was provided by the battleships and cruisers of TG.52.2 which included the veterans *Minneapolis*, *San Francisco* and *New Orleans*, together with the USS *Baltimore*, lead ship of a new class of heavy cruisers then entering service. Makin was finally subdued after three days of fighting but the island of Tarawa was the scene of some of the most desperate fighting of the war. Here fire support was provided by TG.53.4 which included the heavy cruisers *Portland* and *Indianapolis*.

It will be seen from the foregoing that the US Navy's heavy cruisers, no longer faced with strong surface opposition, were now mainly deployed as escorts for the carrier task forces or in the fire support role where their 8in guns provided the heavy firepower needed against well fortified defences. This pattern was repeated in subsequent amphibious operations of which the next, Operation Flintlock (Marshall Islands), occurred at the end of January 1944. In contrast to the assault on Tarawa, American casualties were relatively light, thanks in part to the accurate work of the fire support groups. Following this success, planning then began for Operation Forager, the assault on the strategically important Marianas which began on 15 June 1944. Where the Japanese Navy had not contested the earlier assaults, the importance of the Marianas could not be ignored and the stage was set for one of the major actions of the Pacific war. Inevitably, it was a carrier battle and, in terms of numbers of aircraft involved, far and away the biggest ever fought. The US Navy fielded no less than fifteen carriers including six *Essex* class, and these were organised into four task groups (TG.58.1 to 58.4.) with over 900 aircaft embarked. To guard against a possible attack by Japanese surface units, the six battleships available were formed into a separate task group (TG.58.7) escorted by heavy cruisers *Wichita*, *Minneapolis*, *New Orleans*, *San Francisco* and fourteen destroyers. With the battleships thus deployed, the defence of the carrier groups reverted to the cruiser force. TG.58.1 had no less than three new *Baltimore* class heavy cruisers (*Boston*, *Baltimore*, and *Canberra*) while TG.58.3 included the *Indianapolis* amongst its escort of five cruisers and thirteen destroyers.

For some months the Japanese Combined Fleet had been relatively inactive due to a lack of aircraft and trained aircrews for the carriers. It was not until the spring of 1944 that Admiral Toyoda in Tokyo decided that enough were available to form a force capable of meeting the US Navy on equal terms. Like Yamamoto before him, he looked for the elusive, decisive victory which would annihilate the US Pacific Fleet. This planned offensive operation was code named A-GO and was immediately put into operation when news of the American assault on Saipan was received. Command of the newly constituted First Mobile Fleet was given to Vice Admiral Ozawa and his force included nine aircraft carriers embarking a total of 473 aircraft, and these were to be backed up by some 100 land based aircraft. The carriers were organised into three groups each with an escort of cruisers and destroyers. In fact the Vanguard group also included four battleships of which two were the 64,000 ton monster *Yamato* class armed with 18in guns. The heavy cruisers *Atago*, *Maya*, *Takao*, and *Chokai* were attached to this group. Group A was accompanied by the heavy cruisers *Myoko*, and *Haguro* while *Mogami* was attached to Group B. By Japanese standards this was substantial force but unfortunately for Ozawa, the US Pacific Fleet had in the previous twelve months been completely transformed by the addition of ever increasing numbers of new ships as American industrial might got into its stride.

By June 1944, the task force sent to cover Operation Forager included no less than 15 aircraft carriers as already outlined.

The task of assaulting and capturing the islands was given to the US V Amphibious Corps and over 125,000 troops and their supplies were transported across the Pacific by Task Force 52 which comprised 551 warships, transports and auxiliaries. It was the largest trans-ocean amphibious operation ever conducted up to that time. This great armada was preceded by Task Force 58 under Admiral Raymond Spruance who had risen to prominence in the Battle of Midway two years earlier. As the assault groups went ashore on Saipan, Spruance took his task force to the west of the Marianas where he could forestall any Japanese counter attack.

Although details of Japanese movements were known from Magic intercepts, the first positive sighting came from US submarines in the Philippine Sea and the stage was now set for the greatest carrier battle of the war. Ozawa held one advantage over the Americans in that his strike aircraft had the longer range. He was therefore able to launch his first strike of sixty-nine aircraft at 08:30 while still out of range of any counter attack and this was followed by three more waves of 130, 47 and 82 aircraft. These were all total failures and most of the aircraft were shot down by the defending fighters and escorts. The US carriers were undamaged but the Japanese lost the brand new carrier Taiho and also the veteran *Shokaku* to submarine attacks. As darkness fell that evening, it was clear that the American fleet had won a great victory. In all Ozawa had lost over 340 aircraft as well as two of his largest aircraft carriers. The jubilant American pilots quickly named this the "Great Marianas Turkey Shoot". Their own losses amounted to 30 aircraft and, apart from a hit on *South Dakota* which had not put her out of action, none of their ships had been even scratched.

However, the battle was not quite over.

At dawn on the 20th, Mitscher flew off extensive search patrols but it was not until 15:40 that he finally got a positive sighting report of the enemy ships 275 miles to the west. A strike of 216 aircraft from ten carriers was launched at extreme range and darkness was falling as they reached the Japanese force. Nevertheless, they attacked and sank the 24,000 ton carrier *Hiyo* and two oilers. The carrier *Zuikaku* was damaged but was able to make it back to Okinawa, while the carrier *Chiyoda*, battleship *Haruna* and heavy cruiser *Maya* were also damaged. In addition Ozawa lost another sixty-five aircraft in the course of this attack so that by the time his battered force reached Okinawa there were only thirty-five serviceable aircraft left aboard his remaining carriers.

The Americans had lost twenty aircraft and the exhausted survivors now faced a gruelling night flight back to their carriers. In the next few hours seventy-two aircraft were lost either by ditching when they ran out of fuel or in crash landings aboard the carriers, and many of the remainder landed on the first carrier they saw. Two hundred and nine aircrew ended up in the sea but over three-quarters were eventually located and rescued.

Despite these final losses, a decisive victory had been won by the US Navy. It had effectively wiped out Japanese naval aviation and their remaining carriers would never again present a serious threat to American seapower. With the Central Pacific now secure, attention turned to one of the major objectives of US policy, the reoccupation of the Philippines where US forces had been comprehensively defeated in the aftermath of Pearl Harbor. To support this massive operation an armada totalling 738 ships comprising 157 fighting ships, 420 amphibious warfare vessels, 84 patrol and mine warfare vessels and 73 support and auxiliary ships was assembled. Of these, 17 fleet carriers, 6 battleships, 17 cruisers, and 64 destroyers formed Task Force 38 whose carriers would provide the air support for the operation.

The liberation of the Philippines began with landings at Leyte Gulf which took place on 20 October 1944 (A-Day) and, in contrast to the fierce battles which followed, went ahead with almost textbook precision against relatively light opposition. By midnight on the second day, no less than 132,400 troops and 200,000 tons of supplies had been landed and most of the transports had been unloaded and withdrawn.The Japanese had, of course, anticipated an American assault on the Philippines and had devised a series of SHO plans to be put into effect when the precise objectives were known. Despite the defeat in the Philippine Sea, the Japanese high command still dreamt of a decisive battle in which the US Navy would be defeated and forced to halt its seemingly unstoppable advance across the Pacific. Plan SHO-1 was activated on 18 October when the initial American preparations for the Leyte landings became known but as the Combined Fleet was widely dispersed it took almost a week to achieve the necessary concentrations and begin to put the complex plan into action. As with most Japanese plans, SHO-1 was complicated and involved diversions and deceits, to be exploited by widely spread surface forces. The vital element was a Northern Force under Admiral Ozawa which

The Japanese heavy cruiser Chikuma *frantically manoeuvres to avoid air attacks by aircraft of TG.77 off Samar during the Leyte Gulf battles. She eventually succumbed to several torpedo hits.* US Navy Historical Branch

would sail north of the Philippines with the express intention of luring Halsey's Third Fleet well away from the main attacks. Including four aircraft carriers, it was confidently expected that Halsey would take the bait offered by Ozawa, as indeed he did with almost fatal consequences.

With the American carriers out of the picture, the First Striking force under Admiral Kurita would be split into two groups. Force A under Kurita himself would come north of Leyte through the San Bernardino strait while Force C under Vice Admiral Nishimura would come up south of Leyte through the Surigao Strait between Leyte and Mindanao. These powerful forces, made up of virtually every remaining effective warship available to the Combined Fleet, would then trap and destroy all the American forces to the west of the Philippines and isolate the troops ashore who would then be defeated at leisure. Had this plan succeeded, as it very nearly did, it would have been a major setback for the allies and at the very least would have lengthened the war by years. The ensuing naval actions took place over several days and it is generally recognised that there were four distinct phases or battles which are now described.

The Centre Force under Vice Admiral Kurita included the two 64,000 ton battleships *Yamato* and *Musashi*, each armed with nine 18in guns, and no less than ten 8in heavy cruisers *Atago, Takao, Chokai, Maya, Myoko, Haguro, Kumano, Suzuya, Chikuma,* and *Tone*). This was a formidable surface fleet but unfortunately, from the Japanese point of view, it was almost completely devoid of air cover. Kurita planned to bring this force up the South China Sea then south of Mindoro and into the Sibuyan Sea, an expanse of water almost completely enclosed by islands of the Philippine archipelago. The Japanese force was spotted by US submarines early on 23 October as it headed up the Palawan passage towards Mindoro. Between them they torpedoed and sank the cruisers *Atago* (Kurita's original flagship) and *Maya* while *Takao* was seriously damaged. Information on the movements of the remaining ships was passed to Halsey's TF38 which had three carrier groups deployed to the west of the Philippines. These were ordered to prepare for strikes against the advancing Japanese ships on the following day as they came within range.

The American attacks were planned in several waves which were flown off during the course of the morning but while these were airborne CTG38.3, the most northerly of the three carrier groups, was subjected to a heavy attack by Japanese aircraft based on Luzon. One aircraft got through and placed a bomb squarely on the after flightdeck of the light carrier *Princeton*. This penetrated several decks before exploding and starting an uncontrollable fire. The cruiser *Birmingham* closed to assist the stricken carrier but, as she did so, the torpedo magazine blew up, tearing the *Princeton* apart and seriously damaging the *Birmingham* killing 229 of her crew. The hulk of the *Princeton* was later dispatched by torpedoes from the cruiser *Reno*.

Revenge was not long in coming. The first wave of forty-five aircraft from *Intrepid* and *Cabot* found Kurita's force just entering the Sibuyan Sea and went into the attack, although the results were indecisive. The cruiser *Myoko* was hit by a torpedo and was forced to turn back, and one bomb and one torpedo hit the *Musashi* although the massive battleship shrugged off these relative pinpricks. Another wave of forty-two aircraft from the same carriers managed another four bomb and torpedo hits on the *Musashi*, which was now acting as a magnet for the attacking American aircraft, but she was still able to make 27 knots. At 13:25 a third wave of aircraft, this time from the *Enterprise* and *Lexington*, pressed home their attack and put three torpedoes into *Musashi*, all of them along the starboard bow. These caused the ship to slow to 22 knots and her forward sections began to flood, causing the bow to settle deeper in the water and slowing her still further. A fourth attack developed around 14:30 by aircraft from the *Essex* and *Enterprise* and more torpedo hits reduced her speed to only 12 knots. In view of the damage she had sustained, Kurita reluctantly ordered her to break off and attempt to return to Brunei escorted by two destroyers. It was too late. Another massive American attack put ten more torpedoes into the mortally wounded ship and she began to take a heavy list to starboard. Despite every effort by her crew, she could not be saved and rolled over and sank at 19:35 in the evening.

By the time the last attack died away at around 15:30, several of Kurita's other ships were damaged including the battleship *Nagato* which had been torpedoed twice. Consequently, he was forced to reduce speed to 18 knots in order to keep his ships together for mutual protection and at around 15:55 he decided to reverse course and head away to the west. His reasons for so doing were complex but were influenced by the fact that the other Japanese forces were behind schedule and he would have to delay passing through the San Bernardino Strait if his subsequent advance was to be co-ordinated with their attacks. However, as the Americans observed his battered ships turning away, they assumed that he was breaking off the action and would not risk a return. Consequently, no aircraft were ordered to shadow his force which then effectively disappeared from view. From the American point of view they had won a major victory, sinking one of the world's largest battleships together with two heavy cruisers, and apparently causing serious damage to other ships.

Meanwhile, a further action was being fought to the south. Intending to operate in synchronisation with Kurita's Centre Force, Vice Admiral Nishimura also left Brunei on 22 October and headed towards the Surigao Strait, south of Leyte through the Sulu Sea. Here he was joined by Vice Admiral Shima's Second striking force and the two groups were detected late in the morning by American aircraft on 24 October. Their combined force included two battleships, the heavy cruisers *Nachi*, *Ashigara* and *Mogami*, and seven destroyers. An air strike from the *Franklin* sank the destroyer *Wakaba* although little else was achieved. Admiral Kinkaid had earlier ordered Rear Admiral Oldendorf to take his fire support battleships and other available forces to block the Strait and its approaches to prevent the Japanese force breaking through. As well as six battleships, Oldendorff also had a substantial force of heavy cruisers which, as well as the American *Minnieapolis*, *Portland* and *Louisville*, also included the *County* class cruiser *Shropshire* which had been transferred to the RAN as a replacement for HMAS *Canberra* lost at Savo Island. As darkness fell Nishimura led his ships into the Bohol Sea where the first of several groups of American warships were waiting for him.

The first line of defence comprised small PT boats although their spirited attacks had little success and petered out at around 02:15 but their actions had alerted Oldendorf and given him accurate information regarding the progress of the Japanese ships. The next American ships to engage were destroyers of Desrons 54 and 24 which scored some notable successes with their torpedoes and sank two destroyers and the battleship *Fuso*, while the *Yamashiro* took several hits. Despite these grevious losses, Nishimura pressed steadily onwards through the narrow waters of the strait in his flagship *Yamashiro*, now only accompanied by the cruiser *Mogami* and destroyer *Shigure*. He appeared to be unaware of the massive concentration of firepower which awaited him in the form of Oldendorf's six battleships, not to mention nine heavy and light cruisers. Steaming steadily on an east-west patrol line, Oldendorf's ships were perfectly placed the cross the enemy's T, the classic naval manoeuvre which enables a naval force to concentrate all its firepower onto the head of an advancing column. At 03:53, the battleships opened fire and the *Yamashiro* quickly became a battered wreck. Remarkably, she was still under control and turned away making 12 knots but was eventually finished off by torpedoes from American destroyers and she sank at 04:20. The *Mogami* was also hit but turned and started to make good her escape while the *Shigure*, always a lucky ship, was undamaged and was eventually to be the sole Japanese survivor of this bloody battle. Following Nishimura was Vice Admiral Shima's Second striking Force which ran into the same ambushes. The PT boats managed a hit on the light cruiser *Abukuma* which was put out of action, and was sunk by aircraft on the following day. Shima continued only halfway up the Surigao Strait before he decided that his mission was futile and turned back to the south-west. He was joined by *Mogami* and *Shigure* and headed out into the Bohol Sea. At 04:30, just as Shima was turning away, Oldendorf signalled some of his cruisers and destroyers to follow the retreating enemy. Cruisers *Louisville*, *Denver* and *Portland* had a sharp exchange with the *Mogami* but the Japanese ship escaped and continued away to the west. A little later, *Denver* and *Columbia* caught up with the damaged Asagumo and sank her but Oldendorf now called the pursuing ships off and concentrated his forces back towards Leyte.

A close up of the bridge and fore funnel of HMAS Australia *showing damage sustained in a kamikaze attack off Luzon in January 1945.* US Navy Historical Branch

Later in the day, aircraft from the escort carriers of TF77 finally put paid to Mogami and also caught and sank the Abukuma. It was a clear cut victory for the American ships, from their point of view, the action was particularly satisfying as five of Oldendorf's battleships were survivors from Pearl Harbor, now repaired and back in action with a vengeance.

To the north of the Philipines another element of the Japanese plan was falling into place. It was a basic component of the SHO-1 plan that Vice Admiral Ozawa's carrier force act as bait to draw away the American carriers. Whatever happened, his ships were on a one-way mission as the four carriers between them could only muster 108 aircraft. The staggering losses in the Marianas coupled with further losses around the Philippines had virtually eliminated Japanese naval aviation. Starting from their base in Japan's Inland Sea, Ozawa's force sailed on 20 October but were not spotted for several days and consequently did not initially have any effect on the disposition of the opposing American forces. On the morning of 24 October, Ozawa launched a strike of 76 aircraft against the carriers of TF38.3 operating east of Luzon. This mission was a total failure and many of the aircraft landed ashore on Luzon and only 29 returned to the carriers. However, this activity did alert Halsey to the presence of Ozawa's carriers and, true to form, he immediately ordered all three available carrier groups (TF38.1 had previously been detached to Ulhiti to refuel and was too far away to make the rendezvous) northwards to intercept. Pounding north through the night, the ten carriers embarked no less than 787 aircraft and even before dawn had broken, scout aircraft from Independence had located Ozawa's ships 200 miles east of Cape Engaño. The first strike was flown off at dawn and began attacking at around 08:00. With virtually no air opposition they had only to brave the intense AA fire of the Japanese ships although this was not inconsiderable. During the course of the day the carriers *Chiyoda*, *Zuikaku* and *Zuiho* were sunk, together with a destroyer and light cruiser. On the other hand the battleships *Hyuga*, *Ise* and cruiser *Oyodo* (plus 5 destroyers) all made good their escape and returned to Okinawa on 27 October. The light cruiser Tama, hit during the air attacks, was finished off by a submarine as she also headed towards Okinawa.

Despite the loss of his carriers, Ozawa had performed his mission exactly as planned and had succeeded in diverting Halsey's overwhelming air power at a critical time. While the Americans were throwing everything they had at Ozawa's toothless tigers, they very nearly suffered a major defeat further to the south. As the various elements of the Leyte Gulf battle were being fought, support of the actual landings and continued protection of the transports and troops ashore was vested in Task Force 77 under Rear Admiral Sprague USN. The air element of this was provided by three task groups each consisting of six small escort carriers accompanied by a screen of destroyers. On the morning of 26 October, the most northerly of these was TG77.4.3 (Taffy 3) which was to the east of Samar. Next was TG77.4.2 (Taffy 2) to the north east of Leyte Gulf while TG77.4.1 (Taffy 1) was even further south and too far away to play any part in the forthcoming action. As far as the Americans were concerned, the advancing Japanese surface forces had been decimated and repelled and Halsey's carriers were off to the north to finish off Ozawa's carrier force. Sprague ordered dawn patrols to be flown off from his Taffy 3 carriers and other aircraft were prepared for support missions ashore. At 06:45 one of the patrolling aircraft reported that it was being fired on by a force of ships, including battleships, twenty miles to the north. A radar contact in that position was quickly followed by a visual sighting of what were unmistakably large Japanese warships. Within minutes Sprague's carriers came under heavy shellfire.The Japanese force now in sight was Vice Admiral Kurita's Centre Force which had received such a mauling the previous day in Sibuyan Sea and had appeared to turn away. Although Halsey had subsequently received reports that Kurita had again reversed course and was heading back towards the San Bernardino Strait, he overestimated the damage which had been caused and assumed that the remaining units were of little fighting value. In fact Kurita still disposed four battleships, six heavy (*Chokai*, *Haguro*, *Kumano*, *Suzuya*, *Chikuma*, Tone) and two light cruisers, as well as several destroyers. Meeting no surface opposition, Kurita had made good time and passed through the straits just after midnight so that he was off the eastern coast of Samar at Dawn on the 26th. When he saw the American ships ahead, he at first thought he had encountered the fleet carriers of TF.38 and immediately gave the order for General Attack.

On sighting the Japanese battleships and cruisers Sprague had no option but to order his carriers to turn away and attempt to escape at best speed. As this was only 18 knots, it would only be a matter of time before the much faster enemy ships caught up, and with nothing larger than a 5in gun between them, the ships of Taffy 3 should have been easy meat for the approaching cruisers and battleships. Steadying onto an easterly course, at least Taffy 3's carriers were headed into wind and could launch aircraft while the occasional passing rain shower hid them from the Japanese. Nevertheless, by 07:05 shellfire was falling thick and fast around the carriers and it was only a matter of time before one of them was hit. Sprague therefore ordered his ships to turn south under cover of the rain while his destroyers laid a smoke screen. Kurita was reluctant to follow and headed east and south, keeping away from the smoke screen but in so doing he was on the outside of the turn and so did not close the range even though his ships were making almost 30 knots. At the same time he was being harassed by air attacks as aircraft scrambled into the air from the carriers and bore in with anything they had. In some cases this was only machine gun fire and, while a few were loaded with bombs, none were armed with torpedoes at this stage. At 07:16 Sprague ordered his three destroyers to attack with torpedoes and they turned bravely towards the enemy. First to get within range was Johnston which managed to put a torpedo into the cruiser Kumano before being hit by three 14in shells. Despite this her guns continued to operate and she managed to frustrate a Japanese destroyer attack before finally succumbing to a hail of shellfire as the Japanese force swept by her. The other two destroyers *Hoel* and *Heerman*, joined in, firing at anything that came within range. *Heerman* launched six torpedoes at the *Yamato* which was forced to turn away for several minutes in order to comb the tracks and this took her out of the battle at a critical time. *Hoel* was less fortunate and was hit over 40 times before finally sinking at 08:55. In compensation, air attacks had crippled the cruiser *Suzuya* which later sank.

Meanwhile, the carriers were still desperately heading south and at 07:42 Sprague ordered three of the destroyer escorts to attempt an attack on the Japanese ships. These small 1,200 ton vessels were never designed for a fleet action although they did carry torpedo tubes. Unsurprisingly, the *Samuel B.Roberts* was sunk while *Dennis* and *Raymond* both survived the ordeal although no torpedo hits were scored on the enemy. Despite this brave effort, the advancing Japanese ships began to score hits on the carriers. *Fanshaw Bay* took several 8in shells, while *Kalinin Bay* was also hit but continued in formation despite fires and damaged steering. Finally the *Chikuma* led three other heavy cruisers against the *Gambier Bay* which was hit several times and began to drop astern. The light cruisers and destroyers joined in and the escort carrier rolled over and sank at 09:07.

By that time the tide of the battle had already begun to turn. Taffy 3 aircraft had been joined by torpedo armed aircraft from Taffy 2, some 130 miles to the south, and together they made some well co-ordinated attacks on the Japanese cruisers. As a result the cruisers *Chikuma* and *Chokai* were both sunk, leaving only *Tone* and *Haguro* in close action. The battleships were still lagging behind and their firing was relatively ineffectual. By 09:10, Kurita was hesitating. Although he had the American force at his mercy, he had lost three cruisers and the intensity of air attacks was steadily increasing. Also, he assumed the powerful Task Force 38 was closing in from the north-east and he did not want to be caught by its aircraft. He, therefore, ordered his ships to break off the action and set course for the San Bernardino Strait which he reached in the early evening and then made good his escape under cover of darkness.

Despite Kurita's withdrawal, the escort carriers had one last ordeal before the day's fighting was over. Far to the south, two carriers of Taffy 1 were hit in the first Kamikaze attacks of the Pacific War although both survived. Taffy 3 came under intense kamikaze attacks later in the morning. One kamikaze hit *Kitkun Bay* but fortunately bounced into the sea before exploding. Several others were shot down but two crashed into *Kalinin Bay* although the damage was not fatal. Eventually, the inevitable happened and a steeply diving kamikaze bored straight through St.Lo's flightdeck before exploding in the hangar. The resulting bomb and torpedo explosions sank the ship with a heavy loss of life. By the end of the day the Americans had lost two escort carriers and three of the escorting destroyers, while many other ships were damaged and total casualties amounted to 1,130 killed and

913 wounded. Nevertheless, they had fought off a greatly superior force, sinking three Japanese heavy cruisers and preventing much greater destruction. It was a hard won result.

The question which inevitably had to be answered was how Kurita had managed to bring his ships through the San Bernardino Strait and into action on the 26th without being sighted or stopped. Halsey was mortified at having been caught out. Belatedly he formed and detached TF34 (made up of the modern fast battleships), accompanied by one of his carrier groups, and set off to intercept Kurita. A carrier strike launched at very long range was a failure and his ships did not reach the Strait until 3 hours after Kurita had already passed through. It was a salutary lost opportunity.

Despite the losses suffered in the Leyte operations, the Japanese were still able to provide stiff resistance to further landings intended to liberate the island of Luzon, largest of the Philippines. A major operation was planned at Lingayen Gulf on the west side of the island. In order to soften up the defences there were two fire-support groups in position on 6 January 1945, three days before the landings were due. The first group included the Australian cruisers *Australia* and *Shropshire* as well as the USS *Minneapolis*, while the second included heavy cruisers *Louisville* and *Portland*. Over the next few days this force was subject to constant kamikaze attacks and both *Australia* and *Louisville* were hit on the 5th. Further attacks developed the next day and *Australia* took another kamikaze as did *Louisville*, the latter losing thirty-two men including the cruiser's flag officer, Rear Admiral Chandler USN. Despite this, the ships remained in the line and the bombardment programme continued. Amazingly *Australia* took two more kamikazes on the 8 of January but was not put out of action. The landings took place on the following day and were virtually unopposed, a tribute to the efficiency and sacrifice of the bombarding ships. After the operation, HMAS *Australia* was withdrawn and headed back to Sydney for repairs, later continuing to the UK for a major refit which was still in progress when the war ended.

The battles around Leyte Gulf and the Philippines were the dying effort of the Imperial Japanese Navy. Those ships which survived were laid up due to battle damage or were immobilised due to lack of fuel supplies. For the allies there was still almost another year of fighting and two major amphibious operations to be carried out. These were the assault and capture of Iwo Jima (Operation Detachment) in February and March 1945, followed by a similar sequence of events at Okinawa (Operation Iceberg), the first of the Japanese homeland islands to be attacked. Both of these met with ferocious resistance including the lethal kamikaze suicide attacks which had first occurred during the Leyte battles.

When Japan had entered the war in 1941 she possessed a total of eighteen heavy cruisers, but after Leyte there were only five remaining. Of these, only Tone remained in home waters and was badly damaged by air attack from aircraft of TF.58 on 19 March 1945. She was finally sunk by a further air attack near Kobe on 24 July and the wreck was broken up after the war. The other cruisers had moved to the relative safety of Singapore after the Leyte battles where attempts were made to repair them. *Myoko* was at sea again in December but was torpedoed by the US submarine *Bergall* on the 12th. She lost power and had to be towed back to Singapore and spent the rest of the war as an immobile floating AA battery. After the war, she was towed out into the Straits of Malacca where she was scuttled on 8 July 1946. *Takao* was extensively damaged during the Leyte battles, having been hit by several torpedoes. Arriving at Singapore on 12 November, she lay unrepaired and was also used as a floating AA battery. An attack by British midget submarines on 31 July 1945 failed to sink her and she was still afloat when Singapore was reoccupied at the end of the war. She was later scuttled, again in the Malacca Straits, on 27 October 1946.

The remaining cruisers, *Ashigara* and *Haguro* were more active and continued to support Japanese forces retreating back through Burma and Malaya. This was to lead to one of the last surface ship actions of the war. It had not been until 1944 that the turn of the tide in Europe enabled the Admiralty to begin sending out more ships with the intention of building up the East Indies Fleet under the command of Admiral Sir John Power. Its main task was to support the British offensive in Burma and this entailed considerable activity in the Bay of Bengal, including air strikes and bombardments against Japanese forces. In the spring of 1945 the Japanese Area Commander, Field Marshall Count Terauchi, decided to withdraw his outlying forces occupying the Nicobar and Andaman Islands and strengthen the defences at Singapore. The heavy cruiser *Haguro*, accompanied by the destroyer *Kamikaze* left Singapore on 9 May bound for Port Blair in the southern Andaman Islands. A British task force (TF61) commanded by Rear Admiral Walker RN sailed from Trincomalee to intercept but this was sighted by a Japanese aircraft and the *Haguro* turned back towards Singapore. The British withdrew to refuel but early on 15th Walker ordered Captain Manley Power and the 26th Destroyer Flotilla to proceed to the north of Sumatra to locate and destroy some enemy transports which had been reported by aircraft. Later that morning an aircraft sighted the *Haguro* and accompanying destroyer, the ships having made another attempt to reach the Andamans. On being sighted they turned back and a strike of three Avengers launched at extreme range failed to effect any damage. However, throughout the remainder of the day the enemy's position, course and speed were constantly updated by shadowing aircraft and Power's destroyer flotilla now appeared ideally placed to intercept.

Captain Power, aware of the potential of the cruiser's 8in guns, decided to wait until nightfall before engaging and therefore headed south-east into the Malacca Straits, keeping ahead of the cruiser's assumed position. At 22:40, a radar operator in *Venus* reported a radar contact at the phenomenal range of 34 miles. Powers continued running ahead of the *Haguro* until 00:15 when he reversed course and the flotilla began to manoeuvre to their appointed sectors. Throughout this period the *Haguro* appeared blissfully unaware that she was running into a carefully planned ambush. At 00:45 she began a random zigzag movement but continued a mean course of south-east and it was not until a few minutes later that she turned away to the north and put on speed, having actually sighted the British destroyers. This put her racing towards the destroyer *Venus* which was unable to fire torpedoes but caused the cruiser to turn back again, this time heading towards *Saumarez* which was engaging the Japanese destroyer *Kamikaze*. *Haguro* joined in and hit the *Samaurez* with 5in shells just as she launched a salvo of torpedoes. Three of these were claimed as hits but the destroyer appeared to be badly damaged with one of her boiler rooms out of action. Nevertheless, her action distracted the *Haguro* and allowed *Verulam* to come in on the cruiser's starboard side and launch her torpedoes without being fired upon. Again, three hits were observed although in the post action analysis it was decided that the two destroyers had achieved a total of only three hits between them. Whoever had scored, the results were decisive. The *Haguro*'s forward 8in turrets were now out of action and her speed fell off to 16 knots. Even as these torpedoes had struck home, *Venus* and *Virago* ran in to attack at 01:24 and 01:27, firing six and seven torpedoes respectively of which at least three were hits. The last destroyer to attack was *Vigilant* which had been plagued with a defective radar and was not able to get into a firing position until 01:51 when all eight torpedoes missed. The *Haguro* was now dead in the water with only a few guns firing, but she remained stubbornly afloat despite the six hits from 37 torpedoes fired. Finally, *Venus* was ordered to close and finish her off with her two remaining torpedoes which both hit from a range of only 1,200 yards. It was enough and the blazing cruiser sank at 02:06. Her consort, the destroyer *Kamikaze*, had been ordered to escape by Captain Sugiura and had been able to slip away while the British ships had concentrated on the main target.

Power now ordered his flotilla to reform and set course to join the rest of the ships of TF.61. The damage to Saumarez was not as great as at first thought and she was able to make 25 knots on her remaining boiler. During the day the task force came under attack from Japanese aircraft and a near miss on Virago caused some damage and killed four of her crew. Eventually, the flotilla made a triumphant entry into harbour at Trincomalee on 21 May. This action was the last major surface action of the war and an almost textbook example of a well co-ordinated destroyer attack. Less than a month later the submarine HMS *Trenchant* torpedoed and sank the cruiser *Ashigara*, a sister ship of the *Haguro*, in the Bangka Strait south of Singapore. Thus in the closing stages of the war the Royal Navy was able to effect some retribution for the terrible losses it had suffered at Japanese hands in 1941 and 42.

CHAPTER XIV

Review

After six years of war, the Allies were finally victorious and it was appropriate that the final act was the signing of the Japanese surrender documents aboard a warship, the battleship USS *Missouri*, in Tokyo harbour on 3 September 1945. The naval war had been totally global in concept with major battles and campaigns having been fought in all the world's oceans. The Allies in particular had crucially relied on the ability to transport mean, materials and armaments across the world's oceans, initially in Britain's case to ensure the nation's survival and then later to allow the build up of the allied forces necessary to fight and defeat the enemy in Europe and the Far East. Germany and Italy had much less reliance on sea borne communications but the former expended great effort in trying to cut the Atlantic lifeline while Italian forces were a constant threat to British lines of communication in the Mediterranean. Alone amongst the Axis powers, Japan as an island nation, relied heavily on sea communications and for that reason had built up a powerful navy before entering the war.

In all these affairs the cruiser was an important element and, as has been recounted, was involved at all levels of naval warfare. Our interest has centred on the heavy cruisers spawned by the 1922 Washington Treaty and now is the time to appraise how they fared in the white-hot crucible of war. The Royal Navy was an early and enthusiastic advocate of the heavy cruiser and quickly laid down and completed several examples before coming round to the idea that its interest could be better served by smaller and more numerous cruisers. Consequently, the *County* class cruisers suffered from the fact that by the time war broke out in 1939 some were already over 10 years old and their design was based on the technology of the 1920s whereas other navies had more modern cruisers which incorporated lessons learnt from the first generation Washington Treaty ships. Even at the time of their building, the *County* class ships were criticised by some for being outdated in concept and certainly their general appearance gave credence to that view. With their high freeboard and three raked funnels they presented a distinctive and easily spotted profile and appeared to hark back to an earlier era. In practice their traditional qualities stood them in good stead as they were excellent sea boats and well capable of keeping the seas even in the worst conditions, attributes very relevant to their worldwide trade protection role. Their high deckheads gave spacious accommodation, again a positive factor in ships which could spend long periods patrolling the seas. The high volume hull, with good internal subdivision gave a degree of protection even though it was generally accepted that their armour protection was not as extensive as some of the foreign vessels.

During the War only one of the eleven County class cruisers was lost as a result of surface action, this being the unfortunate HMAS *Canberra*, surprised and overwhelmed by gunfire and torpedoes from Japanese heavy cruisers at the Battle of Savo Island in 1942. Even in this case, she did not sink immediately despite mortal damage and only sank some 12 hours later. However, their great weakness was insufficient protection against air attack and this was demonstrated at an early stage when HMS *Sussex* was seriously damaged by a single bomb off Norway in 1940. When subjected to a concentrated attack by Japanese dive bombers off Ceylon in 1942, the *Dorsetshire* and *Cornwall* quickly succumbed, both ships going down in minutes as the result of numerous hits. However, apart from these losses, the *County* class generally stood up well to the rigours of war service and perhaps the accolade should go to HMAS *Australia* which had an exceptionally busy war in the Pacific culminating in being hit by no less than four kamikazes off Luzon in 1945. Despite this damage she remained in action and completed her bombardment missions before being withdrawn for repairs.

The two smaller British heavy cruisers, *Exeter* and *York* were ultimately less fortunate. Although *Exeter* had her moment of glory in the battle of the River Plate, standing up to hits from the *Graf Spee*'s 11in guns, she was outclassed by the large Japanese cruisers which sank her in early 1942. Her sister ship, HMS *York*, had little chance to prove her mettle before being disabled in a highly unusual and brave attack by Italian explosive motorboats and subsequently had to be abandoned.

At the start of the War in 1939 Britain's only European ally was France but her ships saw little action before the country was overrun by German forces in May and June 1940. Consequently, the effectiveness of her cruisers was never tested and four out of the seven were scuttled at Toulon in November 1942. From a technical point of view this was unfortunate as the last to be completed, *Algérie*, is generally agreed by many observers to have been the best of the European heavy cruisers. Certainly she was a well balanced design keeping within the treaty limitations and introduced several technical advances as well as being armoured.

France's great rival in the Mediterranean was Italy and the inter-war years had been marked by a mini arms race in which Italy was determined to maintain parity with her neighbour even though France could claim the need for more ships due to her extensive colonial responsibilities. Nevertheless, Italy also completed seven heavy cruisers and in general these were faster and more heavily armoured than the French (or British ships) although this was only achieved by exceeding the 10,000 ton limit. Like the French ships, they were designed mainly for deployment in the Mediterranean and were therefore short on range. Although the Italian Navy was aggressive in purpose and mounted many operations, these were often not pressed home even when they held the advantage and, consequently, the individual ships rarely achieved their full capabilities. In particular the cruiser force suffered a crushing defeat at the Battle of Matapan when no less than three heavy cruisers were sunk, battered by the 15in gunfire of the British battleships which had surprised them in the night. In the second battle of Sirte, heavy Italian forces including the heavy cruisers *Gorizia* and *Trento* were turned away by a force of British light cruisers and another significant failure was in August 1942 when Italian heavy cruisers failed to intercept the remnants of the Pedestal convoy which was critical to the survival of Malta. By the time of the Italian surrender five heavy cruisers had been lost, three at Matapan, another torpedoed by submarines and the fifth destroyed by air attack. The remaining two, already badly damaged were sunk in harbour by allied human torpedo attacks.

The other European power with heavy cruisers was Germany with the three *Hipper* class. In appearance these were fine ships but in practice they were something of a disappointment. Certainly their armament was of the highest standards and coupled with excellent fire control systems they were capable of highly accurate fire. Their AA armament was, at the time of their completion, far and a way the best of any heavy cruiser. Unfortunately, they were let down by over complex machinery which was plagued with problems and proved unreliable in service. Their war record was undistinguished with Blücher being sunk early in the Norwegian campaign and the *Prinz Eugen*, despite being involved in high profile actions such as the *Bismarck* chase and the Channel Dash, subsequently achieved little and ended her war career as a training ship in the Baltic. The name ship of the class, *Admiral Hipper*, had a much more active career which was effectively ended in 1942 when she was bested by two British light cruisers in the Battle of the Barents Sea. Noticeably, her armour did not prove effective against the British 6in gunfire.

However, it was in the Pacific that the greatest tests of the cruisers occurred and no more than in the vicious fighting around Guadalcanal in 1942 and 1943. Things got off to a bad start for the allies at the battle of Savo Island where a Japanese cruiser force comprehensively defeated a combined Australian and American force, sinking no less than four heavy cruisers without loss to themselves.

It took almost a year for the Americans to gain the upper hand during the course of which more cruisers were lost or heavily damaged. *Minneapolis* and *New Orleans* both lost their bows to torpedo hits in the Battle of Tassafaronga, this being partly ascribed to their hulls being too lightly constructed in order to keep within treaty limitations.

By contrast, the larger Japanese cruisers proved exceedingly tough birds and virtually all of those lost absorbed considerable damage before finally going down. This was especially true in the Leyte Gulf battles in which the Americans possessed overwhelming air superiority. The only surprise here was that some ships actually survived. Before that the Japanese cruiser force had been well trained and, led by officers with daring and initiative, had pulled of some spectacular victories, noticeably in the Java Sea and at Savo Island. This was despite a lack of sophisticated radar systems such as the allies gradually began to acquire. In terms of enemy ships sunk, the Japanese heavy cruisers had a record far superior to any of the allied cruisers and, coupled with their ability to absorb tremendous battle damage, they must be regarded the most successful. Amongst the various classes the earlier *Myoko* and *Takao* classes were perhaps better balanced than the later *Mogamis* although the two *Tone* class were perhaps the best all rounders of the cruiser fleet. It is impressive to realise that only one of the fourteen large heavy cruisers had been lost prior to the catastrophic events of the Leyte Gulf battles despite being involved in many battles and campaigns. Despite their undoubted merits and successes, it is significant that as completed they were all well in excess of the 10,000 ton limit and, therefore, they cannot strictly be compared with most of their allied counterparts.

The US Navy, although a strong advocate of the Treaty cruisers was slow to build them in significant numbers, but this delay did have the advantage of allowing earlier examples to be evaluated so that changes and improvements could be incorporated in the later vessels. The final Treaty type, The *New Orleans* class was a balanced design optimised for its role in the Pacific. The main armament of nine 8in guns in three triple turrets was a good compromise between the standard eight guns in four twin turrets adopted by the European navies and the ten guns in five turrets on most of the Japanese ships. They carried more aircraft than the European ships, again the result of Pacific requirements, although this was something of a two-edged sword when it came to the close-in night surface actions in which these ships were engaged and in which the presence of aircraft and their volatile fuel stores was a source of all too easily ignited fires. The stern arrangements on the *Wichita* and subsequent ships was an improvement in this respect. Although they were undoubtedly good ships, the New Orleans class suffered badly at Savo Island with no less than three ships being sunk, a disaster similar to that which befell the Italian fleet at Matapan. However the remaining ships, particularly *New Orleans*, *Minneapolis* and *San Francisco*, survived considerable battle damage and served right to the end of the War.

The last of the American Treaty cruisers was the USS *Wichita* which offered several improvements over the *New Orleans* class, noticeably a much better secondary armament with 5in/38 cal dual purpose guns and much better aircraft handling arrangements. However, her stability margins were limited and the ideas pioneered with this ship were not fully realised until the succeeding *Baltimore* class ships which, freed from the Treaty restrictions, were able to increase hull dimensions to improve stability and allow an even heavier armament to be fitted. Although undoubtedly the best heavy cruisers of the war, they were almost 40% larger than those ships built to the strict treaty limitations.

So, in summary, which was the best of the treaty cruisers? From a practical point of view, probably either the Japanese *Takao* or *Tone* classes but, as they significantly exceeded the treaty displacement limits, they should really be excluded from the accolade. In fact, all of the Axis vessels were overweight to some extent so, if we work strictly within the rules then only the Allied vessels should be considered. On paper the French *Algérie* looked to be a very capable ship but she, unfortunately, remains something of an unknown quantity as she was scuttled in 1942 not having had the chance to show her full mettle.

In the Royal Navy, the *County* class ships were incrementally improved with each group and the last pair, *Norfolk* and *Dorsetshire* were certainly better ships than the first examples. However, they had very differing careers. *Dorsetshire* was lost in 1942 to an overwhelming force of Japanese dive bombers in a savage attack which probably would have sunk any of the heavy cruisers of the period. On the other hand *Norfolk* spent years patrolling the Atlantic and Arctic Oceans and contributed significantly to major actions such as the pursuit of the *Bismarck* and sinking of the *Scharnhorst*. Bearing in mind that only three of the eleven *County* class ships were lost to enemy action, their record is actually quite good, although, it must be admitted that they were generally deployed where the risk of air attack was limited and this may partly account for this outcome. Nevertheless, in terms of carrying out the tasks for which they were designed they actually did very well despite the fact that their technical specification did not always compare favourably with their foreign contemporaries.

With their improved armour, the *New Orleans* class cruisers were the best of the American Treaty cruisers and in terms of value for money and technical features they probably achieved more than any other class while remaining within the treaty limits. However, as already mentioned, their war record was very mixed. This really only highlights the fact that while a warship may be the best in the world in terms of technology and design, in war there are other factors which are just as important. These include standards of training and leadership as well as the ever present but entirely unpredictable matter of luck. In the end, the best ships are those which have won and survived.

Appendix 1

Technical Data
Notes on Data Tables
These notes apply to the data provided in the description of each warship type listed in the following pages.

Class: The name which refers to the group of ships of the same design. Most are normally named after the lead ship, although a generic designation may be applied.

Data: As there were often variations in specification between ships of the same class, especially when some were modified or modernised, the specific ship or period to which the data table applies is noted.

Displacement: Unless otherwise indicated, the figure given is the Standard Displacement.

Length, Beam and Draught: Measurements given in feet. Unless otherwise specified, length refers to overall length, beam to the widest part of the hull and draught to keel depth at full load.

Armour: Maximum armour plate thickness over the areas indicated.

Machinery: Propulsion type and maximum power output.

Speed: Maximum, unless otherwise specified. Quoted maximum speeds were often those attained under manufacturer's trials when the ship concerned was not fully loaded. Consequently, the maximum speed achieved under wartime conditions would often be less.

Range: Where available, the range in statute or nautical miles at a specified speed is given. In general, cruising at faster speeds would reduce total range.

Complement: Refers to total crew numbers. In wartime the complement could increase by as much as 30%.

Armament : For each type of gun the number and calibre in inches (or millimetres in some cases) is given. Figures in brackets indicate the disposition of the guns. For example, (4×2) indicates a total of eight guns carried in four twin mountings. A similar convention applies to torpedo tubes where fitted.

Aircraft: Figure quoted is normally the maximum number which can be embarked.

Ships in Class: With most classes a list of all ships is given together with the year of their launch.

United Kingdom/Australia

County Class:	Data *Suffolk* 1941
Displacement:	10,800 tons (14,550 tons full load)
Length:	590ft (pp), 630ft (oa)
Beam:	61 ft (hull), 68.5ft (over bulges)
Draught:	21 ft full load
Machinery:	Eight boilers, Parsons SR geared turbines, four shafts. 80,000 shp
Speed:	31.5kts
Range:	10,400 nm at 14kts
Complement:	784
Protection:	Main belt 1in except 4.5in amidships, bulkheads 1in, decks $1^3/_8$ in (2.5in over fore and aft citadels), turret 2in (face and tops) and 1.5in (sides/rear), barbettes 1in. External bulges
Armament:	Guns: Eight 8in (4 × 2), eight 4in AA (4 × 2), eight 2pdr AA (2 × 4), eight 0.5in AA (2 × 4)
Aircraft:	3. Fixed athwartships catapult abaft funnels
Ships in Class:	*Kent*, *Berwick*, *Cornwall*, *Cumberland*, *Suffolk* (1926), *Australia*, *Canberra* (1927),.*Devonshire*, *London* (1927), *Shropshire*, *Sussex* (1928),.*Norfolk* (1928), *Dorsetshire* (1929)

York Exeter Class:	Data *Exeter* as completed 1931
Displacement:	8,390 tons (10,500 tons full load)
Length:	540ft (pp), 575ft (oa)
Beam:	58ft
Draught:	20.5ft (full load)
Machinery:	Eight boilers, Parsons SR geared turbines, four shafts. 80,000 shp
Speed:	32kts
Range:	10,000nm at 14kts
Complement:	630 (peacetime)
Protection:	Main belt 3in, bulkheads 1in, decks 1.5 in–2.5 in, turrets 2in (faces) and 1.5 in (sides), barbettes 1in.
Armament:	Guns: Six 8in (3 × 2), four 4in AA (4 × 1), two 2pdr AA (2 × 1). Six 21in torpedo tubes (2 × 3)
Aircraft:	1. Catapult abaft funnels
Ships in Class:	*York* (1928), *Exeter* (1929)

France

Duquense Class:	Data Dusquense as completed 1928
Displacement:	10,000 tons (12,200 tons full load)
Length:	627ft (oa), 607ft (pp)
Beam:	62ft
Draught:	20ft full load
Machinery:	Nine boilers, Raeau Bretange SR geared turbines, four shafts. 120,000shp
Speed:	33.75kts
Range:	4,500nm at 15kts
Complement:	605
Protection:	Box citadel and magazines 30mm (1.2in), Decks 30mm, Turrets and CT 30mm.

Armament:	Eight 8in (4 × 2), eight 75mm (8 × 1), eight 37mm AA (4 × 2), twelve 13.2mm MGs. Twelve 21.7in (4 × 3) torpedo tubes
Aircraft:	2. One catapult
Ships in Class:	*Duquesne* (1925), *Tourville* (1926)

Suffren Class:	Data *Suffren* as completed 1930
Displacement:	10,000 tons (12,780 tons full load)
Length:	636.5ft (oa), 607ft (pp)
Beam:	63ft
Draught:	21ft full load
Machinery:	Nine Guyot boilers, Rateau Bretange SR geared turbines, four shafts. 90,000 shp
Speed:	31kts
Range:	4,500nm at 15kts
Complement:	773 (war)
Protection:	Main belt 2in (50mm), bulkheads 1in (25mm), Main deck 1in (25mm), Turrets and CT 1.2in (30mm)
Armament:	Eight 8in (4 × 2), eight 75mm (8 × 1), eight 37mm AA (4 × 2), twelve 13.2mm MGs. Six 21.7in (2 × 3) torpedo tubes
Aircraft:	2 (3 on other three). Two catapults
Ships in Class:	*Suffren* (1927), *Colbert* (1928), *Foch* (1929), *Dupleix* (1930)

Algérie Class:	Data as completed 1934
Displacement:	10,000 tons (13,500 tons full load)
Length:	611ft (oa), 591ft (pp)
Beam:	66ft
Draught:	20ft full load
Machinery:	Six Indret boilers, Raeau Bretange SR geared turbines, four shafts. 84,000 shp
Speed:	31kts
Range:	8,700nm at 15kts
Complement:	748
Protection:	Main belt 4.25in (110mm), bulkheads 2.75in (70mm), Main deck 3.125in (80mm), Turrets and CT 3.875in (100mm)
Armament:	Eight 8in (4 × 2), twelve 3.9in (6 × 2), eight 37mm AA (4 × 2), Twelve 21.7in (4 × 3) torpedo tubes
Aircraft:	3. One catapult
Ships in Class:	*Algérie* (1932)

Germany

Admiral Hipper Class:	Data *Admiral Hipper* 1939
Displacement:	13,900 tons (18,600 full load)
Length:	640ft (wl), 676ft (oa)
Beam:	70ft
Draught:	25ft full load
Machinery:	Twelve high pressure boilers, Blohm und Voss/AG Weser geared turbines, three shafts. 132,000 shp
Speed:	32kts

Range:	6,800nm at 19kts
Complement:	1,600
Protection:	Main belt 3.25in, decks 1.25in–2.5in. Turrets 6.5in, Barbettes 3.75in. Externally bulged
Armament:	Eight 8in (4 × 2), twelve 4.1in AA (6 × 2), twelve 37mm AA (6 × 2), four 20mm AA (4 × 1) Twelve 21in torpedo tubes (4 × 3)
Aircraft:	Three. One catapult
Ships in Class:	*Admiral Hipper* (1937), *Blücher* (1937), Prinz Eugen (1938), Seydlitz and *Lützow* (1939) not completed

Italy

Zara Class:	Data Zara 1940
Displacement:	11,680tons (14,300 tons full load)
Length:	547.5ft (pp), 557ft (oa)
Beam:	63ft
Draught:	20ft (mean)
Machinery:	Eight boilers, Parsons SR turbines, two shafts. 95,000 shp
Speed:	32
Range:	5,361nm at 16kts
Complement:	830
Protection:	Main belt 6in, decks 2.75in, turrets 6in (max).
Armament:	Eight 8in (4 × 2), twelve 3.9in AA (8 × 2), eight 37mm AA (4 × 2), eight 0.5in AA.
Aircraft:	2. Single bow catapult
Ships in Class:	*Zara, Fiume, Goriza* (1931), *Pola* (1932)

Trento / Bolzano Classes:	Data Trento 1942
Displacement:	10.500 tons (13,550 tons full load)
Length:	623ft (pp), 646ft (oa)
Beam:	67.5ft
Draught:	22ft (mean)
Machinery:	Twelve boilers, Parsons SR turbines, four shafts. 150,000 shp
Speed:	35kts
Range:	4,160nm at 16kts
Complement:	781
Protection:	Main belt 2.75in, decks 2in, turrets 4in
Armament:	Eight 8in AA (4 X 2), twelve 3.9in AA (6 X 2), eight 37mm AA (4 X 2), four 20mm AA (4 X 1), eight 0.5in AA (4 X 2)
Aircraft:	3. One fixed bow catapult
Ships in Class:	*Trieste* (1928), *Trento* (1929), *Bolzano* (1932)

Japan

Furutaka / Aoba **Class:**	Data *Aoba* 1939
Displacement:	7,100 tons (8,900 tons full load)
Length:	585ft (pp), 607.5ft (oa)

Beam:	52ft
Draught:	18.5ft (mean)
Machinery:	Twelve Kanpon boilers, geared turbines, four shafts. 102,000 shp
Speed:	34.5kts
Range:	6,000nm at 14kts
Complement:	c.770
Protection:	Main belt 3in, decks $1^3/_8$ in, magazines 2in, turrets 1in
Armament:	Six 8in (3 × 2), four 4.7in AA (4 × 1), eight 25mm AA (4 × 2), four 0.5in AA (2 × 2) Eight 24in torpedo tubes (2 × 4)
Aircraft:	2. One catapult
Ships in Class:	*Furutaka, Kako* (1925), *Aoba, Kinugasa* (1926)

Myoko / **Takao** **Classes:**	Data *Myoko* 1940
Displacement:	10,000 tons (13,300 tons full load)
Length:	631ft (pp) 668.5ft
Beam:	68ft
Draught:	20ft (mean)
Machinery:	Twelve boilers, Kanpon geared turbines, four shafts. 130,000 shp
Speed:	35kts
Range:	8,000nm at 14kts
Complement:	773
Protection:	Main belt 4in, bulkheads 3-4in, decks 1.5in, turrets 1in, barbettes 3in. Internal anti torpedo bulges
Armament:	Ten 8in (5 × 2), eight 5in AA(4 × 2), eight 25mm AA (4 × 2), four 0.5in AA (2 × 2). Sixteen 24in torpedo tubes (4 × 4)
Aircraft:	3. Two catapults abaft funnels
Ships in Class:	*Myoko, Nachi* (1927), *Haguro, Ashigara* (1928), *Takao, Maya, Atagao* (1930), *Chokai* (1931)

Mogami Class:	Data Mogami 1941
Displacement:	12,400 tons (13,887 tons full load)
Length:	620ft (pp), 661ft (oa)
Beam:	66.25ft
Draught:	19.5ft (mean)
Machinery:	Ten boilers (eight in *Suzuya* and *Kumano*), Kanpon geared turbines, four shafts. 152,000 shp
Speed:	34.5kts
Range:	8,150 at 14kts
Complement:	850
Protection:	Main belt 1–4in, decks 1.25–23/8in, turrets 1in, barbettes 3-4in.
Armament:	Ten 8in (5 × 2), eight 5in DP (4 × 2), eight 25mm AA (4 × 2), four 0.5in AA Twelve 24in torpedo tubes (4 × 3)
Aircraft:	4. Two catapults
Ships in Class:	*Mogami, Mikuma, Suzuya* (1934), *Kumano* (1936), *Tone* (1937), *Chikuma* (1938)

Tone Class:	Data *Tone* as completed 1938
Displacement:	11,215 tons (15,200 tons full load)
Length:	620ft (pp), 661ft (oa)

Beam:	66.5ft
Draught:	21ft (mean)
Machinery:	Eight Kanpon boilers, geared turbines, four shafts. 152,000 shp
Speed:	35kts
Range:	9,000nm at 18kts
Complement:	850
Protection:	Main belt 1–4in, decks 1.375–2.5in, turrets 1in, barbettes 3-4in.
Armament:	Eight 8in (4 × 2), eight 5in DP (4 × 2), twelve 25mm AA (6 × 2), four 0.5in AA Twelve 24in torpedo tubes (4 × 3)
Aircraft:	5. Two catapults
Ships in Class:	*Tone* (1937), *Chikuma* (1938)

United States

Pensacola Class:	Data as completed 1930
Displacement:	9,097 tons (11,510 tons full load)
Length:	586ft (oa), 570ft (wl)
Beam:	65ft
Draught:	22ft full load
Machinery:	Eight boilers, Parsons geared turbines, four shafts. 107,000 shp
Speed:	32.5kts
Range:	10,000nm at 15kts
Complement:	c.653
Protection:	Main belt 3in, bulkheads 2–3in, Decks 1–2in, Turrets 1.5in, barbettes 1.5in. CT, 8in
Armament:	Ten 8in (2 × 3, 2 × 2), four 5in AA (8 × 1), two 3pdr, eight 0.5in MG (8 × 1)
Aircraft:	4. Two catapults
Ships in Class:	*Pensacola*, *Salt Lake City* (1929)

Northampton / **Portland Class**	Data *Northampton* 1942
Displacement:	9,050 tons (12,150 tons full load)
Length:	569ft (wl), 600.5ft (oa)
Beam:	66ft
Draught:	24ft full load
Machinery:	Eight boilers, Parsons geared turbines, four shafts. 107,000 shp
Speed:	32.5kts
Range:	10,000nm at 15kts
Complement:	c.1100
Protection:	Main belt 3in, bulkheads 2–3in, Decks 1–2in, Turrets 1.5–2.25in, barbettes 1.5in
Armament:	Nine 8in (3 × 3), eight 5in AA (8 × 1), sixteen 1.1in AA (4 × 4), fourteen 20mm AA (14 × 1)
Aircraft:	4. Two catapults
Ships in Class:	*Northampton*, *Chester*, *Houston* (1929), *Louisville*, *Chicago*, *Augusta* (1930) *Indianapolis* (1931), *Portland* (1932)

New Orleans / **Wichita Class:**	Data Astoria 1941
Displacement:	9.950 tons (13,500 tons full load)

Length:	574ft (wl), 588ft (oa)
Beam:	61.75ft
Draught:	25ft
Machinery:	Eight boilers, Westinghouse geared turbines, four shafts. 107,000 shp
Speed:	32.75kts
Range:	10,000nm at 15kts
Complement:	c.1100
Protection:	Main belt 1.5–5in, bulkheads 5in, decks .5–3in, turrets 3–5in, barbettes 5in.
Armament:	Nine 8in (3 × 3), eight 5in AA (8 × 1), sixteen 1.1in AA (4 × 4)
Aircraft:	4. Two catapults abaft the funnels (One onstern, *Wichita*)
Ships in Class:	New Orleans, *San Francisco, Minneapolis, Tuscaloosa, Astoria* (1933), *Quincy* (1935), *Vincennes* (1936), *Wichita* (1937)

Baltimore Class	Data Baltimore as completed
Displacement:	13,600 tons (17,070 tons full load)
Length:	664ft (wl), 675ft (oa)
Beam:	71ft
Draught:	26ft full load
Machinery:	Four boilers, General Electric geared turbines, four shafts. 120,000 shp
Speed:	33kts
Range:	10,000nm at 15kts
Complement:	1,700
Protection:	Main belt 6in, bulkheads 6in, decks 2–3in, turrets 3–6in, barbettes 6in.
Armament:	Nine 6in (3 × 3), twelve 5in DP (6 × 2), forty eight 40mm AA (12 × 4), twenty-four 20mm AA (24 × 1)
Aircraft:	4. Two catapults
Ships in Class:	*Baltimore, Boston* (1942), *Canberra, Quincy* (1943), *Pittsburgh, St. Paul, Columbus, Bremerton, Fall River, Macon, Los Angeles, Chicago* (1944), *Helena, Toledo* (1945)

Appendix II

Construction Programmes

British and Commonwealth Navies

Ship	Class	Builder	Ordered	Laid Down	Launched	Completed
Berwick	Kent	Fairfield, Glasgow	1924	15 Sep 24	30 Mar 26	12 Jul 27
Cornwall	Kent	Devonport Dockyard	1924	09 Oct 24	11 Mar 26	06 Dec 27
Cumberland	Kent	Vickers Armstrong, Barrow	1924	18 Oct 24	16 Mar 26	08 Dec 27
Kent	Kent	Chatham Dockyard	1924	15 Nov 24	16 Mar 26	25 Jun 28
Suffolk	Kent	Portsmouth Dockyard	1924	30 Jul 24	16 Feb 26	07 Feb 28
Australia (RAN)	Kent	John Brown, Clydebank	1925	26 Aug 25	17 Mar 27	24 Apr 28
Canberra (RAN)	Kent	John Brown, Clydebank	1925	09 Sep 25	31 May 27	10 Jul 28
Devonshire	London	Devonport Dockyard	1925	16 Mar 26	22 Oct 27	18 Mar 29
London	London	Portsmouth Dockyard	1925	23 Feb 26	14 Sep 27	31 Jan 29
Shropshire	London	Beardmore, Dalmuir	1926	24 Feb 27	05 Jul 28	12 Sep 29
Sussex	London	Hawthorn Leslie, Hebburn	1926	01 Feb 27	22 Feb 28	19 Mar 29
Dorsetshire	Norfolk	Portsmouth Dockyard	1926	21 Sep 27	29 Jan 29	30 Sep 30
Norfolk	Norfolk	Fairfield, Glasgow	1926	08 Jul 27	12 Dec 28	30 Apr 30

Last of the line. The USS Newport News *was the last 8in heavy cruiser in service, being finally decommissioned on 27 June 1975. This photo was taken in 1969.* MPL

Ship	Class	Builder	Ordered	Laid down	Launched	Completed
Northumberland	Norfolk	Devonport Dockyard	15 May 29	Cancelled 14/01/30		
Surrey	Norfolk	Portsmouth Dockyard	15 May 29	Cancelled 14/01/30		
York	York	Palmers Shipbuilding, Jarrow	1927	16 May 27	17 Jul 28	01 May 30
Exeter	York	Devonport Dockyard	1928	01 Aug 28	18 Jul 29	27 Jul 31
(17 ordered, 15 completed)						

France

Ship	Class	Builder	Ordered	Laid down	Launched	Completed
Duquesne	Dusquense	Brest Navy Yard	1924	30 Oct 24	17 Dec 25	06 Dec 28
Tourville	Dusquense	Lorient Navy Yard	1924	04 Mar 25	24 Aug 26	01 Dec 28
Suffren	Suffren	Brest Navy Yard	01 Nov 25	17 Apr 26	03 May 27	01 Jan 30
Colbert	Suffren	Brest Navy Yard	01 Mar 27	12 Jun 27	20 Apr 28	04 Mar 31
Foch	Suffren	Brest Navy Yard	1928	21 Jun 28	24 Apr 29	15 Sep 31
Dupliex	Suffren	Brest Navy Yard	01 Apr 29	14 Nov 29	09 Oct 32	20 Jul 32
Algérie	Algérie	Brest Navy Yard	Aug 30	19 Mar 31	21 May 32	15 Sep 34
(7 ordered, all completed)						

Germany

Ship	Class	Builder	Ordered	Laid down	Launched	Completed
Admiral Hipper	Hipper	Blohm & Voss, Hamburg	30 Oct 34	06 Jul 35	06 Feb 37	29 Apr 39
Blücher	Hipper	Deutsche Werke, Kiel	30 Oct 34	15 Aug 35	08 Jul 37	20 Sep 39
Prinz Eugen	Prinz Eugen	Germania Werft, Kiel	16 Nov 35	23 Aug 36	22 Aug 38	01 Aug 40
Seydlitz	Prinz Eugen	AG Weser, Bremen	18 Jul 36	29 Dec 36	19 Jan 39	–
Lützow	Prinz Eugen	AG Weser, Bremen	18 Jul 36	02 Aug 37	01 Jul 39	–
(5 ordered, 3 completed)						

Italy

Ship	Class	Builder	Ordered	Laid down	Launched	Completed
Trento	Trento	OTO, Livorno	18 Apr 24	08 Feb 25	04 Oct 27	03 Apr 29
Trieste	Trento	STT, Trieste	11 Apr 24	22 Jun 25	24 Oct 26	21 Dec 28
Fiume	Zara	STT, Trieste	15 Sep 28	29 Apr 29	27 Apr 30	23 Nov 31
Goriza	Zara	OTO, Livorno	16 Oct 29	17 Mar 30	28 Dec 30	23 Dec 31
Pola	Zara	OTO, Livorno	1930	17 Mar 31	05 Dec 31	21 Dec 32
Zara	Zara	OTO, La Spezia	27 Sep 28	04 Jul 29	27 Apr 30	21 Dec 32
Bolzano	Bolzano	Ansaldo, Genoa	25 Oct 29	11 Jun 30	31 Aug 32	19 Aug 33
(7 ordered, all completed)						

Japan

Ship	Class	Builder	Ordered	Laid down	Launched	Completed
Furutaka	Furutaka	Mitsubishi, Nagasaki	22 Mar 22	05 Dec 22	25 Feb 25	31 Mar 26
Kako	Furutaka	Kawasaki, Kobe	22 Jun 22	17 Nov 22	10 Apr 25	20 Jul 26
Aoba	Aoba	Misubishi, Nagasaki	Jun 23	04 Feb 24	25 Sep 26	30 Sep 27
Kinugasa	Aoba	Kawasaki, Kobe	Jun 23	23 Jan 24	24 Oct 26	30 Sep 27
Myoko	Myoko	Yokosaka Dockyard`	1923	25 Oct 24	16 Apr 27	31 Jul 29
Nachi	Myoko	Kure Dockyard	1923	26 Nov 24	15 Jun 27	26 Nov 28
Haguro	Myoko	Mitsubishi, Nagasaki	1924	16 Mar 25	24 Mar 28	25 Apr 29
Ashigara	Myoko	Kawasaki, Kobe	1924	11 Apr 25	22 Apr 28	20 Aug 29
Takao	Takao	Yokosuka Dockyard	1927	28 Apr 27	12 May 30	31 May 32
Atago	Takao	Kure Dockyard	1927	28 Apr 27	16 Jun 30	30 Mar 32
Maya	Takao	Kawasaki, Kobe	1928	04 Dec 28	08 Nov 30	30 Jun 32
Chokai	Takao	Mitsubishi, Nagasaki	1928	26 Mar 28	05 Apr 31	30 Jun 32
Mogami	Mogami	Kure, Dockyard		27 Oct 31	14 Mar 34	28 Jul 35
Mikuma	Mogami	Kure Dockyard		24 Dec 31	31 May 34	29 Aug 35
Suzuya	Mogami	Yokosuka Dockyard		11 Dec 33	20 Nov 34	31 Oct 37
Kumano	Mogami	Kawasaki, Kobe		05 Apr 34	15 Oct 36	31 Oct 37
Tone	Tone	Mitsubishi, Nagasaki	1934	01 Dec 34	21 Nov 37	20 Nov 38
Chikuma	Tone	Mitsubishi, Nagasaki	1934	01 Oct 35	19 Mar 38	20 May 39
Ibuki	Ibuki	Kure Dockyard	1941	24 Apr 42	21 May 43	-
No.301	Ibuki	Mitsubishi, Nagasaki	1941	01 Jun 42	Not launched.	
(20 ordered, 18 completed)						

Ship	Class	Builder	Ordered	Laid down	Launched	Completed
United States						
CA24 *Pensacola*	Pensacola	New York Navy Yard		27 Oct 26	25 Apr 29	06 Feb 30
CA25 *Salt Lake City*	Pensacola	New York Shipbuilding		09 Jun 27	23 Jan 29	11 Dec 29
CA26 *Northampton*	Northampton	Bethlehem, Quincy		12 Apr 28	05 Sep 29	17 May 30
CA27 *Chester*	Northampton	New *York* Shipbuilding		06 Mar 28	03 Jul 29	24 Jun 30
CA28 *Louisville*	Northampton	Puget Sound Navy Yard		04 Jul 28	01 Sep 30	15 Jan 31
CA29 *Chicago*	Northampton	Mare Island Navy Yard		10 Sep 28	10 Apr 30	09 Mar 31
CA30 *Houston*	Northampton	Newport News		01 May 28	07 Sep 29	17 Jun 30
CA31 *Augusta*	Northampton	Newport News		02 Jul 28	01 Feb 30	30 Jan 31
CA33 *Portland*	Portland	Bethlehem, Quincy		17 Feb 30	21 May 32	23 Feb 33
CA35 *Indianapolis*	Portland	New York Shipbuilding		31 Mar 30	07 Nov 31	15 Nov 32
CA32 *New Orleans*	New Orleans	New York Navy Yard		14 Mar 31	12 Apr 33	15 Feb 34
CA34 *Astoria*	New Orleans	Puget Sound Navy Yard		01 Sep 30	16 Dec 32	28 Apr 34
CA36 *Minneapolis*	New Orleans	Philidelphia Navy Yard		27 Jun 31	06 Sep 33	19 May 34
CA37 *Tuscaloosa*	New Orleans	New York Shipbuilding		03 Sep 31	15 Nov 33	17 Aug 34
CA38 *San Francisco*	New Orleans	Mare Island Navy Yard		09 Sep 31	09 Mar 33	10 Feb 34
CA39 *Quincy*	New Orleans	Bethlehem, Quincy		15 Nov 33	19 Jun 35	09 Jun 36
CA44 *Vincennes*	New Orleans	Bethlehem, Quincy		02 Jan 34	21 May 36	24 Feb 37
CA45 *Wichita*	Wichita	Philidelphia Navy Yard		28 Oct 35	16 Nov 37	16 Feb 39
(18 ordered and completed)						

Post Treaty Cruisers

Ship	Class	Builder	Ordered	Laid down	Launched	Completed
CA68 *Baltimore*	Baltimore	Bethlehem, Quincy	01 Jul 40	26 May 41	28 Jul 42	15 Apr 43
CA69 *Boston*	Baltimore	Bethlehem, Quincy	01 Jul 40	31 Jun 41	26 Aug 42	30 Jun 43
CA70 *Canberra*	Baltimore	Bethlehem, Quincy	01 Jul 40	03 Sep 41	19 Apr 43	14 Oct 43
CA71 *Quincy*	Baltimore	Bethlehem, Quincy	01 Jul 40	09 Oct 41	23 Jun 43	15 Dec 43
CA72 *Pittsburgh*	Baltimore	Bethlehem, Quincy	09 Sep 40	03 Feb 43	22 Feb 44	10 Oct 44
CA73 *St. Paul*	Baltimore	Bethlehem, Quincy	09 Sep 40	03 Feb 43	16 Sep 44	17 Feb 45
CA74 *Columbus*	Baltimore	Bethlehem, Quincy	09 Sep 40	28 Jun 43	30 Nov 44	08 Jun 45
CA75 *Helena*	Baltimore	Bethlehem, Quincy	09 Sep 40	09 Sep 43	28 Apr 45	04 Sep 45
CA130 *Bremerton*	Baltimore	New York Shipbuilding	07 Aug 42	01 Feb 43	02 Jul 44	29 Apr 45
CA131 *Fall River*	Baltimore	New York Shipbuilding	07 Aug 42	12 Apr 43	13 Aug 44	01 Jul 45
CA132 *Macon*	Baltimore	New York Shipbuilding	07 Aug 42	14 Jun 43	15 Oct 44	26 Aug 45
CA133 *Toledo*	Baltimore	New York Shipbuilding	07 Aug 42	13 Sep 43	05 May 45	27 Oct 46
CA135 *Los Angeles*	Baltimore	Philidelphia Navy Yard	07 Aug 42	28 Jul 43	20 Aug 44	22 Jul 45
CA136 *Chicago*	Baltimore	Philidelphia Navy Yard	07 Aug 42	28 Jul 43	20 Aug 44	10 Jan 45
CA137 *Norfolk*	Baltimore	Philidelphia Navy Yard	07 Aug 42	27 Dec 44	Not launched, cancelled 12 Aug 45	
CA138 *Scranton*	Baltimore	Philidelphia Navy Yard	07 Aug 42	27 Dec 44	Not launched, cancelled 12 Aug 45	
CA122 *Oregon City*	Oregon City	Bethlehem, Quincy	07 Aug 42	08 Apr 44	09 Jun 45	16 Feb 46
CA123 *Albany*	Oregon City	Bethlehem, Quincy	07 Aug 42	06 Mar 44	30 Jun 45	11 Jun 46
CA124 *Rochester*	Oregon City	Bethlehem, Quincy	07 Aug 42	29 May 44	28 Aug 45	20 Dec 46
CA125 *Northampton*	Oregon City	Bethlehem, Quincy	07 Aug 42	31 Aug 44	27 Jan 51	07 Mar 53
CA126 *Cambridge*	Oregon City	Bethlehem, Quincy	07 Aug 42	16 Dec 44	Not launched, cancelled 12 Aug 45	
CA127 *Bridgeport*	Oregon City	Bethlehem, Quincy	07 Aug 42	13 Jan 45	Not launched, cancelled 12 Aug 45	
CA128 *Kansas City*	Oregon City	Bethlehem, Quincy	07 Aug 42	Not laid down, cancelled 12 Aug 45		

Ship	Class	Builder	Ordered	Laid down	Launched	Completed
CA129 *Tulsa*	Oregon City	Bethlehem, Quincy	07 Aug 42	Not laid down, cancelled 12 Aug 45		

(24 Baltimore/Oregon City class ordered. 18 completed)

Ship	Class	Builder	Ordered	Laid down	Launched	Completed
CA134 *Des Moines*	Des Moines	Bethlehem, Quincy	25 Sep 43	28 May 45	27 Sep 46	16 Nov 48
CA139 *Salem*	Des Moines	Bethlehem, Quincy	14 Jun 43	04 Jul 45	27 Mar 47	14 May 49
CA140 *Dallas* (ii)	Des Moines	Bethlehem, Quincy	14 Jun 43	15 Oct 45	Not launched, cancelled 06 Jun 46	
CA141	Des Moines	Bethlehem, Quincy	14 Jun 43	Not laid down, cancelled 12 Aug 45		
CA142	Des Moines	Bethlehem, Quincy	14 Jun 43	Not laid down, cancelled 12 Aug 45		
CA143	Des Moines	New York Shipbuilding	15 Jun 43	Not laid down, cancelled 12 Aug 45		
CA148 *Newport News*	Des Moines	Newport News	15 Jun 43	01 Oct 45	06 Mar 48	29 Jan 49
CA149	Des Moines	Newport News	15 Jun 43	Not laid down, cancelled 12 Aug 45		
CA150 *Dallas* (i)	Des Moines	New York Shipbuilding	22 Feb 45	Not laid down, Cancelled 28 Mar 45		
CA151	Des Moines	New York Shipbuilding	22 Feb 45	Not laid down, Cancelled 28 Mar 45		
CA152	Des Moines	New York Shipbuilding	22 Feb 45	Not laid down, Cancelled 28 Mar 45		
CA153	Des Moines	New York Shipbuilding	22 Feb 45	Not laid down, Cancelled 28 Mar 45		

(12 Des Moines class ordered. 3 completed)

Appendix III

Eight Inch Guns

The one common factor in all the various treaty cruisers was that they were armed with 8 inch (203mm) calibre guns (apart from the Japanese *Furutaka* and *Aoba* classes which originally carried 7.9in/200mm guns). As already related, the 8 inch treaty limit was an arbitrary figure resulting from the British desire to retain the *Hawkins* class cruisers armed with 7.5in guns. In most of the navies which were signatories of the Washington Treaty, the 8in gun was not an existing calibre at that time and new weapons had to be specially developed. Below are technical descriptions of the 8in guns developed by each navy together with details of the various mountings in which they were carried.

British and Commonwealth Navies

All the British and Australian *County* class cruisers, together with the two *York* class, were armed with the same 8in Mk.VIII guns carried in twin mountings although there were variations in the design of the mountings. The gun itself had a standard bore of 8in and a barrel length of 400 inches (50 cal). It fired a 256 lb (116.1 kg) shell over a maximum range of 30,650 yards (28,030m) with the

A Fairey IIIF floatplace aboard HMS York*. The trainable catapult and aircraft handling crane was just some of the equipment necessary to operate an aircraft.* Maritime Photo Library

guns at an elevation of 45 degrees. Ships normally carried Semi Armour Piercing Capped (SAPC) shells but High Explosive (HE) shells were also available and at least 20 rounds per gun were normally stowed. The latter were useful for shore bombardments or AA barrage fire.

The original design specification for the *Kent* class called for an anti-aircraft capability which required the Mk.I mountings to have a maximum elevation of 70 degrees and high rates of training and laying. The guns had to be lowered to 10 degrees elevation for the loading cycle but, nevertheless, a rate of fire of around 5 rounds per minute could be achieved for each gun. This was amongst the highest of any of the treaty cruisers. However the power necessary to achieve the specified rates of training and laying could not be adequately met and the mountings suffered a progression of teething troubles although reliability was much better by the outbreak of war in 1939. The revolving mass of the Mk.I mounting, including the two guns which weighed 17.2 tons each, was 183 tons.

The Mk.I mounting was fitted to the five British *Kent* class and also to the two RAN vessels while the later *London* class had the *Mk.I** mounting which had a higher geared elevation drive and increased magazine capacity. The final two ships of the *Norfolk* class, and HMS *York* carried the Mk.II mounting which featured several design changes intended to simplify the handling of shells and charges. There were two hydraulic pumps, instead of one, driven by a more powerful electric motor and the loading mechanism was altered. Although these changes solved several problems experienced with the earlier design, the MK.II was heavier than its predecessor and this was a serious issue in the context of trying to keep within the treaty tonnage limitations.

HMS *Exeter*, the last Royal Navy heavy cruiser was armed with the *Mk.II** mounting in which the maximum elevation was reduced to 50 degrees, a final admission that the concept of using heavy 8in guns in the AA role was not a practical proposition. To be fair, it was not a reflection on the guns but on the increasing performance of aircraft and the lack of a suitable high-angle-fire control system.

Although no more British heavy cruisers were built, some work was done on guns and mounting for the projected Hawke class. Designated Mk.IX and Mk.X, the guns would have fired a heavier 290 lb (131.5 kg) projectile over a maximum range of 31,300 yds (28,620m). They were intended to be carried in a new triple mounting similar to that utilised by the US Navy but very little design work had been done when the whole project was cancelled in October 1942.

France

The two *Dusquense* and four *Suffren* class heavy cruisers were all armed with the 8in/50cal M1924 gun which fired a variety of Armour Piercing and HE shells. The earliest rounds weighed 271 lb (123.5 kg) but later versions were slightly lighter at 263 lbs (119.5 kg). Subsequently, the M1936 *AP* shell which was in service in 1939 was much heavier at 295 lb (134 kg). Maximum range was 32,800 yds (30,000m) when fired at 45 degrees elevation. All six ships had the same twin mounting which weighed in at 180 tons, each gun weighing 20.39 tons and carried in a separate cradle so that they could be elevated individually or locked together as required. Maximum elevation was 45 degrees so that the mounting design was considerably simpler than the British equivalent and the loading cycle could be carried out at any point between −5 and + 10 degrees. Rate of fire was between 4 and 5 rounds per minute for each gun.

The last of the French Treaty cruisers, *Algérie*, was armed with the 8in/55cal M1931 gun which was similar to the earlier models except for a longer barrel. There was very little difference in performance and the maximum range was calculated at 33,000 yds (31,000m) at 45 degrees elevation. Each gun was slightly heavier, weighing in at 21.69 tons. The twin mounting was similar to that in the earlier ships except that the heavier guns and increased armour protection increased the total weight.

Although not relevant to the subject of this book, it is interesting to note that the submarine *Surcouf* was armed with two 8in/50cal M1924 guns in a twin mounting which had only limited training capability and a maximum elevation of 30 degrees.

Germany

The standard German weapon which armed all the *Hipper* class cruisers, including *Prinz Eugen* and was also intended for the uncompleted *Seydlitz* and *Lutzow*, was the 8in/57cal SKC/34 gun. This fired a 269 lb (122 kg) shell over a maximum range of 36,680 yds (33,540m) at an elevation of 37 degrees, the maximum possible in the twin Drh LC/34 mountings. Available ammunition included APC and HE, as well an illuminating shell, each ship stowing 40 of the latter. Rate of fire was 5 rounds per minute for each gun. The rotating mass of the twin mounting was 244 tons.

The German 8in guns were the longest ranged of any of these weapons and were backed up by an efficient and accurate fire control system, as the *Prinz Eugen* demonstrated in the engagement with the British battleships *Prince of Wales* and *Hood* on 25 May 1941 during the pursuit of the *Bismarck*. Her 8in guns actually outranged the 15in guns of the *Hood*, on whom she scored several hits, although the 14in guns of the *Prince of Wales* had a greater range.

A complete main armament set of guns and mountings was built for the cruiser *Seydlitz* but these were never fitted and two of the turrets were installed on the *Ile de Croix* on the French Atlantic Coast to boost the defences. The remaining pair were intended for the *Ile de Re* but were never installed. The Lutzow was sold to Russia in an incomplete state in 1940 and towed to Leningrad for completion. It is believed that only two or three guns had actually been fitted, two in A turret foreward, and the other possibly in D turret aft.

Italy

The first Italian Treaty cruisers, *Trieste* and *Trento*, were armed with the 8in/50cal Ansaldo 1924 gun in twin M1924 mountings. Each gun weighed 21.06 tons and fired a 276 lb (125.3 kg) AP shell over a range of 34,256 yards (31,324m) at an elevation of 45 degrees, this being the maximum for the mounting. The HE shell was slightly lighter at 244 lb (110.6 kg) although, surprisingly, the maximum range for this is quoted as slightly less. Loading took place at 15 degrees elevation and at near this figure the rate of fire was just over 3 rounds per minute. However at the higher angles of elevation the loading cycle rose to 40 seconds so that only 3 rounds could be fired in 2 minutes.

A feature of the mounting was that the two guns were mounted very close together on a common cradle. The interaction between the two guns caused an undesirable dispersion of the shells and in an effort to solve this effect the propellant charge was reduced so that muzzle velocity fell from almost 3,000 ft.sec to 2,750 ft/sec. Naturally, this also reduced maximum range, to around 30,600 yds (28,000m), but actually did little to improve the dispersion of shot.

The subsequent *Pola* class of four cruisers were armed with the 8in/53cal Ansaldo 1927 gun. With a slightly longer barrel, it fired the same 276 lb shell over a range of 33,400 yds (30,547m). Maximum elevation was again only 45 degrees. The M1927 was similar to the earlier version except that loading could be carried out at any elevation angle, effectively maintaining the rate of fire at almost 4 rounds per minute. The revolving mass of the mounting was 178.1 tons (181.0 tonnes) but the two guns were still close together, only one metre between bores, and the shot dispersion problems remained.

The last Italian heavy cruiser, *Bolzano*, was armed with the M1929 8in gun which was essentially a lightened version of its predecessor. The M1929 mounting was similar to the M1927 except that it was much lighter by virtue of reduced armour (100mm maximum against 150mm in the *Pola* class).

Japan

Japan's earliest heavy cruisers, conceived before the signing of the Washington Treaty, were armed with 7.9in (200mm)/50cal I 3rd Year Type guns but these were subsequently replaced by the standard 8in (203mm)/50cal II which armed all subsequent heavy cruisers, including the *Mogami* class when their triple 6in mountings were replaced by twin 8in. The Model II gun fired a 277.5 lb (125.85 kgs) shell to a maximum range of 32,150 yards (29,400m) at an elevation of 45 degrees. The standard twin mounting was produced in several variations, differing mainly in the maximum elevation of the guns.

Types C and D were carried in the *Aoba* and *Nachi* classes respectively and in these maximum elevation was only 40 degrees so that maximum range of the guns was slightly less than that quoted above. The Type E mountings fitted in the *Atago* class were capable of 70 degrees elevation but difficulties with these meant that the last ship *Maya* was given modified mountings with 55 degrees elevation. This became standard in subsequent Type E mountings which armed the *Mogami* and *Tone* class cruisers, as well as the *Kako* and *Furutaka* when they were rearmed. The revolving weight of these mountings was around 170 tons and rate of fire varied between 2 and 5 round per minute depending on the angle of elevation. It was rather ironic that the lowest rates of fire were achieved at high angles of elevation for use in the anti-aircraft mode when maximum rate of fire was most desirable!

United States
In contrast to many other navies, the USN was an enthusiastic advocate of the 8in gun although prior to the Washington Treaty it had not built any heavy cruisers. Nevertheless, the treaty limitations were very much in line with US Navy thinking and an 8inch gun had already been produced for use in pre-dreadnoughts and armoured cruisers built at the end of the 19th Century. This was 45cal weapon with a range of 22,500 yards. However a much more effective weapon, the 8in/55cal Mk9, was produced for use by the Treaty cruisers, and also for the battlecruisers *Lexington* and *Saratoga* when they were completed as aircraft carriers. The gun was actually produced in various versions designated Mks 9, 10, 11, 13 and 14 and was fitted in the *Pensacola*, *Northampton*, and *Portland* classes, as well as the first three *New Orleans* class. All of these featured triple mountings apart from the *Pensacola* which was fitted with twin mountings, identical to those on the two carriers.

The Mk.14 gun weighed 30 tons and fired a 260 lb (118 kg) shell over a maximum range of 31,860 yards (29,130m) at 41 deg elevation. The triple mounting in a New Orleans class cruiser had a revolving mass of 294 tons (299 tonnes) and a rate of fire of just over 3 rounds per minute per gun. By comparison the twin mounting weighed in at around 187 tons although rate of fire was similar.

The last four *New Orleans* class (*Tuscaloosa, San Francisco, Quincy, Vincennes*) carried the much lighter 8in/55cal Mk12 or Mk.15. Each gun weighed only 17.17 tons (17.45 tonnes) although maximum range was slightly less at 30,050 yards (27,480m). This weapon also armed the USS *Wichita* as well as subsequent *Baltimore* and *Oregon City* classes. In a typical Baltimore class installation, the triple mounting had a revolving mass of 297tons (302 tonnes) and rate of fire was 4 rounds per minute per gun.

The final evolution of the American 8in gun was the Mk.16 carried by the three post war *Des Moines* class. Although the individual guns were lighter, at 16.68 tons (16.95 tonnes), the triple mountings were much heavier at 451 tons (458 tonnes) revolving mass due to the complexity of the automatic loading system which enabled rates of fire as high as 10 rounds per minute per gun. Capable of a tremendous weight of fire in a relatively short time, these ships provided invaluable fire support during the Korean and Vietnam wars although none were completed until well after the Second World War.

Appendix IV

Aircraft Deployed Aboard Heavy Cruisers

At the start of the First World War the aircraft was little more than a fragile novelty but by 1918 it had become a viable and effective military weapon. From the naval point of view, one of its most useful roles was as a means of scouting and reconnaissance. Land based aircraft and airships provided useful information to ships at sea and by 1918 the aircraft carrier was already evolving. Specialist seaplane carriers had been introduced and one of these, HMS *Engadine*, had been involved in the Battle of Jutland, one of her aircraft providing the first sighting of the German fleet. When the first of the treaty cruisers were being constructed all navies designed them to carry one or more seaplanes in order to assist with the cruisers traditional scouting role. Although it was possible to launch aircraft from a warship by means of a catapult or short flying-off deck, it was not feasible for a conventional aircraft to land on any ship except a dedicated aircraft carrier with a long flight deck. The only option was to land on the sea and then be hoisted aboard the parent ship by means of a crane. This method of recovery therefore dictated that the cruiser would carry seaplanes which from a technical point of view fell into two categories, floatplanes or flying boats. The former was by far the most common and, although some were purpose designed, others were adaptations of landplanes in which the wheeled undercarriage was replaced by floats. These would either be in a

The Curtiss SOC Seagull *was the standard US Navy cruiser floatplane for most of the Second World War, despite the advent of more modern types.* US Navy Historical Branch

twin float configuration or else a large single float under the fuselage with a smaller stabilising float at each wingtip. On the other hand, the flying boat, as its name implies, had a boat shaped hull and actually sat in the water when at rest. With a few exceptions, notably the British Walrus amphibian and French Loire 130 flying boat, most of the aircraft deployed aboard the cruisers were floatplanes.

Aircraft handling facilities were a significant part of the ship's equipment and contributed materially to the weight. As a minimum, two aircraft were required in order to provide an acceptable degree of operational readiness and to increase search areas when required. The American and Japanese navies, operating in the vast expanses of the Pacific, laid considerable emphasis on the provision of air search capabilities and their ships were designed to handle up to six aircraft. To launch the aircraft at least one catapult was required and this needed sufficient space to train and launch. Some aircraft were stored in readiness already mounted on a catapult but spare aircraft were either parked on deck (taking up more space), or in dedicated hangars which also provided cover for maintenance and repairs. Recovery of the aircraft after landing, and general positioning of aircraft around the deck and onto the catapults, was normally carried out by one or more cranes which sometimes also had the task of handling the ship's boats. The aircraft required a supply of highly inflammable aviation fuel as well as ordnance and spare parts, while the aircrew and maintainers required accommodation and facilities aboard the ship. As has been described elsewhere, considerable ingenuity went into providing these facilities and several variations evolved.

As the war progressed some of the cruiser's aircraft functions were carried out by newly fitted ships radar sets or by carrier-borne aircraft. At the same time there was an ever present need to increase AA defences so that in many cases the aircraft and its associated facilities were removed or reduced in order to make room for AA guns and their fire control systems. With less effective radars, and an ever decreasing carrier force, the Imperial Japanese Navy retained aircraft aboard most of their cruisers to the end of the war.The following sections lists the main aircraft types which were embarked aboard the treaty cruisers from the mid 1920s until the end of the Second World War. Technical data and a brief description are given in each case.

Britain and Commonwealth

Fairey IIIF Mk.IIIB
Reconnaissance twin float biplane
Power: One Napier Lion XIA, 570hp
Armament: One fixed forward firing Vickers 0.303 machine gun. One manually operated Lewis gun in rear cockpit
Performance: Max speed 120mph, Endurance up to 4 hrs, Service Ceiling 20,000ft
Crew: Pilot, Observer, Telegraphist/Air Gunner
Size: Span: 45ft 9in. Length: 36ft 4in. Height: 14ft 3in
Weights: Empty: 3,923 lb. Loaded: 6,301 lb

The Fairey first flew in 1926 and a total of 610 were produced in various forms for the RAF and Fleet Air Arm. Most of these had a conventional wheeled undercarriage but 177 of the float equipped Mk.IIIB were produced and this variant was intended to equip the catapult flights aboard the various *County* class cruisers although in the event it was only shipped by *Norfolk* and *Dorsetshire*, and also *Exeter* and *York*, as initial equipment when they first commissioned but were replaced by 1935.

Fairey Seafox
Reconnaissance twin float biplane
Power: One Napier Rapier VI sixteen cylinder H-type inline, 395hp
Armament: One .303in Lewis gun on a flexible mount
Performance: Max speed 120mph, Cruising Speed 106mph, Endurance 4.15hrs, Range 440 miles, Service Ceiling 11,000ft
Crew: Pilot and Observer
Size: Span: 40ft. Length: 35ft 3.5in. Height: 12ft 1in
Weights: Empty: 3,805 lb, Loaded: 5,420 lb

The Seafox was designed specifically for use aboard cruisers and entered service in 1936 and served aboard all *York* and *Exeter*. A Seafox from the light cruiser HMS *Ajax* played a vital role in the Battle of the River Plate which led to the destruction of the *Graf Spee*. The type remained operational until early 1943.

Hawker Osprey
Fighter-reconnaissance twin float biplane
Power: One Rolls Royce Kestrel V liquid cooled inline, 640hp
Armament: One fixed forward firing Vickers 0.303 machine gun. One manually operated Lewis gun in rear cockpit.
Performance: Max speed 169mph, Cruising Speed 109mph, Endurance 2.5hrs, Service Ceiling 22,000ft
Crew: Pilot and Observer
Size: Span: 37ft. Length: 29ft 4in. Height: 12ft 5in
Weights: Empty: 3,405 lb. Loaded: 5,570 lb

The Osprey was a naval version of the Hawker Hart two-seat day bomber produced for the RAF and first flew in 1930. The floatplane version started equipping the catapult flights of the 2nd and 5th Cruiser squadrons from 1932 onwards and was eventually carried by all *County* class cruisers and *Exeter* and *York*. A total of 129 Ospreys, both wheeled and float equipped versions, were produced although the type had been withdrawn from all cruiser flights by the outbreak of war in 1939.

Supermarine Walrus
Single engine biplane general purpose amphibious flying boat
Power: One Bristol Pegasus nine cylinder air cooled radial engine, 775hp
Armament: One Vickers 0.303 K machine gun in bow and dorsal positions. Light bombs and depth charges on underwing racks
Performance: Max speed 135mph, Cruising Speed 95mph, Range 600 miles, Service Ceiling 18,500ft
Crew: Pilot, Observer, Telegraphist/Air Gunner
Size: Span: 45ft 10in. Length: 37ft 7in. Height: 15ft 3in
Weights: Empty: 4,900 lb. Loaded: 7,200 lb

The Walrus, or Shagbat, as it was affectionately known, was standard equipment aboard all British heavy cruisers during the Second World War. Unlike most contemporary shipboard catapult aircraft, it was a flying boat rather than a floatplane and any pretence of performance was abandoned in favour of a general purpose capability. Uniquely, it was an amphibian so that its retractable undercarriage enabled it to land ashore or on a carrier's flight deck. Although only carrying a normal crew of three, its capacious fuselage was capable of carrying more so that it was often used to rescue survivors from sunken ships or ditched aircraft. The prototype, originally named Seagull, first flew in 1933 and the first orders materialised from the Australian Navy although the Royal Navy subsequently placed orders in 1935 and from 1936 onwards it gradually equipped all British and RAN heavy cruiser flights.

France

Gourdou-Leseurre GL-810
Observation and Scout twin float monoplane
Power: One Gnome-Rhone 9Ady Juptier nine cylinder radial engine, 420 hp
Armament: One fixed forward firing Vickers 7.7mm Vickers macine gun. Two 7.7mm Lewis guns on a flexible dorsal mounting. Two 165lb G2 bombs.
Performance: Max speed 112mph, Cruising Speed 98mph, Endurance 4hrs, Service Ceiling: 18,000ft
Crew: Pilot, Observer, gunner/radio operator
Size: Span: 52ft 6in. Length: 34ft 5in. Height: 14ft
Weights: Empty: 3,682 lb. Loaded: 5,423 lb

Although it flew in prototype form in 1926, the production version incorporated several improvements including larger floats and a more powerful engine. The type initially equipped the *Dusquense* and *Suffren* classes but was replaced by the Loire 130 before the outbreak of war. Sub variants included the GL-811 and GL-812 which incorporated folding wings as opposed to the fixed wing of the GL-810.

Loire 130
Reconnaissance single engined monoplane flying boat
Power: One Hispano-Suiza 12Xirsl twelve cylinder liquid cooled engine, 720hp
Armament: Two 7.5mm Darne machine guns in flexible bow and dorsal mountings. Two 165 lb bombs
Performance: Max speed 137mph, Cruising Speed 102mph, Endurance 7.5hrs, Service Ceiling: 19,600ft
Crew: Pilot, Observer, gunner/radio operator
Size: Span: 52ft 6in. Length: 37ft 1in. Height: 12ft 7in
Weights: Empty: 4,519 lb. Loaded: 7,716 lb

An Arado Ar.196 *floatplane being hoisted aboard a German cruiser.* Author's collection

First flown in 1934, the Loire 130 was similar in concept to the British Walrus although did not possess an amphibian capability. By the outbreak of the Second World War in 1939 the type was serving aboard all major French warships including heavy cruisers. The *Dusquesne* class carried one, while the *Suffren* class and the *Algérie* carried two. Those ships which remained in allied service after November 1942 landed their aircraft and equipment so that the AA armament could be augmented, Nevertheless, a few Loire 130s remained in service at seaplane bases until the end of the war.

Germany

Arado Ar196
Reconnaissance single engined twin float monoplane
Power: One BMW132K nine cylinder radial engine, 970 hp
Armament: Two 7.9mm MG17 machine guns, one fixed forward firing and one on a flexible mounting in the rear cockpit
Performance: Max speed 193mph, Cruising Speed 157mph, Endurance 4.5hrs, Service Ceiling: 23,000ft
Crew: Pilot, observer/gunner
Size: Span: 40ft 10in. Length: 36ft 1in. Height: 14ft 5in
Weights: Empty: 6,580 lb. Loaded: 8,200 lb

The Gourdon Leseurre 810 *was the standard French cruiser floatplane in the 1930s. A* Suffren *class cruiser can be seen in the background.* Marius Bar

A highly successful design of which 593 examples were built although most of these were the more heavily armed A3 variant designed for coastal reconnaissance from seaplane bases. The shipboard variant equipped all three *Hipper* class cruisers as well as most other German capital ships where it replaced the earlier He60 biplane.

Italy

I.M.A.M Ro.43
Reconnaissance single float biplane
Power: One Piaggio PXR nine cylinder radial engine. 700 hp
Armament: Two 7.7mm Breda machine guns, one fixed forward firing and one on a flexible mounting in the rear cockpit
Performance: Max speed 186mph, Cruising Speed 149 mph, Endurance 4.5hrs, Service Ceiling: 22,000ft
Crew: Pilot, observer/gunner
Size: Span: 37ft 11in. Length: 31ft 10in. Height: 11ft 6in
Weights: Empty: 3,924 lb. Loaded: 5,291 lb

The Italian Navy's standard ship-based seaplane during the Second World War and operated from all the heavy cruisers. A single seat version, the Ro.44, was also produced and was armed with two fixed forward firing machine guns. Intended to operate as a fighter, it had a poor performance and was not deployed aboard the cruisers.

Japan

Aichi E13A1 (Jake)
Long range reconnaissance twin float monoplane
Power: One Mitsubishi MK8 Kinsei 43 fourteen cylinder radial engine, 1,080 hp
Armament: One flexible 7.7mm machine gun, one 550 lb or four 132 lb bombs
Performance: Max speed 234mph, Cruising Speed 138mph, Endurance 14.5hrs, Service Ceiling: 26,100ft
Crew: Three
Size: Span: 47ft 6in. Length: 37ft 11in. Height: 15ft 8in
Weights: Empty: 5,824 lb. Loaded: 8,047 lb

A very successful design which entered service at the end of 1941 and was widely used throughout the rest of the war. It was E13A1 floatplanes from the cruisers *Chikuma*, *Tone* and *Kinugasa* which carried out reconnaissance missions over Pearl Harbor before the fateful attack on 7 December, 1941. Jake was the reporting code name applied to the type by the allies.

Kawanishi E7K1 and E7K2 (Alf)
Reconnaissance twin float biplane
Power: One Mitsubishi MK2 Zuisei 11 fourteen cylinder radial engine, 870 hp
Armament: One fixed and two flexible 7.7mm machine guns, four 132 lb bombs.
Performance: Max speed 171mph, Cruising Speed 115mph, Endurance 10 hrs, Service Ceiling: 23,160ft
Crew: Three
Size: Span: 45ft 11in. Length: 34ft 5in. Height: 14ft 11in
Weights: Empty: 4,375 lb. Loaded: 6,614 lb

The original E7K1 first flew in 1933 and operated from heavy cruisers (*Atago* and *Nachi* classes) in the 1930s until replaced by the E7K2 fitted with a more powerful engine. This version, to which the above data relates, entered production in 1938 and some 347 were built. From 1941 onwards it was progressively retired to second line duties as the Achi E13A1 entered service.

United States

Vought O3U Corsair
Scout observation single float biplane
Power: One Pratt and Whitney R-1340-12 Wasp nine cylinder radial engine. 550 hp
Armament: One fixed and one flexible 0.3in machine guns
Performance: Max speed 164mph, Endurance 5 hrs, Service Ceiling: 18,000 ft
Crew: Two
Size: Span: 36ft 0in. Length: 27ft 3in. Height: 11ft 6in
Weights: Empty: 2,938 lb. Loaded: 4,451 lb

The O3U was an inmproved version of the earlier O2U and first entered service in 1930. It initially equipped the *Pensacola* and *Northampton* classes but from 1935 onwards it was progressively replaced by the Curtiss Seagull and none were operational by 1941.

Curtiss SOC Seagull
Scout observation single float biplane
Power: One Pratt and Whitney R-1340-18 Wasp nine cylinder radial engine. 600 hp
Armament: One fixed and one flexible 0.3in machine guns, two 100 lb bombs.
Performance: Max speed 165mph, Cruising Speed 133mph, Endurance 5 hrs, Service Ceiling: 14,900 ft
Crew: Two
Size: Span: 36ft 0in. Length: 31ft 5in. Height: 14ft 9in
Weights: Empty: 3,788 lb. Loaded: 5,437 lb
The SOC-1 Seagull first flew in 1934, entered service in 1935 and was produced in both floatplane and landplane versions. Production terminated in 1938 although the type served aboard most US heavy cruisers and many examples were still operational at the end of the war, despite the introduction of more modern types.

Vought OS2U Kingfisher
Scout Observation single float monoplane
Power: One Pratt and Whitney R-985-AN Wasp Junior nine cylinder radial engine. 450 hp
Armament: One fixed and one flexible 0.3in machine guns, two 100 lb or 350 lb bombs
Performance: Max speed 164mph, Cruising Speed 125mph, Endurance: up to 8 hours Service Ceiling: 13,000 ft
Crew: Two
Size: Span: 35ft 10in. Length: 33ft 10in. Height: 15ft 1in
Weights: Empty: 4,123 lb. Loaded: 5,600 lb

Over 1200 Kingfishers were built between 1937 and 1942 and both floatplane and landplane versions were built. Several were deployed aboard heavy cruisers, notably the newer *Baltimore* class. 100 were delivered to the Royal Navy which used them aboard armed merchant cruisers.

Curtiss SC-1 Seahawk
Scout single float monoplane
Power: One Pratt and Whitney R-1820-62 Cyclone nine cylinder radial engine. 1,350 hp
Armament: Two fixed 0.5in machine guns, two 250 lb and two 100 lb bombs
Performance: Max speed 313mph, Economic Cruising Speed 125mph, Endurance 8 hrs (with auxiliary tank in the central float), Service Ceiling: 37,300 ft
Crew: One
Size: Span: 41ft 0in. Length: 36ft 4in. Height: 18ft 0in
Weights: Empty: 6,320 lb. Loaded: 7,936 lb

The single seat Seahawk was considerably larger and heavier than its predecessors, and possessed a startling performance for a seaplane. However, the prototype did not fly until February 1944 and it did not enter operational service until early 1945 when it began to equip some heavy cruisers including *Pensacola*. Production ceased in October 1946 after a total of 577 had been delivered.

Index

Page numbers in *italics* refer to illustrations.

Abe, Vice Admiral 129–130, 131
Abukuma 138, 143, 144
Achates, HMS 100, 109
Achilles, HMS 89, 90
Admiral class proposal 37
Admiral Graf Spee 4, 36, 89, 90, 115, 150
Admiral Hipper 15, *45*, *46*, 47, 48, 91, 92, 93, *93*,
   99–100, *99*, 150
Admiral Hipper class cruisers 45–49, *45*, *46*, *47*, *99*,
   150
   armament 47
   armour 47
Admiralty 89, 94, 147 *see also* Royal Navy
Agano 135
Agar, Captain A.W.S., VC 98, 118
Ainsworth, Rear Admiral 133
aircraft
   Arado Ar 196: *172*
   Avro Lancaster 102
   Boeing B-17 121, 128, 131
   Bristol Beaufort 111
   Bristol Blenheim 108
   Consolidated B-24 Liberator 136
   Consolidated Catalina 117–118, 121
   Curtiss SOC Seagull *168*
   Douglas SBD Dauntless 119, 122, 129
   Fairey IIIF *164*
   Fairey Albacore 108, 117
   Fairey Fulmar 95, 108, 117, 118
   Fairey Swordfish 95, 96, 105, 108, 117
   Gourdou-Leseurre GL810 *38*, *173*
   Gourdou-Leseurre GL812 41, 44
   Gourdou-Leseurre GL832 41
   Grumman Avenger 148
   Grumman Wildcat 117
   Hawker Hurricane 95
   Hawker Sea Hurricane 117, 118
   Junkers Ju 88: 110
   Junkers Stuka 91
   kamikaze 146, 147, 150
   Loire-Nieuport 130: 41
   Mitsubishi Zero 121, 122
   North American B-25 Mitchell 119
   Piaggio P6 52
   Short Sunderland 105–106
   Supermarine Spitfire 113

   Supermarine Walrus 91, 97
   Vickers Wellington 111
aircraft carriers 11
Ajax, HMS 89, 90, 106
Akagi 122
Akagi class battlecruisers 9
Akatsuki 131
Albany, USS 84
Aleutian islands 120, 137–138
Alexandria 103
Alfieri 109
Algérie *42*, 43–44, *44*, 103, *103*, 105, 150, 151
Almirante Brown 54
Amagi 68
American, British, Dutch and Australian (ABDA)
   command 75, 115–116
Amethyst, HMS 30–31
Andaman Islands 148
Anglo German Naval Treaty (1935) 3, 14–15, 46
Antiope 114
Aoba 60, *60*, 124, 126, 128
Aoba class cruisers 13, 60–61
Archer, HMS *5*
Arethusa, HMS 94
Arethusa class cruisers 37
Argentinean Navy 54
Ark Royal, HMS 91, 92, 94, 95
Armstrong shipyard 4
Asagumo 143
Ashigara *62*, 63, 117, 143, 147, 148
Astoria, USS 77, 82, 115, 119, 121, 122, 123, 126
Atago 63, 64, 65, 120, 127, 132, 135, 136, 139,
   142
Atago class cruisers 64–65
Athelstone, RFA 118
Atlanta, USS 130, 131
Atlanta class light cruisers 139
Atlantis (Raider 16) 97–98
atomic bomb trials 48, 73, 97
Attendolo 113
Augusta, USS *70*, *71*, 74–75, 102, 114
Austin, Commander B.L. 135
Australia, HMAS 23, *24*, 26, 92, 119, 123, 127, *144*,
   147, 150
Australian, British, Dutch and American (ABDA)
   command 75, 115–116

Australian ships 23, 24, 26
Ayanami 132

B class cruisers 35–36, 77
Bailey, USS 137, 138
Baltimore, USS 84, *138*, 139
Baltimore class cruisers 15, *80*, 83–84, *138*, 151
Barents Sea, Battle of the 99–100, 150
Barham, HMS 92, 108, 109
Barton, USS 131
Beatty, Admiral 9
Belfast, HMS 101
Bergall, USS 147
Berwick, HMS *19, 20, 22*, 23, 25–26, 89, 91, 92, 93, 105
Bévésiers 92
Bikini Atoll 48, 73, 97
Birmingham, HMS 89, 94, 111
Birmingham, USS 7, 142
Bismarck 4, 33, 48, 93–94, *93*, 95, 97, 101, 150, 152
Blücher 6, 15, 47, *47*, 48, 91, 150
Blue, USS 123, 124
Boise, USS 128, 129
Bolzano *55*, 56–57, 105, 108, 109–110, *112*, 113, 114
Bonaventure, HMS 92–93
Boston, USS 84, 139
Bougainville 133–134
Breconshire 110, 111
Brest 93, 96
Brest Navy Yard 43
Brisbane Star 113
British 8th Army 113, 114
British Emperor, SS 97
Brooklyn class light cruisers 14, 66, *77, 79*, 83–84
Buchanan, USS 128
Burke, Captain Arleigh 135
Burnett, Rear Admiral R.L. 98, 100, 101

C class cruisers 5, 7
Cabot, USS 142
Cairo, HMS 111, 113
Callaghan, Rear Admiral 130, 131
Canaris 33, 96
Canberra, HMAS 23, *23*, 26, 28, 123, 124, *124, 125*, 143, 149
Canberra, USS 84, 139
Cape Esperance, Battle of 60, 61, 73, 128–129
Cape Matapan, Battle of 106, 108–109, 150
Caradoc, HMS *7*
Carducci 109
Carlisle, HMS 110
Casablanca 114

Cesare 105
Chandler, Rear Admiral 147
Chester, USS 75, 115, 119, 121, 139
Chicago, USS (*Northampton* class) 74–75, 115, 119, 123, 124, 133
Chicago, USS (*Baltimore* class) *80*
Chikuma 15, 67, 115, 120, 121, 127, 130, 135, *141*, 142, 145, 146
Chiyoda 140, 145
Chokai 63, *63*, 64, 65, 118, 120, 124, 126, 135, 139, 142, 145, 146
Churchill, Winston 90, 92, 103
Clan Campbell 111
Cleopatra, HMS 110
Cleveland class light cruisers 49, 135
Coghlan, USS 137, 138
Colbert 41, 43, 103, 105
Colombo 118
Columbia, USS 143
convoys
    Harpoon 111, 113
    JW51A 98–99
    JW51B 98–99, 100
    JW55B 100–101
    Malta 110–111, 113–114, 150
    MW10 110
    PQ17 98
    PQ18 98
    QP14 98
    Russian 98–102
    Vigorous 111, 113
    WS5A 92–93
    WS-12X 98
Coolidge, President Calvin 12, 77
Coral Sea, Battle of the 119–120, 123
Cornwall, HMS *22*, 25–26, 89, 97, 117, 118, 149
County class cruisers 4, 12, 13, 70, 102, 149–150, 151–152 *see also Kent* class cruisers; *London* class cruisers; *Norfolk* class cruisers
    funnels 21, 23
Crace, Rear Admiral 119
Craven class destroyers 73
cruisers
    Armed Merchant 5
    armoured 4–5
    evolution of 4–8
    First Class Protected 4
    protected 4
    Scout 5, 7–8, 69
    Second Class Protected 4
    Third Class Protected 4
    Type A 13–14
    Type B 13–14

Crutchley, Rear Admiral Victor 123
Cumberland, HMS *21*, 26, 89, 90, 92, 98
Cunningham, Vice Admiral John 92, 103, 106, 108, 109
Cushing, USS 130–131

D class cruisers 5
D-Day landings 102
Dakar 92
Dale, USS 137
Darwin 117
de Gaulle, General Charles 92
De Ruyter 116
Defence, HMS 4–5
Denmark Strait 94
Dennis, USS 146
Denver, USS 135, 143
Des Moines, USS 85
Des Moines class cruisers 85, *160*
Deutschland class *panzerschiffe* (armoured ships – pocket battleships) 45, 46, 48, 89
Devonshire, HMS *27*, 28, 89, 91, 92, 97, 98
Diadem class cruisers 4
Dido class cruisers 37
Doolittle, Lt. Col James 119 *see also* Tokyo raid
Doorman, Rear Admiral Karel 115, 116
Doric Star 89
Dorsetshire, HMS 31, 33, 89, 95, 98, 117, 118, 149, 151–152
Duguay Trouin class cruisers 38
Duke of York, HMS 101
Duncan, USS 128
Dunedin, HMS 92–93
Dunkerque 46
Dunkirk 92
Dupleix *40*, 43, 89, 103, 105
Dusquense 38, 39, 41, 103, 105
Dusquense class cruisers 38–39, *38*, *39*, 41

E class cruisers 5
Eagle, HMS 89, 105, 113
Eastern Naval Task Force 102
Eastern Solomons, Battle of the 127–128
Eckholt 100
Egusa, Lt.Cdr. 118
Electra 116
Elswick cruisers 4
Emden 91
Encounter, HMS 116, 117
Enterprise, USS 61, 115, 119, 121, 122, 123, 127, 128, 129, 130, 131, 142
Esmonde, Lt.Cdr. Eugene 96
Essex, USS 142

Essex class aircraft carriers 139
Euryalus, HMS 110
Evertsen 117
Exeter, HMS 4, 35–36, *36*, 89–90, 115, 116, 117, 150

Fanshaw Bay, USS 146
Farenholt, USS 128–129
Fiji class cruisers 37
First World War 5, 7, 50
Fiume *54*, 56, 103, *104*, 105, 109, 114
Fleet Air Arm
  815 Squadron 108
  825 Squadron 96
Fletcher, Admiral Jack 119, 121, 122, 123, 127, 130
Fletcher, USS 132
Foch *42*, 43, 89, 103, 105
Foote, USS 135
Forbes, Admiral 91
Forester, HMS 113
Formidable, HMS 108, 110, 117, 118
Four Power Pact 11
Franklin, USS 143
Fraser, Admiral 101
French cruiser development 6–7
French government 11
French Navy 150
Frigates 4
Fubuki 128
Furious, HMS 113
Furutaka 58, *59*, 60, 61, 124, 128
Furutaka class cruisers 8, 11, 12, 13, 58–61, *59*, *60*
Fuso 143

Gambier Bay, USS 146
Geneva Conference 12–13
German air force (*Luftwaffe*) 91
German Navy (*Kriegsmarine*) 6, 15, 46, 89, 90–91, 93, 96
  auxiliary cruisers disguised as merchant ships 97–98
German-Russian pact 48
Ghormley, Admiral 127, 128
Gilbert Islands 139
Glorious, HMS 91, 92
Gloucester, HMS 106, 108
Glowworm, HMS 91
Gneisenaü 46, 48, 92, 93, 96
Godfrey, Vice-Admiral 103, 105
Gorizia 56, 57, 103, *104*, 105, *107*, 109, 110, 111, 113, 114, 150
Goto, Rear Admiral 128
Graf Spee see *Admiral Graf Spee*

'Great Marianas Turkey Shoot' 140
Greyhound, HMS 109
Griffin, HMS 109
Guadalcanal 84, 123, 127, 128, 129, 130, 132, 133
  Henderson Field 128, 129, 130, 131, 132
Gwin, USS 133

Haguro 62, 116, 117, 120, 135, 139, 142, 145, 146, 147, 148
Halsey, Admiral 130, 132, 133, 142, 145, 147
Hara, Rear Admiral 127
Harding, President Warren 9
Haruna 129, 140
Harwood, Commodore 89, 90
Hasty, HMS 111
Hatsukaze 135
Hatsuyuki 128
Havock, HMS 109, 111
Hawkins, HMS 8
Hawkins class cruisers 3, 5–6, 8, 11, 13, 19, 69
Heerman, USS 146
Helena, USS 128, 131, 133
Hermes, HMS 117, 118
Hermione, HMS 111
Hiei 130, 131
Highflyer class cruisers 4
Hiraga, Vice-Admiral Yuzuru 58
Hiryu 122
Hitler, Adolf 46, 49, 96, 100, 105
Hiyo 131, 140
Hoel, USS 146
Holland, Vice Admiral 94
Hollyhock, HMS 118
Honolulu, USS 132, 133
Hood, HMS 9, 94, 95
Hoover, President J. Edgar 13
Hoover, Captain 131
Hornet, USS 73, 118, 119, 121, 122, 128, 129, 130
Hosogaya, Vice Admiral 137, 138
Houston, USS 66, 74–75, 115, 116, 117
Hughes, Secretary 10
Hyuga 145

I-58 81
Ianchino, Admiral 105, 108, 109, 110
Ibuki 68
Ibuki class cruisers 68
Ijuin, Rear Admiral 135
Illustrious, HMS 105
Independence, USS 145
Indianapolis, USS 72, 77, 81, 139
Indomitable, HMS 113, 117, 118
Intrepid, USS 142

Ironbottom Sound 123, 130, 131, 132–133
Ise 145
Italian Navy 50, 55, 103, 105, 113, 114, 150
  Division, 1st 105, 109
  Division, 3rd 105, 109, 110, 111
Iwo Jima 147

Jamaica, HMS 98–99, 100, 101
Japanese Army, Imperial 132
Japanese Navy, Imperial 7, 61, 63, 65, 117, 124, 135, 147, 151
  Carrier Division, 5th 117
  Cruiser Squadron, 4th 63, 64–65, 135
  Cruiser Squadron, 5th 62
  Cruiser Squadron, 6th 60, 61
  Cruiser Squadron, 7th 66, 67, 135
  Cruiser Squadron, 8th 67, 135
  First Carrier Strike Force 120
  Fleet, First Mobile 139
  Fleet, 2nd 130, 131, 135
  Fleet, Fourth 67
  Fleet, 8th 130
  Fleet, Combined 129, 139, 141, 142
  Naval Staff 66
  Vanguard Force 129–130
Java, HMS 116
Java Sea, Battle of the 36, 62, 75, 115–117
Jean Bart 114
Jervis, HMS 109
Jintsu 133
Joffre class aircraft carrier project 41
Johnston, USS 146
Joshima, Rear Admiral 128, 129
Juneau, USS 131
Junyo 129, 130, 131
Jupiter, HMS 116

Kaga 122
Kaga class battleships 9
Kako 58, 59, 60, 61, 124, 127
Kako, Baron 11
Kalinin Bay, USS 146
Kamikaze 148
Kent, HMS 22, 26, 89
Kent class cruisers 19–21, *19*, *20*, *21*, *22*, 23–26, *23*, *24*, *25*, 33–37, *33*, *34*, *36*, *124*, *125*, *144*
  aircraft arrangements 25, 26
  armament 21, 25, 26, 31
  armour 20
  displacement 24–25
  magazines 20
  modifications 25–26
Kenya, HMS 113

King, Admiral 123
King George V, HMS 95
Kingston, HMS 111
Kinkaid, Rear Admiral 129, 130
Kinkaid, USS 143
Kinugasa 60, *60*, 61, 124, 127, 128, 131, 132
Kirishima 130, 131, 132
Kirk, Rear Admiral 102
Kitkun Bay, USS 146
Komandorski Islands, Battle of the 73, 137–139
Komoran 97
Kondo, Admiral 130, 131, 132
Kongo 129
Kortenaer 116
Kula Gulf, Battle of 133
Kumano 65, 66, 118, 120, 127, 135, 142, 145, 146
Kummetz, Admiral 99, 100
Kurita, Vice Admiral 142, 143, 145, 146, 147

L'Audacieuse 92
Labour Government 24
Laffey, USS 128, 130, 131
Lanciere 111
Langsdorff, Kapitan zur See Hans 89, 90
League of Nations 12, 14
Leander, HMNZS 133
Leander class cruisers 36–37
Lee, Rear Admiral 'Ching' 132
Legion, HMS 111
Lexington, USS 62, 115, 119, 120, 142
Lexington class battlecruisers 9
Leyte Gulf 140, 141, 142, 145
Leyte Gulf, Battles of 66, 145, 151
Littorio 110, 111
London, HMS 23, *23*, 28, 29–30, *29*, *30*, 89, 98
London class cruisers 27, 28–31, *29*, *30*, 31, *31*, 32–33
    armament 28
    radar 28
London Naval Conference, first 13, 15
London Naval Conference, second 14, 15
London Treaty, First 13–14, 15, 58, 65, 66–67, 77, 83
Louisville, USS 75, 143, 147
Lütjens, Admiral Gunther 93, 95
Lützow 47, 48–49, 91, 93, 99, 100
Luzon 147

Makin island 139
Malaya, HMS 105
Malta 110, 111, 113, 150
Manchester, HMS 94, 113
Manxman, HMS 109
Marblehead, USS 115

Mariana Islands 137, 139, 140
Mars, Lt. Alastair, VC 113
Massachusetts, USS 114
Matapan, Battle of 106, 108–109, 150
Maya 63, 64, 65, 120, 127, 131, 135, 136, 137, 138, 139, 140, 142
MacArthur, General 137
McCalla, USS 128
McCoy, Captain 101
MacDonald, Ramsey 13
McMorris, Rear Admiral 137, 138
Meisel, Kapitan zur See 93
Melbourne Star 113
merchant ships, German auxiliary cruisers disguised as 97–98
Merrill, Rear Admiral 'Tip' 135
Midway, Battle of 66, 121–122
Midway Island 120, 121
Mikawa, Vice Admiral 123–124, 126, 127, 131
Mikuma 65, 66, 67, 117, 118, 120, 122
Minneapolis, USS 76, 77, *78*, 82, 119, 120, 121, 127, 132, 133, *134*, 139, 143, 147, 151
Minotaur, HMS 4–5
Missouri, USS 149
Mitscher, Admiral 140
Mogami 64, 65, 66, 67, 117, 118, 120, 122, 135, 136, 139, 143, 144
Mogami class cruisers 15, *64*, 65–67, *65*, *141*, 151
Monaghan, USS 137, 138
Monssen, USS 131
Montevideo 90
Montpelier, USS 135
motor boats, explosive (EMBs) 109
Murakumo 128
Musashi 142
Mutsu 11
Mutsu class battleships 11
Myoko 62, 117, 120, 127, 135, 139, 142, 147
Myoko class cruisers 12, 34, 61–62, *62*, 151

Nachi 62, 66, 116, 117, 120, 137, 138, 143
Nagato 143
Nagumo, Vice Admiral 117, 118, 120, 121–122, 127, 128, 130
Natsugomo 128
Nelson, HMS 11, 12, 113
Neosho 119
Nestor, HMS 111
Netherlands Navy 115, 116
New Georgia 133
New Guinea 119, 123
New Orleans, USS *74*, 77, *77*, 82, 115, 119, 120, 121, 127, 132, 133, 139, 151

New Orleans class cruisers *74*, *76*, 77, *77*, *78*, *79*, 81–83, *125*, *126*, *134*, 151, 152
  armament 81–82
  armour 81
Newcastle, HMS 111
Newport News, USS 85, *160*
Nigeria, HMS 113
Nishimura, Vice Admiral 142, 143
Norfolk, HMS 31, *32*, 33, 89, 94, 95, 98, 101, 102, 151–152
Norfolk class cruisers 31, 33–34
Normandy landings 102
Northampton, USS (*Northampton* class) 75, 115, 119, 121, 129, 130, 132, 133
Northampton, USS (*Oregon City* class) 84
Northampton class cruisers *70*, *71*, 73–75, 77
Norwegian campaign 91–92
Nubian, HMS 109

O'Bannon, USS 130
Obdurate, HMS 100
Obedient, HMS 100
Ohio 113
Okinami 66
Okinawa 147
Oldendorf, Rear Admiral 143, 144
Oliver, Captain R.D., DSC 97, 98
Omaha class light cruisers 7, 9
Omori, Rear Admiral 135
Onslow, HMS 100
operations
  A-GO 139
  Catapult 103
  Detachment 147
  Dragoon 102, 114
  Flintlock 139
  Forager 139–140
  Galvanic 139
  Harpoon 111, 113
  Husky 114
  Iceberg 147
  KA 127
  M1 120
  Menace 92
  Mincemeat 109
  MO 119
  Overlord 102
  Pedestal 150
  Rheinübung 93–94
  Torch 75, 114
  Vigorous 111, 113
  Watchtower 123
Oran 103

Oregon City, USS 84
Oregon City class cruisers 84–85
Orion, HMS 106, 108
Orwell, HMS 100
Oslofiord 91
Osugi, Rear Admiral 135
Oyashio 75, 133
Oyodo 145
Ozawa, Vice Admiral 118, 139, 140, 141, 142, 145

Pampas 111
Patterson, USS 124
Pearl Harbor 115, 118
Peary, USS 117
Penelope, HMS 110
Pensacola, USS *69*, 70, *71*, 73, 121, 129, 132, 133, 139
Pensacola class cruisers 34, *69*, 70–73, *71*, 74
  armour 72
Perth, HMAS 75, 115, 116, 117
Perth, HMS 66, 106
Phelps, USS 120
Philippine Sea, Battle of the 140
Philippines 140–142
Pinguin (Raider 33) 97
Pittsburgh, USS 84
Plan SHO-1 140, 145
Pola 55, 56, *104*, 105, 109, 114
Pope, USS 117
Port Chalmers 113
Port Moresby 119, 120, 123
Porter, USS 130
Portland, USS 77, 80–81, 115, 119, 127, 130, 131, 132, 139, 143, 147
Portland class cruisers 77–78, 80–81
Power, Admiral Sir John 147
Power, Captain Manley 148
Powerful, HMS 4
Pridham-Whippel, Vice Admiral 106, 108
Primauget 114
Prince of Wales, HMS 94, 95, 115
Princeton, USS 142
Prinz Eugen 15, 47, 48, *49*, 93–94, 95, 96–97, 150
Python 98

Quincy, USS 77, 81, 82, 84, 98, 102, 123, *125*, 126–127, *126*

Ralph Talbot, USS 123
Ramilles, HMS 94, 105
Ranger, USS 98
rating system 4
Ray, USS 66

Raymond, USS 146
Rennell Island, Battle of 133
Reno, USS 142
Renown, HMS 94, 105
Repulse, HMS 94, 115
Resolution, HMS 92
Reuben James, USS 98
Revenge, HMS 94
Richelieu 92
Richmond, USS 137, 138
River Plate, Battle of the 4, 36, 89, 90, 115, 150
Rochester, USS 84
Rochester Castle 113
Rodney, HMS 11, 12, 94, 95, 113
Rogge, Kapitan Bernhardt 98
Rommel, General Erwin 113
Roosevelt, President Franklin D. *71*
Royal Air Force, 209 Squadron 95
Royal Navy 19, 23, 24, 33, 34, 35, 36, 70, 93, 94,
    96, 105, 106, 109, 149 *see also* Admiralty; Eastern
    Naval Task Force; Western Naval Task Force
    construction programme 34–35
    Cruiser Squadron, 1st 89, 92
    Cruiser Squadron, 5th 89
    cruiser strength 1919 9
    Destroyer Flotilla, 4th 95
    Destroyer Flotilla, 26th 148
    East Indies Fleet 147–148
    Eastern Fleet 117, 118
    Force F 89
    Force G 89
    Force H 89, 94, 105, 110, 113
    Force I 89
    Force M 89
    Force W 111
    Home Fleet 98
    Mediterranean Fleet 103, 106, 108, 111
    Task Force 61: 148
Royal Sovereign, HMS 105
Ryujo 127, 128

S-44 127
St. Lo, USS 146
St. Louis, USS 133
St. Paul, USS 84
Salem, USS 85
Salt Lake City, USS 4, *69*, 70, 73, 115, 119, 128,
    137, 138, 139
Samidare 135
Samuel B. Roberts, USS 146
San Bernadino Strait 145–147
San Francisco, USS 77, 81, 82, 115, 128, 129, 130,
    131, 132, 139, 151

San Juan, USS 130
Santa Cruz, Battle of 67, 80, 129
Saratoga, USS 123, 127, 130, 136
Saumarez, HMS 148
Savo Island, Battle of 4, 26, 64, 75, 82, 123–124,
    125, 126–127, 149, 150, 151
Scapa Flow 98
Scharnhorst 4, 33, 46, 48, 92, 93, 96, 100–102, 152
Scirocco 111
Scott, Rear Admiral Norman 128, 129, 130, 131
Sendai 132, 135
Seydlitz 47, 49
Shannon, HMS 4–5
Sheffield, HMS 94, 95, 98–99, 100, 101
Sherbrooke, Captain R.St.V., VC 99, 100
Shigure 143
Shima, Vice Admiral 143
Shiratsuyu 135
Shoho 119, 120
Shokaku 119, 120, 127, 128, 129, 140
Shropshire, HMS 28, *31*, 89, 143, 147
Sibuyan Sea 142
Sicily 114
Sims, USS 119
Singapore 147
Sirte, First Battle of 110
Sirte, Second Battle of 150
Slot, the 123, 127, 128, 130, 131, 133
Somerville, Admiral James 117, 118
Soryu 122
South Dakota, USS 129, 130, 132, 140
South Dakota class battleships 9
Southampton class light cruisers 37, 66
Sprague, Rear Admiral 145, 146
Spruance, Rear Admiral Raymond 81, 121, 122,
    140
Sterett, USS 130, 131
Strasbourg 46, 103
Strong, USS 133
Stuart, HMS 109
Suffolk, HMS *21*, *25*, 26, 89, 91–92, 94, 95, 98
Suffren *40*, 41, 43, 103, 105
Suffren class cruisers *40*, 41, *42*, 43, *173*
Sugiura, Captain 148
Surabaya 115–117
Surigao Strait 143–144
Sussex, HMS 28, 89, 149
Suzaya 65, 66, 118, 120, 127, 131, 135, 142, 145
Sydney, HMAS 97

Taiho 140
Takagi, Rear Admiral 115–116, 119
Takanami 133

Takao 63, 64, 65, 120, 127, 132, 135, 136, 139, 142, 147

Takao class cruisers 63–64, 151

Talabot 111

Tama 145

Tamerlane, SS 97

Tanaka, Rear Admiral 116, 127, 131, 132, 133

Taranto raid 105

Tarawa Atoll 139

Tassafaronga, Battle of 73, 75, 82, 132–133, *134*, 151

Tenedos, HMS 118

Tenryu 124

Terauchi, Field Marshal Count 148

Terrible, HMS 4, *6*

Tirpitz 98, 102

'Tokyo Express' 128, 129, 132, 133

Tokyo raid 73, 75, 118–119

Tomozuru 67

Tone 15, 67–68, 115, 118, 120, 121, 127, 135, 142, 145, 146, 147

Tone class cruisers 67–68, 151

torpedoes, Long Lance 124, 135

Toulon 43, 105, 150

Tourville 39, *39*, 41, 103, 105

Tovey, Admiral 94, 95, 99

Toyoda, Admiral 139

treaties, end of 15–16

Trenchant, HMS 62, 148

Trento 50, *52*, 53, 55, 57, 105, 108, 109, 110, 111, 113, 114, 150

Trento class cruisers 50–54, *50, 51, 52, 53*, 56, *107*

Trieste 50, *50*, *51*, 53, *53*, 57, 105, *107*, 108, 109, 110, 113, 114

Triumph, HMS 57, 110

Tulagi 123

Turner, Rear Admiral Kelly 123, 130

Tuscaloosa, USS 77, 81, 82, 98, 102, 114

U-73 113

U-boats 92, 98

Umbra, HMS 111

Unbroken, HMS 57, *112*, 113

United States Army
  Amphibious Corps, V 140
  Infantry Regiment, 164th 128

United States government 9–10

United States Marine Corps
  Marine Amphibious Corps, I 133–134

United States Navy 7, 12, 69, 72, 77, 83, 84, 98, 118–119, 137, 140, 151 *see also* Eastern Naval Task Force; Western Naval Task Force

Asiatic Fleet 115–116

Carrier Task Group 38.3: 142

carriers 118

General Board 8, 9, 10, 12

Pacific Fleet 139

Task Force (TF) 16: 121, 130

TF.17: 119, 121

TF.34: 147

TF.36.1: 133

TF.38: 140, 142

TF.38.1: 145

TF 38.3: 145

TF.39: 135

TF.44: 119

TF.52: 140

TF.58: 140, 147

TF.61: 127

TF.62.4: 130

TF.64: 128, 130, 132

TF.67: 132

TF.67.4: 130

TF.77: 144, 145

Task Group (TG) 50.1: 139

TG.50.2: 139

TG.50.3: 139

TG.52.2: 139

TG.53.4: 139

TG.58.1 to 58.4: 139

TG.58.7: 139

TG.77.4.1: 145, 146

TG.77.4.2: 145, 146

TG.77.4.3: 145, 146

Third Fleet 142

United States Senate 9

Utmost, HMS 110

Valiant, HMS 106

Vampire, HMAS 118

Veinticinco de Mayo 54

Venus, HMS 148

Versailles Treaty 45, 46

Verulam, HMS 148

Vian, Rear Admiral 110, 111

Victorious, HMS 94–95, 113

Vigilant, HMS 148

Vincennes, USS 77, *79*, 81, 82, 83, 98, 119, 121, 123, 126, 127

Virago, HMS 148

Vittorio Veneto 105, 106, 108, 109, 111

Wakaba, USS 143

Wake Walker, Rear Admiral 94

Walker, Rear Admiral 148

Warspite, HMS 105
Washington, USS 130, 132
Washington Conference 3, 9–11
    aftermath 12
Washington Naval Treaty for the Limitation of
    Armament 3, 9–12, 15, 70, 149
Wasp, USS 123, 127
West Virginia class ships 11
Western Naval Task Force 102
Wichita, USS 77, *79*, 83, 84, 98, 114, 139, 151\
Wilson, President Woodrow 9
Witte de With 116
Worcester, HMS 96
Wright, Rear Admiral 132

Yamamoto, Admiral 119, 120, 129, 130
Yamashiro 143

Yamato 120, 142, 146
Yamato class battleships 139
York, HMS *34*, 35, 36, 89, 105, 106, 109, 150, *164*
York class cruisers *34, 164*
Yorktown, USS 119, 120, 121, 122
Yubari 58, 124
Yudichi 131
Yunagi 124

Zara *52, 53*, 55, 56, 103, *104*, 105, 109, 114
Zara class cruisers *52, 53, 54*, 55–56, *104, 107*
Zuiho 129, 145
Zuikaku 119, 120, 127, 128, 140, 145